How to be an Effective Supervisor

How to be an Effective Supervisor

Best practice in research student supervision

Adrian Eley and Rowena Murray

 Open University Press

Open University Press
McGraw-Hill Education
McGraw-Hill House
Shoppenhangers Road
Maidenhead
Berkshire
England
SL6 2QL

email: enquiries@openup.co.uk
world wide web: www.openup.co.uk

and Two Penn Plaza, New York, NY 10121-2289, USA

First published 2009

A catalogue record of this book is available from the British Library

ISBN-13: 978-0-33-522295-7 (pb) 978-0-33-522296-4 (hb)
ISBN-10: 0-33-522295-1 (pb) 0-33-522296-X (hb)

Library of Congress Cataloging-in-Publication Data
CIP data applied for

Typeset by RefineCatch Limited, Bungay, Suffolk
Printed in the UK by Bell and Bain Ltd, Glasgow.

Mixed Sources
Product group from well-managed
forests and other controlled sources
www.fsc.org   Cert no. TT-COC-002769
© 1996 Forest Stewardship Council

FSC

The McGraw·Hill Companies

Adrian wishes to dedicate this book to the memory of his mother, Jean Dorothy Eley (1931–2005)

Contents

Figures and tables

Figures

Tables

Foreword

Since the late 1990s there has been an exponential growth of interest in graduate education inspired by and generating policy, code, canon and edict at institutional, national and international levels. Thus supervisors are subject to an unprecedented rapid and comprehensive change in their role and remit. Many such academics, midst the turmoil of multiplying demands, view with trepidation the changes themselves and/or the thought of engaging with them. Such reactions are understandable: reconstruing one's role in response to a plethora of evolving and expanding expectations is never going to be comfortable.

In this book, the authors adopt a novel approach with which to decrease such discomfort by focusing on and exploring the practical import and potential impact of the precepts in the most recent version of the Code of Practice for graduate education produced by the UK Quality Assurance Agency. Through the provision of explanatory examples, perspectives from students and fellow academics, fictional (but eminently recognizable and relevant) problems and suggested solutions, the reader is enabled to make informed decisions about critical areas of professional practice so that they can continue to be intellectually and vocationally rewarding. The coverage is comprehensive, though key texts for further reading are supplied, and the presentation of each chapter is, as one would expect from these authors, engagingly accessible. Based on the several pages of notes that I have made myself for my own practice and for supervisors' workshops, I predict that this will become a well-thumbed, frequently consulted resource for conscientious supervisors.

Pam Denicolo
Director of the Graduate School for the Social Sciences,
University of Reading, and Vice-Chair of the
UK Council for Graduate Education

Preface

Since becoming Lecturer in Medical Microbiology in 1987 and Senior Lecturer in 1995 at the University of Sheffield and Professor of Bacteriology at the United Arab Emirates University (2006–07), Adrian has successfully supervised more than 30 home-based or overseas students for PhD or master's degrees. Following the award of MEd in 2001 in which his thesis was on the student–supervisor relationship, Adrian took on the roles of Founding Chair of the School of Medicine's Graduate Research Committee, Sub-Dean for Postgraduate Affairs in the Faculty of Medicine and Chair of the Faculty Graduate Research Committee. A growing interest in postgraduate research supervision led to the co-authorship of *Effective Postgraduate Supervision: Improving the Student–Supervisor Relationship* (with Roy Jennings), which was published by Open University Press in 2005.

Adrian was very aware of the impact the Quality Assurance Agency (QAA) Code of Practice for Postgraduate Research Degree Programmes (QAA 2004) would have on the future management of doctoral programmes. Although the aims and objectives of the Code were praiseworthy, they were written as 27 precepts which, even though expanded by the QAA for a degree of clarity, were mostly beyond the general comprehension of the average supervisor. Adrian considered that what would be useful for academic staff would be to write an up-to-date text on postgraduate student supervision based on these precepts to allow them to be put into context. He was delighted when Rowena Murray accepted the invitation to co-write *How to be an Effective Supervisor: Best practice in research student supervision*. Our intention was to bring these precepts into life so that they became of practical use. We hope that we have gone some way in achieving these objectives.

Since her appointment as Lecturer in the Centre for Academic Practice at the University of Strathclyde in 1989, and Visiting Professor at Swinburne University in Melbourne (2002–05), Rowena has supervised five PhDs and MPhils to successful completion, along with other research projects (EdD, MSc, Certificate and Diploma). She developed the first supervisor training programmes at Strathclyde, in collaboration with the Vice-Deans (Research) in each faculty, and created the first module on research supervision in the accredited course on teaching and learning in higher education. In 2005 she moved to the Faculty of Education, where she is now Associate Dean (Research). She has published extensively on academic writing and other aspects of postgraduate training, including *How to Write a Thesis* and *Teaching at University: A Guide for Postgraduates and Researchers* (with Kate Morss), and co-authoring a book on research supervision was a logical extension of her work.

Using the QAA precepts for this book is a novel idea. It involves interpreting a set of general statements and combining them with current research and, crucially, student voices, to make them meaningful to supervisors across the disciplines. In writing chapters for this book Rowena had in mind new academics attending modules on research supervision, for whom this combination of policy, practice, current research and student perspectives will be relevant. She also hopes that experienced supervisors will find this book useful in their own work and for mentoring new supervisors.

Adrian Eley and Rowena Murray
Universities of Sheffield and Strathclyde
August 2008

Acknowledgements

In the preparation of this book, we would like to thank a number of people and institutions. First, we are grateful to the Quality Assurance Agency for Higher Education for allowing us to publish the Precepts from the *Code of Practice for the Assurance of Academic Quality and Standards in Higher Education, Section 1: Postgraduate Research Programmes* (QAA 2004) and to include material from the *Report on the Review of Research Degree Programmes: England and Northern Ireland. Sharing Good Practice* (QAA 2007b), and a diagram of the Bologna process in Higher Education (Appendix 1). We are also grateful to the Office of the Independent Adjudicator for allowing us to use selected case studies from its website and to the Higher Education Academy to include tables from Chris Park's *Redefining the Doctorate* (Park 2007).

We thank Peter Mertens from the Institute for Animal Health for permission to use a figure of the Training and Accreditation Programme for Postgraduate Supervisors (TAPPS), and John Wakeford from the Missenden Centre for permission to use the case studies in Appendix 2.

At the University of Strathclyde, Rowena wishes to thank Christine Sinclair of the Centre for Academic Practice and Learning Enhancement for generously giving us the benefit of her experience and expertise in reading and discussing draft chapters. Likewise, there were many others who listened to ideas for chapters and gave their views. This was invaluable for testing the relevance of our material across the disciplines, and our thanks go to them. To the many participants in the Research Supervision module of the Advanced Academic Studies course, we offer thanks for their insightful, thought-provoking and astute contributions to discussions of research supervision policy, practice and research.

At the University of Sheffield, Adrian is grateful to his wife, Penelope, from the Department of French for the acronym PIP (Precept into Practice) which we use to illustrate the precepts. He also thanks Liz Buckton from Student Services for discussions of material in Chapter 9, Claire Taylor and Geof Tomlinson from the Graduate Research Office and Senior Management Group respectively, for giving permission to use tables and figures originating from the University of Sheffield, and to Peter Fearnley, also from the Graduate Research Office, for reading a draft of the complete text and for providing helpful feedback. Adrian also wishes to thank his colleagues Ian Geary and Brenda Price for help with some of the figures and tables used in the book.

Finally, our thanks go to Open University Press, especially Melanie Havelock, for help and encouragement and for keeping this project alive.

Disclaimer

The authors wish to state that there are no intended references in this book to people, alive or dead, and any such associations are purely coincidental.

1

Introduction

Origins of the doctorate • Criticisms of doctoral education and the drivers for change • The response of the QAA to the changing nature of the doctorate • How the precepts have been interpreted in this book • Students' views and precepts into practice • Why use the precepts in supervisor training and development? • Talking points and key texts • List of precepts

Origins of the doctorate

Universities have awarded doctoral degrees, which are the highest academic degrees that a university can award to a student who has successfully completed a defined programme of work in particular field of study, in Europe since medieval times. However, the early doctorates were not awards for research but were a licence to teach. The most common form of doctorate, the Doctor of Philosophy (PhD, from the Latin *Philosophiae Doctor*) which is research based, has its origins in early nineteenth-century Germany. The idea for the PhD was to increase the supply of scientists and other researchers by providing students with an opportunity to carry out a research project under the guidance of an experienced researcher. In 1861 the first PhD was awarded in the USA and the degree was quickly transformed into requiring a programme of study leading to cutting-edge knowledge, understanding and skills in addition to appropriate training in the research skills relevant to the area of interest. Both had to be successfully completed before the student could proceed to the research project stage. In the UK the doctorate (although not initially called a PhD) was introduced in 1917 and was seen to be much more specialized within subject areas than the US model. The importance of this degree is highlighted in the following:

'over the last century the PhD has established itself as a qualification recognised internationally, as the standard qualification for entry into the research and academic professions, and as an important qualification for other labour markets' [Advisory Board of the Research Councils (ABRC) 1996]. There is little doubt that, for most people in most countries, the doctorate is the research degree of choice.

(Park 2005: 4)

In the UK the nature of what we know as the traditional PhD has changed over the years from being a research project which led to the submission of a thesis followed by an oral examination of the work, to a much more structured (and closely monitored) programme of activities including the need to acquire research training skills; thesis submission and oral examination have essentially remained the same.

Criticisms of doctoral education and the drivers for change

Since the 1980s, as governments around the world started to scrutinize their spending in some detail, it became apparent that doctorates would be put under the microscope like never before. It was during this time period that doctoral statistics attracted attention and revealed that surprisingly only about 50 per cent of doctoral candidates graduated with a doctorate and that of those who did complete the degree, few did so within the specified time (Taylor and Beasley 2005: 10). These findings further intensified questioning of the doctorate's fitness for purpose. Particular topics that were explored included:

• Whether the purpose of education was to further economic growth, and whether doctoral research topics should be relevant to the real world
• Whether a doctorate should be more interdisciplinary, to reflect the needs of society, where wide-ranging expertise is increasingly required
• Whether doctoral programmes were catering for an increasing number of doctoral students who were entering employment in professions other than academia.

More recently in the UK there have been several drivers for change, including a new emphasis on skills and training (which we discuss in detail in Chapter 6), submission rates and quality of supervision (discussed in Chapter 4), changes in the examination of the thesis and the introduction of national benchmarking (Park 2005). Of course, one of the principal changing contexts has been the revised Quality Assurance Agency (2004) Code of Practice for Postgraduate

Research Programmes, which forms the basis for this book. Another significant factor for change is the Bologna Process, including the idea of a European doctorate, which we discuss in some detail in Appendix 1.

In the UK, as described by Park (2007: 9), there are several key stakeholder groups who have different interests, expectations and agendas, and these groups should be widely consulted as the nature of the doctorate begins to change (Table 1.1). Indeed, the Higher Education Academy has now offered to sponsor a national debate, as there is widespread agreement that the time is right for it (Park 2007). This means that the above major stakeholder groups can come together and discuss the future of doctoral education in the UK.

Table 1.1 Key stakeholder groups

- Funding Councils for England (HEFCE), Wales (HEFCW), Scotland (Scottish Funding Council) and Northern Ireland (Department for Employment and Learning)
- Quality Assurance Agency (QAA)
- Research Councils UK (RCUK)
- National Postgraduate Committee (NPC)
- UK Council for Graduate Education (UKCGE)
- Universities UK (UUK) and Guild HE
- Vitae
- Higher Education Academy (HEA)
- Higher Education Institutions (HEIs)
- Employers

Source: Adapted from Park (2007: 9)

However, it is not only the UK where questions have been raised about the fitness for purpose of doctoral education. In one study (Powell and Green 2007), the views of 17 countries were summarized as follows:

- Although assumptions have been made, there is no clear understanding of the purpose of the doctorate.
- There seems to be a clear division in that some countries have a broad range of doctoral awards, in terms of both title and nature of the award (for example, in the UK: see Table 1.2), while others have retained the traditional PhD.
- There is an enormous potential in some countries, for example, China and India, in terms of providing students and training programmes.
- Funding is a central issue, whether there is direct involvement of the state, whether it is linked to the quality of the degree process or, in exceptional circumstances, where doctoral education is free to all students.
- Delivery of postgraduate education can be divided into those countries where the structure of higher education gives autonomy to institutions and those in which higher education is more strictly controlled and managed by the state.

- The majority of graduate programmes are associated with graduate schools in some shape or form.
- A number of countries have moved or are moving towards a national system of quality frameworks and auditing, such as in the UK with the QAA.

Table 1.2 Summary of the most common types of doctoral award in the UK

Award	Characteristics
Traditional PhD	Based largely on the supervised research project, examined on the basis of the thesis
PhD by publication	Based on the (sometimes supervised) research project but examined on the basis of peer-reviewed academic papers which have been published or accepted for publication, usually accompanied by an overarching paper that presents the overall introduction and conclusions
New Route PhD or PhD with Integrated Studies	Contains significant taught elements (which are examined and must be passed) and initially developed to provide international students with an integrated doctoral training scheme
Professional doctorate	Based on a combination of taught modules (which are examined and must be passed) and the supervised research project which is often smaller than the traditional PhD, is more applied and is work-based or focused
Practice-based doctorate	Based on a supervised research project, usually in the performing arts where the output involves both a written piece (which is usually much shorter than the traditional PhD thesis) and one or more other forms such as portfolio of work (for art and design) or one or more performance pieces (for theatre studies or music). Both forms of output are examined

Source: Adapted from Park (2007: 33)

It is clear, therefore, that global factors will have a major impact on how doctoral education develops in the future.

The response of the QAA to the changing nature of the doctorate

Since the late 1990s the QAA has produced a suite of interrelated documents that forms an overall code of practice for the assurance of academic quality and standards in higher education for the guidance of higher education institutions. Initially, the code was a response to the reports of the National Committee of Inquiry into Higher Education and its Scottish Committee (the

Dearing and Garrick Reports: National Committee of Inquiry into Higher Education 1997a, 1997b). Concerning postgraduate research degree programmes, the most recent edition (second) was published in 2004, following the first edition in 1999 (QAA 2004 and QAA 1999a respectively). Essentially the Code consists of a comprehensive series of system-wide principles (called 'precepts'), which the higher education community has identified, covering matters relating to the management of academic quality and standards in higher education. The aim is that individual institutions should be able to demonstrate that they are addressing matters covered by these precepts through their own management and organizational processes. The Code, which is a statement of good practice endorsed by the higher education community, therefore provides an authoritative reference point for institutions, as they try to assure and improve the academic quality and standards of their programmes, awards and qualifications.

Interestingly, the Code applies to a wide range of qualifications, including the PhD (incorporating the New Route PhD [see Chapter 10] and PhD awarded on the basis of published works), the DPhil, which is essentially a PhD under another name awarded at a small number of institutions, all forms of taught or professional doctorates, and research master's degrees, where the research component is larger than the taught component.

The second edition of the Code was developed by a working group that included representatives from academic institutions, UK funding councils, research councils and national organizations, such as the UK Council for Graduate Education, the Society for Research into Higher Education and the National Postgraduate Committee. The development of the Code incorporated considerable feedback from institutions, in addition to the findings of a number of national reports, such as the *SET for Success* report (Roberts 2002), the report on *Improving Standards in Postgraduate Research Degree Programmes* (Higher Education Funding Council for England [HEFCE] 2003) and 'Skills training requirements for research students' (published as Annexe A to HEFCE 2003), which have provided new information and guidelines in certain areas.

How the precepts have been interpreted in this book

The revised Code published by the QAA (see Appendix 3) consists of the precepts and a brief explanation of their context. However, although the explanations are useful they do not allow for detailed comments, nor do they provide examples to explain their practical applications and uses. We considered that these would be important in helping academics understand the applications of the precepts and establish how they relate to academic practice. So, rather than being entirely prescriptive, in the chapters that follow we aim to show the benefits and advantages of the precepts, in order to encourage best practice, while acknowledging that institutions have some (but not total) discretion in how they are applied. We say 'some discretion' in that in certain instances we are guided by the legal system which has to be adhered to.

We also note that because of their content, some chapters need to be procedural in tone and style, in contrast to others where we can be more discursive. Moreover, we ask readers to be flexible in their interpretation of titles of academic staff who hold key roles in postgraduate education and names of institutional, faculty, school and departmental committees, as the ones we use may differ from those used in other institutions. The same applies to the research training programmes and tables and figures from the Universities of Sheffield and Strathclyde that we have used as examples.

Students' views and precepts into practice

To be helpful to the reader, we provide two types of examples in each chapter which help explain topics within precepts. One example is of students' views, which include anonymized comments made by research students on particular themes and give their side to an issue. The other is the 'Precept into Practice' (PIP), which briefly describes a fictional issue (which is often based on fact) and is then followed by a suggested resolution to the problem.

Of course the PIPs as provided are only examples of a number of issues that might be related to any one precept; there will be others, but we cannot cover them all here. In addition, the issue and resolution provided are our views on a particular theme, which may be approached quite differently by other people. In other words, we do not pretend that our proposed issues and resolutions are the only interpretation of events and course of action.

More detailed case histories, as provided by John Wakeford in Appendix 2, can be very useful as training materials.

Why use the precepts in supervisor training and development?

Focusing on a set of precepts in this way is a novel approach to this topic. It prompts us to access a range of literature, include student and supervisor perspectives and open up key debates. More importantly, the precepts provide a framework for supervisors to pull together current literature and policy, with their personal values, beliefs and experiences, and to put it all under scrutiny. We know from experience of running seminars for academics on research supervision that these are all relevant: both knowledge and beliefs influence supervision practice.

This book provides the basis for the type of graduate-level discussion that occurs in accredited courses and modules on research supervision. To have value for academics across the disciplines, this discussion must be informed by research, and should include the relative merits of such research. It has to take into consideration current policy, and there has to be discussion of the specifics of practice and monitoring in implementing such policy. Above all, these discussions must provide an introduction to the field, so that academics across the disciplines can continue to access literature and other information after the course or module is finished. This is the first book to meet these needs.

Finally, there are three clear – though still debatable – reasons for using these precepts in this way:

- They have been endorsed by numerous bodies and authorities.
- They are comprehensible and accessible.
- They are easily aligned with both current research and common sense.

Talking points and key texts

Each chapter concludes with a list of 'Talking points'. These are issues that have proved contentious and/or are frequently contested in discussions among supervisors and others. They are intended to prompt in-depth consideration and discussion of some of the underlying tensions and complexities in research supervision. The final element of each chapter is one or two 'Key texts'. While the References section has a range of readings in higher education research and policy, these key texts are the ones that we think are the priority readings on each topic. They are the best starting point for new supervisors, and experienced supervisors might find recent publications on, for example, the doctoral examination, to be useful.

This book is not a blueprint for a new bureaucracy, but a framework for improving and maintaining standards. Individuals and institutions still have some discretion in how they define and manage supervision, and how the precepts work at both levels. A full list of precepts now follows, to allow readers to familiarize themselves with them.

List of precepts

1   Institutions will put in place effective arrangements to maintain appropriate academic standards and enhance the quality of postgraduate research programmes.
2   Institutional regulations for postgraduate research degree programmes will be clear and readily available to students and staff. Where appropriate, regulations will be supplemented by similarly accessible, subject-specific guidance at the level of the faculty, school or department.
3   Institutions will develop, implement and keep under review a code or codes of practice applicable across the institution, which include(s) the areas covered by this document. The code(s) should be readily available to all students and staff involved in postgraduate research programmes.
4   Institutions will monitor the success of their postgraduate research programmes against appropriate internal and/or external indicators and targets.
5   Institutions will only accept research students into an environment that provides support for doing and learning about research and where high quality research is occurring.
6   Admissions procedures will be clear, consistently applied and will demonstrate equality of opportunity.
7   Only appropriately qualified and prepared students will be admitted to research programmes.
8   Admissions decisions will involve at least two members of the institution's staff who will have received instruction, advice and guidance in respect of selection and admissions procedures. The decision-making process will enable the institution to assure itself that balanced and independent admissions decisions have been made, that support its admissions policy.
9   The entitlements and responsibilities of a research student undertaking a postgraduate research programme will be defined and communicated clearly.
10   Institutions will provide research students with sufficient information to enable them to begin their studies with an understanding of the academic and social environment in which they will be working.
11   Institutions will appoint supervisors who have the appropriate skills and subject knowledge to support, encourage and monitor research students effectively.
12   Each research student will have a minimum of one main supervisor. He or she will normally be part of a supervisory team. There must always be one clearly identified point of contact for the student.

13 Institutions will ensure that the responsibilities of all research student supervisors are clearly communicated to supervisors and students through written guidance.

14 Institutions will ensure that the quality of supervision is not put at risk as a result of an excessive volume and range of responsibilities assigned to individual supervisors.

15 Institutions will put in place and bring to the attention of students and relevant staff clearly defined mechanisms for monitoring and supporting student progress.

16 Institutions will put in place and bring to the attention of students and relevant staff clearly defined mechanisms for formal reviews of student progress, including explicit review stages.

17 Institutions will provide guidance to students, supervisors and others involved in progress monitoring and review processes about the importance of keeping appropriate records of the outcomes of meetings and related activities.

18 Institutions will provide research students with appropriate opportunities for personal and professional development.

19 Each student's development needs will be identified and agreed jointly by the student and appropriate academic staff, initially during the student's induction period; they will be regularly reviewed during the research programme and amended as appropriate.

20 Institutions will provide opportunities for research students to maintain a record of personal progress, which includes reference to the development of research and other skills.

21 Institutions will put in place mechanisms to collect, review and, where appropriate, respond to feedback from all concerned with postgraduate research programmes. They will make arrangements for feedback to be considered openly and constructively and for the results to be communicated appropriately.

22 Institutions will use criteria for assessing research degrees that enable them to define the academic standards of different research programmes and the achievements of their graduates. The criteria used to assess research degrees must be clear and readily available to students, staff and external examiners.

23 Research degree assessment procedures must be clear; they must be operated rigorously, fairly and consistently; include input from an external examiner; and carried out to a reasonable timescale.

24 Institutions will communicate their assessment procedures clearly to all parties involved, i.e. the students, the supervisor(s) and the examiners.

25 Institutions will put in place and publicise procedures for dealing with student representations that are fair, clear to all concerned, robust and applied consistently. Such procedures will allow all students access to relevant information and an opportunity to present their case.

26 Independent and formal procedures will exist to resolve effectively

complaints from research students about the quality of the institution's learning and support provision.

27 Institutions will put in place formal procedures to deal with any appeals made by research students. The acceptable grounds for appeals will be clearly defined.

2

Institutional environment

Academic standards and quality • Regulations • Code of Practice • Monitoring success • The research environment • Conclusion • Talking points • Key text

In the light of national developments, institutions have had to be active to ensure the quality of postgraduate research degrees and to promote quality enhancements. Such arrangements have included procedures for programme approval, annual and periodic evaluation of research degree programmes, student representation and feedback and 'thematic' reviews of specific areas of activity.

Institutions have also played a key role in supporting national developments, such as the Threshold Standards initiative (HEFCE 2003) and the introduction of the updated Code of Practice, contributing to consultations and taking part in the consideration of early drafts and discussions via the QAA's national corresponding group and follow-up meetings.

An institution's research environment will be determined by many factors. However, its mission is likely to include the maintenance of the highest standards of research excellence and education of students in a research environment. Successful implementation of this mission will be reflected in both QAA Subject Reviews and HEFCE Research Assessment Exercises (now replaced by Research Excellence Framework Monitoring).

In this chapter we will discuss how the institutional environment, in its broadest sense, can have a significant impact on the quality of research degree programmes.

Academic standards and quality

Precept 1
Institutions will put in place effective arrangements to maintain appropriate academic standards and enhance the quality of post-graduate research programmes.

Programme approval

The academic approval process for research programmes can vary between institutions but is often via the relevant faculty or faculties (for joint pro-grammes), the university research committee or equivalent and, finally, the Senate. Where there is a significant taught component, such as in the PhD with Integrated Studies or professional doctorate, the approval process may additionally involve consideration by the appropriate learning and teaching committees. In some instances, where institutions share in the teaching and award of degrees, the approval process needs to be made at both contributing institutions.

There may also be a formal annual approval process for taught units that are offered as part of the university's Research Training Programme (RTP), based on consideration of the proposal forms for the relevant units by faculty deans for postgraduate affairs or equivalents.

Annual student evaluation of research degrees

Many institutions require all departments to undertake regular evaluation of the experience of their research students and provide an annual report on the outcomes of this evaluation, which is discussed in more detail in Chapter 7. An abbreviated sample questionnaire (for full-time research students) is seen in Table 2.1, which covers such core areas as research supervision, research training and support facilities.

Of course, alternative arrangements for gathering student feedback, such as focus groups, are also encouraged where appropriate. However, it has to be remembered that information gained through focus groups could be different from that acquired through anonymous questionnaires. Therefore, the data gained should be interpreted with caution, depending on whether compar-isons are to be made. Focus groups have the potential advantage of revealing information at a deeper level than questionnaires, but they are more labour intensive and because of that, usually include smaller numbers of students.

When questionnaires have been reviewed, departments should receive a relevant summary report, which is considered by the relevant faculty research committee, before being sent to the university research committee and finally Senate. To the latter are sent appropriate recommendations and examples

Table 2.1 Annual student evaluation of research degrees (full-time research students)

Section A – Information about you
What year of your research studies are you in?   1st ☐   2nd ☐   3rd ☐   4th ☐   5th ☐

Section B – Research Supervision
How frequently do you have a formal progress report with your supervisor(s)?

	Every 4–6 weeks	☐
	More often	☐
	Less often	☐
Is the number of meetings:	Too many	☐
	About right	☐
	Too few	☐

Section C – Research Training Programme (RTP)
What year of your research degree are you currently in?   1st or 2nd year ☐
                                                              3rd year+ ☐

Please complete the following questions giving your current view of the RTP
How satisfied are you with the units you have taken as part of the RTP in the following areas?

Choice of units?

	Very satisfied			*Very unsatisfied*	
Departmental	5 ☐	4 ☐	3 ☐	2 ☐	1 ☐
University/Subject-area wide	5 ☐	4 ☐	3 ☐	2 ☐	1 ☐

Quality of delivery

	Very satisfied			*Very unsatisfied*	
Departmental	5 ☐	4 ☐	3 ☐	2 ☐	1 ☐
University/Subject-area wide	5 ☐	4 ☐	3 ☐	2 ☐	1 ☐

Section D – Library, IT and other Research Facilities

Library
How satisfied are you overall with the University Library opening hours?

	Very satisfied			*Very unsatisfied*		*Do not use*
During Semester	5 ☐	4 ☐	3 ☐	2 ☐	1 ☐	☐
During Vacation	5 ☐	4 ☐	3 ☐	2 ☐	1 ☐	☐

Source: University of Sheffield

of good practice. These will then be incorporated in the following year's University Guide for Research Students and Supervisors, which in some institutions may now be called the University's Code of Practice for Research Students and Supervisors. The Code of Practice for student evaluation, sample questionnaire and report pro forma for the following year are also updated to take account of feedback on the evaluation process itself.

Despite different attempts to achieve a satisfactory response from students via questionnaires, typical participation rates of between 20 and 40 per cent can be quite disappointing and could obviously bias feedback. This should also therefore be taken into account. Feedback mechanisms are discussed in detail in Chapter 7.

Independent reviews of research supervision and support

Some institutions develop their own internal review processes to identify strengths in provision and areas for improvement. A flowchart outlining the different stages of an independent review process can be seen in Figure 2.1. Typically, a review undertaken by a panel of assessors may take place over a two-day period, including, for example, the type of agenda found in Table 2.2.

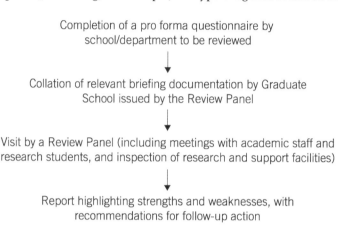

Figure 2.1 Flowchart of independent review stages.

Source: University of Sheffield

Table 2.2 Independent review of research supervision and support

Agenda
Day one
1.00 pm   Lunch
Visits to research support facilities
Review Panel considering pro forma questionnaires and finalizing main areas of questioning
Day two
8.45 am   Private session (Review Panel only)
9.15 am   Meeting with members of the relevant Faculty/School committees (research student strategy)
10.45 am   Private session (Review Panel only)
11.30 am   Meeting with research supervisors
1.00 pm   Lunchtime meeting with PGR students
2.30 pm   Private session (Review Panel only)
Close

Source: University of Sheffield

The review panel would normally consist of members of the university's academic staff plus an external academic nominated by the faculty or school under review. Once a report had been completed, it is usually first considered by the faculty panel's research committee who then draw up an action plan in response to the recommendations. These are then discussed by the university research committee, which considers any university-wide issues raised during the review and monitors action taken by the faculty.

Advantages of regular independent reviews are that they raise awareness among staff of the demands placed upon them, and in theory the quality of research degree programmes should improve over time. Disadvantages are that a review, if comprehensive, can be demanding on resources and, since in higher education as a whole there is increasing auditing in many areas, there is a real possibility that life becomes one round after another of reviews, with a real chance of producing review burnout.

Student representation and feedback

Feedback from students on the quality of their research study experience is an important part of quality assurance arrangements for research degree programmes. In addition to their involvement in the processes described above, research students may contribute to the workings of both the faculty and university research committees. The Students' Union's role in coordinating and supporting research student representation across the university may be channelled through its postgraduate committee or equivalent. In addition, the Students' Union's education officer (or equivalent title for this role) may also attend the university's research committee and play an important part in representing the interests and views of research students. Opportunities for student representation on faculty committees can be promoted at the annual induction meeting for new research students.

Thematic reviews of skills training provision such as the Research Training Programme

The RTP should be reviewed on a frequent basis, typically every few years. Such a review might consider changes to the RTP credits required by students in some institutions, before being awarded a PhD, which could be a consequence of the national developments brought about by the Roberts Skills Training agenda. An RTP review should consult staff and students on the programme, via questionnaires and focus groups.

Reviews have revealed a lack of engagement by some supervisors with the RTP, which has been widely observed across many institutions (Hinchcliffe et al. 2007: 3), and there is an element of student dissatisfaction with certain aspects of the programme, such as its relevance to their specific area of research. Part of the solution to these problems may relate to the need to communicate effectively to students and supervisors the potential benefits of the RTP, which for students can be addressed in part by discussing these issues at an annual induction meeting. Moreover, supervisors should receive greater encouragement to review the skills development needs of their students, and institutions should consider this a priority area. Finally, students have to realize that there needs to be a balance between time spent away from research, such as in RTPs, and time spent directly on research, particularly in the first year of study, if completion rates are not be adversely affected.

Quality enhancement

Of particular importance is the creation of a graduate school or graduate research centre, which acts as a focus for consideration of postgraduate research issues and quality enhancement. It is also a dedicated central resource for research students and should include a workshop or seminar room, study space (including some computing facilities), a library of general study, and other relevant materials and social space. Such a centre could facilitate the improvement of links between graduate schools and research students and provide a central venue for research training sessions, plus workshops on relevant topics such as career management and thesis preparation.

One simple but effective mechanism for ensuring greater consistency in the initial stages of a research degree programme is the use of an induction checklist for research supervisors (Table 2.3), created to help supervisors remember and keep track of the increasing number of activities that need to be addressed. Other institutional publications for both postgraduate research students and their supervisors allow for updating of relevant matters.

Table 2.3 Induction checklist for research supervisors

First supervisor	✓
• Name and contact details	☐
• Date of first supervisory meeting and frequency of further meetings during first six months of research	☐
• Responsibilities of the student relating to supervisory meetings	☐
• Copies and explanations of forms/records to be completed	☐
• Set target dates for update and submission	☐
Supervisory team (other contacts)	✓
• Name and contact details of members of supervisory team	☐
• Date of first meeting and explanation of how the supervisory team will work with the student	☐
• Name and contact details of Postgraduate Tutor (or equivalent) and outline of their role	☐
• Name and contact details for Head of Department	☐
Publications	✓
• *Code of Practice for Research Degree Programmes* incorporating *The RTP Handbook*	☐
• Any departmental literature	☐
• Health and Safety Code of Practice (either printed format or from the web)	☐

Registration and events ✓
- University Registration ☐
- Information session for New Research Students ☐
- RTP registration ☐
- University's Health Service ☐
- Registration for computer passwords/e-mail account etc. ☐
- Compulsory session on copyright and avoidance of unfair means in thesis ☐

Departmental and University resources ✓
- Explanation of what the Department expects from the student ☐
- Opportunity for student to discuss any expectations they may have ☐
- Introduction to Staff/Student Committees and the chance to be a representative on Central University Committees, e.g. Faculty Boards ☐
- Procedures for 'Application to Read' ☐
- Procedures for upgrading (if appropriate) ☐
- Departmental workspace and equipment ☐
- Departmental and University library facilities ☐
- Departmental and University computing facilities ☐
- Departmental safety procedures ☐
- Graduate Research Centre ☐
- The Union of Students including Student Advice Centre and catering facilities ☐
- International Student Services provided by Student Support and Guidance, Department of Student Services ☐
- Introduction to the English Language Teaching Centre (which offers free Writing advisory service to both home and international students) and the Modern Languages Teaching Centre ☐
- Details of other University Welfare Departments, e.g. Counselling Services, Careers Services, Housing Services ☐

Social and networking opportunities ✓
- Details of mentoring scheme, if available ☐
- Details of opportunities for new students to meet other research students and staff ☐
- Details of opportunities that exist for students to share experience and understanding beyond their own study area ☐
- Information on PROGRESS, the Postgraduate Student Society ☐

Source: University of Sheffield

Precept into Practice – 1

Issue

Tony was a part-time research student with a major difficulty. His work and family commitments meant that he had very little free time to visit the university library, apart from late evenings and at weekends. Unfortunately, resource implications had resulted in the library opening hours being cut during the periods when Tony was free. He had mentioned this dilemma a great deal to his supervisory team, and although they were sympathetic, they did not appear to be able to do much about the situation.

Resolution

Tony realized that to stand any chance of encouraging the library to restore later opening hours, including evenings and at weekends, he would need the support of other students, especially those who were influential. So he approached the Union of Students, which had also received similar complaints from other students. The Union of Students thought that questions needed to be raised at a number of key university committees, including those relating to both the library and graduate research. They also felt that the matter was important enough to be included in the annual research student questionnaire, which was circulated to all research students, and in focus group discussions of research students from all faculties. With all the student feedback obtained, and with an institutional audit on the horizon, the Union of Students' representation on key committees made the views of the majority of research students known and convinced the university that library resources and normal opening times should be restored.

Regulations

Precept 2
Institutional regulations for postgraduate research degree programmes will be clear and readily available to students and staff. Where appropriate, regulations will be supplemented by similarly accessible, subject-specific guidance at the level of the faculty, school or department.

Regulations are in place covering all research degree programmes. They are published annually in the university calendar or equivalent, which should be available in the university library and on the university website. The calendar contains a mixture of general and programme regulations.

Regulations are reviewed on an annual basis, with input invited from all staff. Suggested new or amended regulations are considered first at faculty research committee, then the university research committee, followed by Senate. Students are referred to the regulations in documents such as the university's Code of Practice for Research Students and Supervisors, and the Research Training Programme Handbook.

Regulations include coverage of such matters as admission requirements, academic and procedural requirements for particular research degrees, progression requirements and time limits (Table 2.4), assessment methods and degree criteria and procedures relating to discipline and academic complaints and appeals.

Table 2.4 Periods of registration and time limits for research degree programmes

| Degree | Candidate | Time limit | | |
		Minimum	Normal	Maximum
PhD	Full time	2 years	3 years	4 years
PhD with Integrated Studies	Full time	4 years	4 years	5 years
PhD	Part time	4 years	6 years	8 years
PhD	University staff	2 years	2 years	8 years
MPhil	Full time	1 year	2 years	3 years
MPhil	Part time	2 years	3 years	6 years
MPhil	University staff	1 year	1 year	6 years
EdD	Part time	4 years	6 years	8 years
LLM	Full time	1 year	1 year	4 years
LLM	Part time	2 hears	2 years	6 years
DMedSci	Full time	3 years	3 years	4 years
DMedSci	Part time	4 years	6 years	8 years
DMedSci	University staff	4 years	4 years	8 years
MD/DDSc	Full time	2 years	3 years	4 years
MD/DDSc	Part time	4 years	6 years	8 years
MD/DDSc	University staff	2 years	2 years	8 years
MMus	Full time	9 months	1 year	3 years
MMus	Part time	2 years	2 years	6 years

Source: University of Sheffield

Precept into Practice – 2

Issue

Hilary was a successful student, now in the third year of her PhD, when she was given the opportunity of working as a government researcher. This was a great accolade, but she was a full-time student who had not yet completed her PhD, so she discussed her predicament with her supervisory team, who expressed some concerns about trying to balance the demands of a job with study for a PhD. However, they considered that a possible solution might be to transfer to part-time registration to enable her to take up the new position and to give her more time to complete her PhD. Unfortunately, no one had thought to question her financial situation, as she was currently in receipt of a scholarship that was restricted to full-time study. So, if she changed her registration status, what impact might this have on Hilary's finances, and would she have to give some money back to her sponsors?

Resolution

Typically, time limits for research degrees are specified in the letters from institutions confirming the offer of a place and are reiterated from time to time in formal correspondence relating to a student's academic progress. Details of time limits are also made generally available in booklets and/or on the institutional web pages. This of course is very basic information, and a myriad of circumstances may arise that could potentially affect a student's registration, as shown by one example above. Unfortunately, a registration change can have a knock-on effect on finances and time limits and it is important for institutions to have more detailed information made widely available and not just restricted to one or two university personnel. This would allow students and staff more independence in decision-making and could reduce the likelihood of students getting themselves into further difficulties.

Code of Practice

Precept 3
Institutions will develop, implement and keep under review a code or codes of practice applicable across the institution, which include(s) the areas covered by this document. The code(s) should be readily available to all students and staff involved in postgraduate research programmes.

In many institutions a Code of Practice for Research Degree Programmes will have replaced any previously existing guidance issued to research students and supervisors. These developments will have been the result of consultations and many local meetings to discuss the content and introduction of an institutional Code of Practice, any gaps in procedures, and how they might be addressed. One of the areas that has required more work has been the development of a personal and professional development plan (PPDP) for research students.

Personal and professional development plan

Following the QAA (2001) *Guidelines for Higher Education Progress Files*, the implementation of personal development planning applies to all higher education institutions, and a system needs to be available to all new students. In addition, the QAA's revised Code of Practice for Postgraduate Research Programmes (QAA 2004) now requires that research students be provided with opportunities to maintain a record of personal progress that includes reference to the development of research and other skills (see Chapter 6).

In its review of emerging practice in 2004, UK GRAD (now called Vitae), in association with the National Postgraduate Committee, explored the rationales for current personal development planning (postgraduate) practices in UK universities (National Postgraduate Committee 2005b). These fell into three categories:

- *Developmental*: a focus on student reflection and review, skills development, supporting continuing professional development.
- *Institutional*: the need to comply with policy requirements, a framework for checking progress or storing records.
- *Aspirational*: the desire to provide distinctive provision, to develop a community of practice within and 'beyond the PhD', to promote cultural change.

The idea of cataloguing key learning experiences and reflecting upon them, a vital element in the academic and personal development of researchers, forms the basis of any PPDP. Currently the PPDP is designed to be owned by the individual researcher (student), who will be responsible for completing any documentation.

Precept into Practice – 3

Issue

The institution was proud of its new Joint PhD programme, which it had just launched with an overseas university, and was confident that after much hard preparatory work, all would go well at the start. The Joint programme meant that a student's supervisory team would be split between the two institutions. Unfortunately, through a lack of foresight and a computer server problem, it was not possible for the academic staff at the overseas institution to access the electronic version of the awarding institution's Code of Practice for Research Students and Supervisors. No wonder the overseas academic staff had not fully prepared their students for their first written assignment, which resulted in a few red faces all round.

Resolution

Joint programmes like the one described are becoming more common, as numbers of traditional (fully sponsored) overseas students are on the decline in many institutions, and it is imperative that the overseas academic staff have access to similar high-quality facilities as a prerequisite of any Joint PhD programme. This means that there is an expectation of high-quality electronic services. The awarding institution should have gone through all the procedures necessary for the course to begin properly, before the programme was launched, including access to an electronic version of the Code of Practice or, failing that, hard copies of the Code.

Monitoring success

Precept 4
Institutions will monitor the success of their postgraduate research programmes against appropriate internal and/or external indicators and targets.

All institutions, especially those in receipt of Research Council funding, will want to achieve the submission rates set by those bodies. For example, all full-time doctoral students are expected to submit their thesis within four years. However, the same institutions also need to take into account the needs and expectations of self-funded students who might legitimately wish to study over an extended period.

In an institution, thesis submission rates should be considered at least once a year, first by the relevant faculty, then by the university research committee, before being reported to the Senate. Where departments have poor submission rates, they may be reminded about meeting submission deadlines and advised on how submission rates might be improved. Such a strategy includes careful consideration of any requests for extensions to time limits for the submission of a thesis beyond four years after the start of the doctoral programme.

Completion rates or rates of qualification should also be monitored, taking as completion the date the degree was officially awarded.

Institutions also need to monitor the number and nature of academic complaints and appeals they receive each year from postgraduate research students, as well as cases of plagiarism and fabrication. This information should be considered by the university research committee on an annual basis, with any issues for concern brought to the attention of the relevant faculty officer, such as a dean.

Finally, all examiners' reports should be read by the faculty officer. The report form should provide examiners with the opportunity to comment on issues other than the quality of the thesis and the viva performance, such as, for example, the quality of supervision received by the candidate. Where a specific comment or concern is raised, the matter should be initially dealt with by the faculty officer, who may then decide whether or not to act upon it.

Precept into Practice – 4

Issue

Professor Snook was the Faculty of Science's representative on the university's research committee. The professor was concerned because the faculty's PhD submission rates had decreased again, for the third year in succession. The chair of the research committee would certainly not be pleased as at this rate, research funding for the faculty would be affected, potentially damaging its overall research activities.

Resolution

Ultimate responsibility for submission of a thesis lies with the student. However, the consequences of poor submission rates, including a loss in research and other funding, are too important for an institution to neglect. One possible solution would be to impose financial penalties on students who submit late and/or penalize respective supervisors by denying them rights to apply for certain types of funding, which the university has to approve. Alternatively, financial incentives might be offered to students who submit on time. It might also be relevant to investigate the submission figures, by breaking them down according to department and/or supervisor to see if particular departments and/or individuals should be targeted for improvements.

The research environment

Before looking at Precept 5, let us remind ourselves of the definition of research provided by the funding councils:

> Research for the purpose of the RAE (and presumably similar to that of its replacement, Research Excellence Framework Monitoring) is to be understood as original investigation undertaken in order to gain knowledge and understanding. It includes work of direct relevance to the needs of commerce and industry, as well as to the public and voluntary sectors; scholarship; the invention and generation of ideas, images, performances and artefacts including design, where these lead to new or substantially improved insights; and the use of existing knowledge in experimental development to produce new or substantially improved materials, devices, products and processes, including design and construction. It excludes routine testing and analysis of materials, components and processes, e.g. for the maintenance of national standards, as distinct from the development of new analytical techniques. It also excludes the development of teaching materials that do not embody original research.
>
> (HEFCE et al. 1998: 40)

Precept 5
Institutions will only accept research students into an environment that provides support for doing and learning about research and where high quality research is occurring.

An institution's mission will be to achieve and maintain the highest standards of excellence in research which will be reflected primarily in HEFCE Research Assessment Exercises (now called Research Excellence Framework Monitoring).

As well as research students making an important contribution to the university's culture via departmental seminars, attending conferences is also seen as a valid experience for research students, and the institution should provide resources for such visits. In at least one institution a new concept to have developed from the Roberts (2002) Skills initiative is that of an Excellence Exchange Scheme. This offers funding to enable research students to undertake research visits to known centres of excellence in order to develop and enhance their knowledge or skills.

Often an important topic of debate in institutions is reaching agreement as to what constitutes basic research facilities for every student. For example, should all students have their own desks or office spaces? As there are not unlimited resources, this debate will no doubt run on. However, what should be made available to students is written information from departments on facilities, for example, office space, equipment, computers, so that students know what should be provided. Perhaps, not surprisingly, examples of what constitutes an appropriate research environment in this regard, as quoted by the QAA, are not specific.

Finally, at the heart of the university's research culture is its training of research students, both in subject-specific and generic skills training (see Chapter 6). The Research Training Programme can be a suite of short courses, consisting of taught units or modules, which have been selected as being useful to students undertaking research degrees. Some units can be from approved taught master's degree programmes, while others will have been specifically designed for research students. The aim of the RTP is to provide research students with the skills and experiences necessary to enable them to undertake successfully a sustained period of research. Every unit taken as part of the RTP will provide the skills associated with one or more of the following objectives:

- Development of generic skills that contribute to the understanding of research methods, techniques and the context in which research takes place
- Development of generic skills that contribute to the personal and professional development of a research student
- Broadening or deepening of subject knowledge.

It is the intention that the RTP should be seen as integral to a research student's programme of study. Students are encouraged to view the RTP as a process of continuous training and development and are advised to select elements of training following a training needs analysis (see Chapter 3) with their supervisor(s).

Precept into Practice – 5

Issue

Jill was delighted to be studying at a top class university, but unfortunately her first choice of supervisor was too busy to accept her and instead the more junior Dr Jones offered to be her supervisor. Dr Jones was starting to work in a newly developing field of research involving human tissue. However, Dr Jones had no experience of this type of research, and after a few months' work on her project, Jill was told by the departmental safety officer that her research work would have to stop immediately, as the appropriate ethics approval had not been given.

Resolution

Unfortunately, the topics of human ethics and research governance have become more complicated since the early 2000s, and even the better quality universities can get caught out. As a general precaution against a number of issues that can subsequently become problematic for students, some universities are reviewing all postgraduate research student projects (unless they are externally funded and hence have already been through a peer review process). If any issues are raised in the review, they must be resolved before an offer can be made to a student. In addition, all supervisors should be aware of the need for seeking ethical permission on a whole range of activities that previously did not require such permission. It was no defence that Dr Jones was inexperienced in this new research topic.

Conclusion

It is important that research degree programmes undergo a comprehensive approval process within the institution in order to maintain academic quality. At the same time, institutional independent reviews of research supervision and support, together with student evaluation of research degree programmes and feedback on a regular basis, aim to ensure the maintenance of academic standards and to address any issues as and when they arise. An awareness of research degree submission rates can serve as a useful indicator of research degree programme performance, and these rates therefore need to be taken seriously.

Research Training Programmes and related skills training following the Roberts (2002) report, *SET for Success,* need to be frequently updated and reviewed to ensure their relevance in a rapidly changing work environment. It should be emphasized that at the heart of the university's research culture is its training of research students in both subject-specific and generic skills, which is exemplified by the Research Training Programme and is discussed in detail in Chapter 6.

Since the late 1990s, there has been an increase in the development of graduate schools or their equivalent to provide essential resources for research students. Such a resource should be a local version of the Code of Practice, which needs to be made available to all staff and students. Also, regulations for research degree programmes should be frequently updated and made available to everyone involved.

Talking points

- Feedback from students via annual student evaluations needs to be seriously considered and acted upon, if necessary, or its relevance will diminish.
- Efforts still need to be made regarding the relevance of RTPs, in light of some academic opposition.
- Realistically, how much research can be expected from a first-year PhD student with demands on time from RTPs, the Transfer process and PPDPs? What is the impact of these demands on completion rates?
- Can we over-review our research degree programmes?
- How can we improve departmental submission rates?
- If there have been several complaints from students about the quality of an academic's supervision, at what stage can he/she be prevented from supervising a new student?
- With increasing demands for ethical permission on a wide range of research topics, could they negatively affect the nature of the research conducted?

Key text

Higher Education Funding Council for England (HEFCE) (2003) *Improving Standards in Postgraduate Research Degree Programmes: Formal Consultation.* (www.hefce.ac.uk/pubs/hefce/2003/03_23htm).

3

Selection and admission of students

The need for a legal framework • Special needs • Appropriate qualifications • Admissions decisions • Entitlements and responsibilities • Induction • Conclusion • Talking points • Key text

The need for a legal framework

Institutions are under increasing pressure to admit more students onto degree courses. For postgraduate research degree programmes, this relates especially to accepting more overseas or international students, who are considered a valuable source of funding. However, for there to be a fair process in which only the most appropriate research students are admitted, guidelines have to be in place for their selection. It is particularly important that these guidelines are developed with reference to the relevant legislation.

Once students are accepted onto research degree programmes, it is equally important that they receive all materials and documentation necessary for the admissions process, as well as invitations to induction sessions organized at institutional level and by departments or faculties as appropriate. In 2006 concerns were raised about the accuracy of university documentation in prospectuses (Higher Education Policy Institute [HEPI] 2006). The Fraud Act 2007 includes the possibility for making misrepresentation both orally or written of, for example, information relating to university admissions that can be classified as fraud; this is a criminal offence.

Since the early 2000s, there have been increasing demands placed on postgraduate research students, and knowledge and an awareness of all matters related to admissions are fundamental to their progress in the early stages of their research programme and beyond. In this chapter we will give an update on factors relevant to the procedures of selection and admission of research students onto research degree programmes.

Special needs

Precept 6
Admissions procedures will be clear, consistently applied and will demonstrate equality of opportunity.

To promote equal opportunities, UK legislation outlaws discrimination on the basis of age, disability, sex, sexual orientation, race or religion. Since the introduction of the Special Educational Needs and Disability Act 2001, institutions need to make reasonable adjustments and provide appropriate support for students with a disability. Although the disability discrimination legislation is still considered to be less than perfect (Farrington and Palfreyman 2006: 483), institutions have a responsibility to promote equal opportunities, with respect to disability, and need to publish a Disability Equality Scheme to be implemented by the end of 2009. However, the duty to design and modify buildings so as to accommodate people with disabilities has been around since the Chronically Sick and Disabled Persons Act 1970:

> Any person undertaking the provision of a building shall, in the means of access both to and within the building, and in the parking facilities and sanitary conveniences, make provision, in so far as it is in the circumstances both practicable and reasonable, for the needs of persons using the building who are disabled.

In 1999 the QAA produced the *Code of Practice for Assurance of Academic Quality and Standards in Higher Education: Students with Disabilities* (QAA 1999b) and this makes good practical recommendations to institutions on improving their provision for students with disabilities. In this context, disability refers to any physical or sensory impairment, mental and medical health conditions or specific learning difficulty, such as dyslexia, that necessitate the provision of additional support during a course of study. Interestingly, the Disability Discrimination Act 2005 states that people who have certain types of cancer or HIV infection shall be deemed to have a disability, regardless of symptoms.

After an application form had been completed by a student and received in the Admissions Office, any disability is highlighted, such that it will be identifiable by the receiving admissions tutor or selector. It has to be stressed that applicants are judged primarily on their academic suitability, and that considerations relating to additional support requirements should remain separate. Potential applicants with additional support requirements, such as wheelchair users or those with a mobility impairment, are advised to visit the institution before making a formal application, thus giving both parties time to consider the feasibility of any requests. The purpose of making such an information visit is:

- To allow the applicant to assess their chosen research project, additional support, the facilities and surroundings and to make informed decisions as to whether an application can and should be made
- To allow the institution to assess any additional facilities that will be required for the applicant's disability
- To facilitate any advance planning to cater for the applicant's additional support requirements
- To identify any circumstances where the adjustments that would be needed in order to admit the student are not practicable
- To discuss sources and availability of funding with the applicant.

During such a visit relevant matters for discussion may include:

- Possible physical adaptations to be made to buildings
- Fire evacuation and other safety issues
- Study strategies the applicant has previously found useful
- Personal support requirements, such as specialist equipment
- Access to information, physical access and work placements
- Assessment and examination methods
- The institution's and the applicant's responsibilities.

Once the admissions tutor has made a final decision, taking all the above into account, if the decision is negative, it is advisable that the Admissions Office write to the student, explaining why he or she will not be offered a place. If a student with a disability is offered a place to study, he or she may be eligible to receive a Disabled Student's Allowance from their local funding body, such as a local education authority. This allowance is intended to pay for additional support required for study. However, this type of funding is not guaranteed, and international students are not eligible. It is, therefore, a good idea to discuss a student's funding requirements with specialized units, such as within the institution.

Precept into Practice – 6

Issue

John had recently been awarded a first-class honours degree in electronic engineering and was keen to do a PhD for his career development. John did not suggest a specific PhD supervisor in his application, as he was unsure whether this would limit his opportunities. Nevertheless, the application form was completed correctly and included the fact that he was a wheelchair user and was therefore classed as disabled. When Dr Stringer, the admissions selector, received John's application, he was impressed with John's academic credentials, but became very negative when he realized John was a wheelchair user, as the Department of Electronic Engineering was on the top floor of a high-rise building. Correctly, Dr Stringer was concerned about John's safety should a fire break out in the building. With these important concerns in mind, Dr Stringer rejected John's application. John was disappointed, confused and could not understand why his application had been rejected, as no reasons had been given to him.

Resolution

Although Dr Stringer was rightly concerned about John being a wheelchair user and his ability to escape from the top floor of a high-rise building in a fire, it was a pity that he did not discuss the matter with academic colleagues (and explain in writing why John's application was rejected) to see if there were possible solutions to this problem. Dr Stringer should also have contacted the disability support services, who would have been able to advise him on how best to deal with applications from students with mobility difficulties. It so happened that one of Dr Stringer's colleagues was interested in a collaborative research programme with the Department of Computer Studies, which was based on the ground floor of the same high-rise building. Giving John the opportunity to consider working on such a collaborative project might have led to a resolution of this issue.

Appropriate qualifications

Precept 7
Only appropriately qualified and prepared students will be admitted to research programmes.

The normal requirement for a student to be registered for doctoral study is that they already possess an honours degree at the 2.1 level or above. However, in the current climate, and unlike the situation in the 1980s, the majority of students who graduate now achieve a 2.1 degree. Does this mean that all these students are appropriately qualified for doctoral study? Phillips and Pugh (2005) make the point that we do not really know how best to select students who wish to pursue research, and they question whether judging a student's performance in undergraduate examinations, which are often based on memory, is better than skills based largely on curiosity and exploration. Clearly, this debate will continue.

In the first year of study the student would normally be registered for an MPhil degree or provisionally registered for a PhD, and that a change to registration for a doctorate would happen only following a successful transfer process, also known as 'upgrade'. Of course, if students already possess an MPhil or MRes degree, they would usually register directly for a doctorate. In some cases, a taught master's degree could be considered suitable for direct registration for a doctorate.

In the sciences one of the criteria that has been used to judge research potential is the student's performance in a laboratory-based research project. Although these projects, which are typically undertaken as part of the final year of an undergraduate degree programme, can be rather short, they can give an indication to the supervisor whether a student has an aptitude for research or not. In other fields, prospective supervisors have developed other ways of trying to judge a student's research potential, which may well include a personal interview, where problem-solving or related analytical tasks might be beneficial.

In addition, as an important aid to judging an applicant's command of English, a written test may be useful, where the student is asked to summarize a research report in the presence of an academic member of staff. For students whose first language is not English, there will usually be the additional requirement to demonstrate English language competence across all four language skills – listening, reading, writing and speaking – by reference to an International English Language Testing System (IELTS) or Test of English as a Foreign Language (TOEFL) score. There are different levels of scores, with a suggested minimum of IELTS 6, which equates to a TOEFL score of 550. A middle range score would be an IELTS of 6.5, which is equivalent to TOEFL 575. A high score would be IELTS 7, equating to a TOEFL score of 600. At the same time, institutions might also require a specific total score, but with minimum scores of, for example, IELTS 6 in different components, such as writing or reading. Others might only specify minimum scores in an individual component, such as IELTS 4.5 in written English. The TOEFL test is probably the most common worldwide and has developed from a paper-based test into computer-based and now Internet-based tests. Clearly, this provides flexibility for students who may not have good access to paper-based testing centres. However, total scores for each type of test are very different, and it is important to know how the more recent testing formats compare with the paper-based test (Table 3.1). It is also worth remembering that the three testing formats are not comparable, as they measure different components. For example, the paper-based total score does not include an assessment of writing.

Table 3.1 TOEFL score comparison

Internet-based total	Computer-based total	Paper-based total
78–80	213	550
90–91	233	577
100	250	600–603

It needs to be stressed that often the suggested competency levels are the minimum requirement and that on admission, further English language training, often in specialized fields, is recommended and is usually provided free by the institution. Students should always be encouraged to take advantage of such opportunities.

Precept into Practice – 7

Issue

Walid applied to study for a PhD and was confident about the application, as his home university in the Middle East had a Memorandum of Understanding with the university in the UK that he was applying to. In addition, Walid had an excellent first degree and was one of the brightest students to have made an application from his institution. After several weeks waiting for the expected acceptance letter, Walid was shocked to discover that his application had been rejected on a technicality which was that no certificate of English language competency had been included. Of course the new departmental selector was only doing his job, and according to the institutional guidelines, all international students without English as their first language had to produce evidence of competency in English. However, this had not been the case with Walid's previous colleagues, as it was known that some of their teaching had been in English, and most students got by without too many difficulties. Moreover, until recently it had not been possible to take a TOEFL test in Walid's home town. Walid went immediately to his tutor in his home university to complain and to see what could be done.

Resolution

For a number of reasons it has been the case that some international students, especially those on collaborative programmes, have not had to meet institutional guidelines for competence in English. However, this is not to be recommended and can be risky. In the minds of the students it also reduces the importance of being competent in English, and for many international students this can be a significant factor in delays to thesis submission times. The departmental selector in this situation was right, and unless English is the first language, all international students should provide some documentary evidence of English competency, especially as Internet-based and computer-based versions are now available, which remove the necessity of having to travel long distances to take the paper-based test. Of course, the crisis which developed above could have been avoided if the overseas institution had been forewarned of the necessity of such documentation.

Admissions decisions

Precept 8
Admissions decisions will involve at least two members of the institution's staff who will have received instruction, advice and guidance in respect of selection and admissions procedures. The decision-making process will enable the institution to assure itself that balanced and independent admissions decisions have been made, that support its admissions policy.

Although one of the best ways of assessing a student's potential for doctoral study is the formal interview, this is often problematic for an international student. Sometimes there are instances where the student is already studying in the UK, or the student might visit the UK at the same time as making the application, so they can meet prospective supervisors. In both cases, there is the opportunity to invite them to attend for a formal interview. However, this is not a common occurrence, and the student might be based thousands of miles away.

One possibility is that an academic might be visiting an overseas institution, and although there is the chance for an interview, more often than not a decision will be based on one person's judgement, which is not ideal. A more common possibility is that a telephone interview might be arranged, which could involve more than one academic. However, this can be problematic regarding time differences and quality of the telephone connection. Furthermore, how do you know whether you really are talking to the applicant? Another more recent opportunity is the videoconference interview, and although this can be expensive, is not available everywhere and is not an ideal format for interviewing, it has the advantage that you will know who has been interviewed, and as interviews are recorded, others can see the interview, even if they could not be there at the designated time.

An alternative is podcasting, where guidelines are given to a potential applicant and a deadline set to receive audio material in which an applicant describes his or her academic background and indicates why he or she should be considered for admission. Of course, this is not a replacement for an interview, but it could be an opportunity for providing additional material that could be used for screening inappropriate applicants in the selection process.

Data Protection Act 1998

One important matter is the Data Protection Act 1998, which came into force on 1 March 2000. Regarding personal information that is collected by telephone, callers should be advised on how that information will be used and what their rights are, according to the Act. Personal and/or confidential information should not be discussed in an open area, and ideally meetings should take place in a private meeting room. Any notes taken at a meeting should be filed in a legible and coherent manner, while informal notes should be placed in confidential waste.

This Act is also of particular note for references that are made on behalf of applicants. The Act allows applicants to access their references which have been received by the institution. Therefore, referees need to be reminded about the Act when they are asked to supply a reference, and that references should be factually accurate and fair. Matters of opinion should be based on factually accurate data. It is particularly important that overseas referees are given guidelines about producing a reference so that it complies with the Act.

In line with many institutions' desire to encourage equal opportunities, and with reference to the rehabilitation process of ex-offenders, for some areas of work, such as teaching, health, social work or work with children or vulnerable adults (Farrington and Palfreyman 2006: 237), details of criminal records are required by the Rehabilitation of Offenders Act 1974. In this case, applicants need to be checked by the Criminal Records Bureau before an offer can be made. Although most higher education students are over 18 years of age, some are not, and institutions should seek information on past convictions and carry out Criminal Records Bureau checks on any member of staff who may come into contact with these younger students.

Academic Technology Approval Scheme

As of 1 November 2007, the British government, like other governments around the world, introduced the Academic Technology Approval Scheme (ATAS) to stop the spread of knowledge and skills that could be used in the proliferation of weapons of mass destruction and their means of delivery. This means that non-EU/EEA (including Switzerland) nationals planning to undertake postgraduate study in the UK in certain science, engineering or technology subjects need to acquire an ATAS certificate from the Foreign and Commonwealth Office before making a visa application. An ATAS certificate is specific to the programme of study and to the institution, so that an applicant holding a number of offers from different institutions needs to obtain separate ATAS certificates for each programme of study or institution.

An area that can be difficult for academic staff judging international students is the standard of qualifications they possess. Around the world educational systems and standards differ, such that it can be problematic trying to compare qualifications for a bachelor's degree equivalent to that of a 2.1 or above. Unless one has specific country and/or area knowledge, it is recommended that selectors seek advice, often from the institution's International Office or equivalent. Other sources of useful information are the British Council and the National Academic Recognition Information Centre (NARIC 1996) *International Guide to Qualifications in Education*.

As mentioned in Precept 7, the normal requirement for entry to a research degree is a first degree at the minimum level of 2.1 or an international equivalent. However, in general, selectors are asked to consider applications on their academic merit and in accordance with the regulations governing admission to the university. Often the university's higher degree regulations also enable candidates with relevant experiential learning, but without a first degree, to be admitted for a higher degree, typically an MPhil in the first instance. This means that professional qualifications and/or relevant employment details should also be considered in non-standard applications, which demonstrate the candidate's ability to complete the intended programme of study. In such cases admission can be granted only following written faculty approval by the relevant university authorities or officers.

Precept into Practice – 8

Issue

Rashid from Bangalpindi wanted to do a PhD with Prof. Woolley, who also happened to be the new departmental selector. This made the decision process easier and quicker, as Prof. Woolley did not have to send on the application form to one of his colleagues. Prof. Woolley was quite impressed with Rashid's application, and Rashid made the point of emailing Prof. Woolley on a regular basis to ask how his application was going and to keep him informed of activities brought about by gaining a vacation scholarship to work at a famous research institute close to Bangalpindi. Prof. Woolley was also under pressure to start some new research, and as Rashid had a first class degree from his local university (although not highly rated), he decided to make him an offer. It was only later on, after discussing Rashid's proposed offer letter with a colleague, that Prof. Woolley became concerned, as he had not realized that a first class degree in India can be awarded for marks over 60 per cent and not 70 per cent as is the case in the UK.

Resolution

Prof. Woolley was rather embarrassed about his error. First, it could have been avoided if he had looked at the degree transcript for the overall exam marks, rather than taking a cursory glance at the application form, where it indicated that Rashid had been awarded a first class degree. Second, the error might also have been avoided if he had formally shared the information with a colleague, rather than just making the decision himself, which was in breach of the university's admissions policy and code of practice. Fortunately, there was a delay in sending out offer letters from the central office, so he was able to stop it before it left the institution. Rashid would now have to be told that because his degree was not equivalent to a UK first class degree and was not from a well-recognized university, he failed to meet the entry requirements for a research degree at Prof. Woolley's institution.

Entitlements and responsibilities

Precept 9
The entitlements and responsibilities of a research student undertaking a postgraduate research programme will be defined and communicated clearly.

Offer letters

Offer letters usually include the scope of the proposed research for which admission is being offered, the start date, the academic fees and, where applicable, details of any conditions, such as English language requirements, that the applicant must fulfil. It is important to remember that the offer letter is a legally binding contract that must be honoured in order to avoid action for breach of contract. It is vitally important, therefore, that selectors make sure that all details on the offer letter are correct.

University–student contract

The notion of a university–student contract was discussed by Samuels (1973). An example of a university–student contract as used by Massey University in New Zealand is outlined below.

The University will:

1 Use best endeavours to provide the Student with tuition and supervision of a professional standard in the course(s) in which the Student is enrolled.
2 Act reasonably and fairly in exercising its powers under the regulatory framework and this Contract.
3 Give reasonable notice of any changes in the course(s) required because of changes in funding, staffing or other reasonable cause.

The Student will:

4 Use best endeavours to fulfil the requirements prescribed by the University for the course(s).

5 Observe the regulations and rules of the University and accept the jurisdiction of the University in all matters connected with academic progress and with discipline.

6 Pay the fees prescribed by the University for the course(s).

The University and the Student also agree:

7 The Contract is formed when a Confirmation of Enrolment Form is issued for the course(s).

8 The Contract will continue for the period for which the Student is enrolled by the University and will then end. However, clause 12 will continue to apply after the Contract ends.

9 The University and the Student may enter into further contracts, in subsequent periods, by repeating the process in clause 7.

10 The relevant Admission Form, Enrolment Form, Confirmation of Enrolment Form and material published in the Calendar also form part of this Contract, but nothing else shall be incorporated into the contractual relationship between the Student and the University.

11 Liability for failure to perform this Contract is excluded where that failure has been caused by circumstances beyond the control of the University or the Student.

12 Any dispute arising out of or in connection with this Contract, or otherwise relating to the performance by the University or its staff of their responsibilities to the Student, shall be resolved through the Grievance Procedures prescribed by the University, which shall be the exclusive procedures for resolution of such a dispute.

A less formal development of this type of contract used at many institutions is often known as the Student Charter, and it provides helpful information on what is expected of students, supervisors and institutions.

Scholarships

Students who are to receive scholarships or bursaries must have submitted an application to the institution before they can be considered for such an award. It is important that relevant details are sent to the appropriate offices in the institution, to make sure that at student registration, fee processing is smooth running and trouble free.

Students employed as teachers

The opportunity for a postgraduate student to teach should be encouraged. However, the employment of such students as part-time teaching assistants needs to be without detriment to the research programme. In many institutions there are teaching training programmes, including the more comprehensive Postgraduate Certificate in Higher Education. Of course, not all departments can offer teaching opportunities on a regular basis. Where possibilities do arise, the institution may wish to follow the following principles regarding the employment of graduate students as teachers:

1 All graduate students employed by the institution should be assessed for their suitability before employment.
2 Full-time research students will be restricted to a maximum number of teaching duties per annum, including preparation time and marking, as based on rules relating to Research Council studentships.
3 Students involved in teaching should be given a written specification detailing their duties, including the total number of hours required in preparation, class contact hours, marking and payment. Payment should be based on institutional recommended rates of pay.
4 All students involved in teaching should receive guidance and help regarding course content and delivery methods from an appropriate member of academic staff. Students are to be encouraged to attend relevant training courses covering the teaching skills required.
5 Students involved in demonstrating will be given prior experience with equipment to be used and guidance on expected results and potential problems.
6 Each department should have a member of academic staff responsible for coordinating teaching undertaken by graduate students.
7 Responsibility for delivery and examination of modules taught by graduate students remains with the member of academic staff concerned.
8 Graduate students formally employed by the institution should be covered by the institution's professional indemnity insurance policy in the same way as academic staff members.

Precept into Practice – 9

Issue

Jane had applied to do a PhD with Integrated Studies in the Department of Biochemistry and, as she was a former student in that department, her application had been processed easily and quickly. However, the departmental selector, Dr Gibbins, was not familiar with the PhD with Integrated Studies programme. She knew that it included a master's component, but was a little confused about the organization of the fees. However, without consultation, she instructed the Admissions Office to send out an offer letter and suggested the fees that should be charged. When Jane received the offer letter she was rather surprised, as the annual rate for an enhanced fee (including 'bench fees') seemed rather low. However, she was happy, as the PhD programme was not as expensive as she had expected.

Resolution

It was a red-faced Dr Gibbins who received a copy of the offer letter and realized that she had made a mistake over the fees for the PhD with Integrated Studies programme and charged the student at the master's rate for the four-year period, rather than just for the first year only, with the remaining three at the higher, doctoral level. The problem was that the offer letter, should the student accept it, was a legally binding contract, and the institution would have to make up the deficit. Fortunately, Jane's sponsors were happy to abide by a revised offer letter, as they realized that a simple mistake had been made.

Induction

Precept 10
Institutions will provide research students with sufficient information to enable them to begin their studies with an understanding of the academic and social environment in which they will be working.

Induction at the beginning of the academic year can be at a number of levels, from the institution to the supervisor, and each has a relevant role to play (see Chapter 6). At the institutional level such a session is often led by the head of the Graduate School, graduate dean or equivalent. It is usually a general welcome and introduction to the university, as well as providing details of how the Graduate School operates and how to access information from it. As well as general contact information and details of skills training (possibly via a Research Training Programme), there might well be other information on social events and sports facilities. At this event, an induction checklist for students (Table 3.2) might be introduced to help them keep up with all the different demands early on in the programme. At the University of Sheffield, for example, a series of Ten Top Tips (Figure 3.1) on managing your research degree are presented in a light-hearted approach but they give an important message.

Induction at a more local level, such as school or department, gives more practical information on how to get a research project started and what needs

Table 3.2 Postgraduate research (PGR) students – induction checklist

Attended the Information Session for new research students	☐
Completed university registration (see *Registration: The Essential Guide* for exact timings)	☐
Received U-card	☐
Made appointment to register with University Health Service	☐
Completed computer network registration (with CICS), obtained passwords and familiarized self with computing facilities	☐
Visited the Graduate Research Centre and North Campus	☐
Attended compulsory sessions on copyright material and avoidance of unfair means	☐
Familiarized self with university and departmental library facilities	☐
Familiarized self with university's Health and Safety Code of Practice	☐
Checked with supervisor whether ethical approval and/or vaccinations required	☐
Received the Research Training Programme (RTP) Handbook	☐
Completed RTP registration	☐

Source: University of Sheffield

One...
Discuss your expectations with your supervisor and discuss theirs.

Being a research student will be a very different experience to being a taught student and all supervisors work in different ways.

Figure 3.1   Example of a Top Ten Tip used at an induction presentation.

Source: University of Sheffield

to be considered in order to do so. A typical programme for such an event is given in Table 3.3, where a number of key topics are discussed. It is always useful to describe the hierarchical structures of committees, so that students can see how decisions taken at one level, such as the Graduate School, can trickle down to a faculty and then a school and/or department. At the same time this can allow students to input their views upwards through the committee structure via student representation.

An illustration of a new student's feelings at the beginning of a research degree programme is provided opposite:

Table 3.3 Induction session for new graduate students

	Programme in School of Medicine and Biomedical Sciences
11.00	Welcome
	Academic matters
11.05	Use of Library
11.10	Faculty and School Graduate Research Committee
11.15	Student Representatives and Student Committee
11.25	Student Advocate System
11.30	Key Milestones in Year 1
11.45	RTPs in the School
11.55	Research Governance
12.05	Plagiarism
12.15	Lunch
	Management matters
12.40	Management, Technical Teams, Ordering, etc.
	Safety matters
12.50	Health and Safety and Biological Safety
13.00	Discussion

Source: University of Sheffield

I came straight from my undergraduate degree. I knew the department did the subject I was interested in. I didn't know anything about the PhD. I expected a well-defined problem and a well-structured PhD programme. But this was not what I got. I didn't even know which journals to look at . . . or what facilities I could use. So, there's a real lack of structure. There's no support at the start.

One of the first tasks that a student must undertake when starting a research programme is a *training needs analysis* (TNA). This means that students are expected to take responsibility for their own development and to think critically about the skills they will need as they progress through their research programme. A good starting point for the TNA is the UK Research Councils' *Joint Statement of the Skills Training Requirements for Research Students* (Research Councils UK 2001), which gives a common view of the skills and experience required of a research student. The process of analysing training needs involves a consideration of the student's own skills needs and the skills required for successful completion of a doctoral research project. Such an audit is presented in Table 3.4. What is then required is the plan of how to fulfil the training needs within a certain timescale.

Table 3.4 Final skills audit

Please rate your skills from 1 to 4 (1 = basic, 2 = competent, 3 = skilled, 4 = expert, n/a = not applicable)

Research skills and techniques	1	2	3	4	n/a
Ability to define original research problems					
Capacity for independent, critical thinking					
Knowledge of recent advances in your field and closely related links					
Understanding of research methodologies and techniques and ability to apply them within your own field					
Ability to analyse and evaluate critically your own findings and those of others					
Ability to record and reflect on the progress of your research					
Self-reliance, initiative and the ability to work independently					

Research environment	1	2	3	4	n/a
Understanding of the context, national and international, in which research takes place					
Knowledge of intellectual property issues (copyright, attribution, ownership of data, etc.)					
Knowledge of data protection legislation (if relevant to your research)					
Understanding of other legal and ethical issues relating to your research					
Appreciation of standards of good research practice in their institution and/or discipline					
Understanding of relevant health and safety issues and ability to demonstrate responsible working practices					
Understanding of how research is funded and evaluated					
Ability to justify the principles and experimental techniques used in your own research					
Understanding of how research results can be exploited academically and commercially					

Research management	1	2	3	4	n/a
Ability to manage a project by setting goals, prioritising and checking progress					
Ability to identify and access relevant information sources (bibliographic tools, archives, etc.)					
Ability to gather and collate information					
Ability to use IT effectively for storing and presenting information					

Personal effectiveness	1	2	3	4	n/a
Willingness to learn and ability to acquire knowledge					
Creativity and originality in your approach to research					
Flexibility and open mindedness					
Self-awareness and the ability to identify your own training needs					
Recognition of your own limitations and willingness to seek support when necessary					

Communication skills	1	2	3	4	n/a
Ability to write clearly and in a style appropriate to purpose					
Ability to construct coherent arguments and present them clearly to a range of audiences					
Ability to defend your findings in response to constructive criticism					
Ability to make your research interesting and understandable to members of the public					
Teaching ability					

Networking and teamworking	1	2	3	4	n/a
Ability to maintain good working relationships with supervisors and colleagues in your own department and elsewhere					
Understanding of how your behaviour impacts on others					
Ability to listen to others					
Willingness to accept constructive criticism					

(Continued overleaf)

Table 3.4 Continued

Career management	1	2	3	4	n/a
Commitment to continued professional development					
Ability to set realistic career goals and identify ways to increase your employability					
Awareness of how the skills gained through research can be applied in other areas of employment					
Awareness of the range of career opportunities available inside and outside academia					
Ability to present yourself effectively in applications and at interview					

Source: University of Sheffield

A more recent and significant development that has taken place, especially for research involving human participants, including patients, is *research governance*. This is a process to ensure that research involving patients, data or human tissue is scientifically sound, properly financed and ethically approved. The major benefit of doing this is to give greater protection for researchers and participants. Essentially, research governance applies to all UK health care research. In practice, this applies not only to all studies on patients, but also to all studies on volunteers in university-led projects which do not involve the National Health Service. If research governance approval is required for a project it is essential that an application is made well in advance, as the process itself can be quite lengthy. Of course, any project that does require approval cannot start until it is given, thereby potentially having a knock-on effect for the start of a research programme and progress of the student. Part of the research governance process will involve independent ethical scrutiny.

Another key element is *health and safety*. A copy of the institution's Code of Practice for Health and Safety should be given to all research students, and in certain subject areas it is important that specialized advice and training are also provided before a research programme is started.

Although many other topics might be discussed in induction programmes, it is recommended that time should be given to discussing *plagiarism*. With the dramatic rise in availability of electronic information over the last few years, institutions have been faced with a growing problem of student plagiarism. In order to ensure that students understand what is meant by the term, it is important to define what it is. Plagiarism is presenting someone else's own work as if it were your own, whether you mean to or not. 'Someone else's work' means anything that is not your own idea, even if it is presented in your own style. It includes material from books, journals or any other printed source, the work of other students or staff, information from the Internet, software programmes and other electronic material, designs and ideas. It also includes the organization or structuring of any such material.

It should be pointed out to students that if they are caught plagiarizing, penalties can be severe, including disciplinary procedures as well as exam failure. Students should also be made aware that academic staff routinely use search engines to scan and match documents, such as the transfer report, as part of the requirement to transfer from MPhil to PhD. A more recent mechanism for emphasizing the importance of plagiarism, and ensuring that students recognize that they are responsible for their actions, is to demand that students read and sign that they have understood a definition of plagiarism at the beginning of the research programme, so that they cannot claim ignorance if caught.

For a review on plagiarism, see Park (2003). For up-to-date information see Sutherland-Smith (2008), and for software that teaches students how to avoid accidental plagiarism see www.preventplagiarism.co.uk. As the basic principle underlying the preparation of any piece of academic work is that the work submitted must be the student's own work, another possibility for cheating is *fabrication*. Essentially, this means submitting work, such as practical or laboratory work, which is untrue, made up, falsified or fabricated in any way. This is regarded as fraudulent and dishonest, and cases will be treated in the same way as plagiarism, regarding penalties.

One of the problems with induction courses that are typically held at the start of the academic year is that many students start their research programme at different times throughout the year, and it is not always feasible to run these events more than once. Therefore, if possible it might be a good idea if induction events were recorded, so that they can be accessed by students any time of the year.

Precept into Practice – 10

Issue

Paula was very much in awe of her principal supervisor, Prof. Green, who had become quite distinguished in his field. Of course, Prof. Green had supervised many PhD students in the past and knew exactly what to do when Paula started. He sat down with Paula and told her that she had to take several research training modules to fulfil the requirements of her PhD, and that in his opinion, there was essentially no choice, as Prof. Green knew which were the most relevant modules for Paula to study. Paula was slightly taken aback by this, as she had heard about the need for a training needs analysis in the institution's induction session, but was told by Prof. Green that it would not be necessary. Prof. Green was not aware of Paula's plan for the future. Without a TNA it would be hit and miss whether Paula received all the skills training that she should have, and in the long term the only person to miss out would be Paula. Paula realized all this, but did not dare to challenge Prof. Green any further.

Resolution

At the outset, it would have been better if Paula and her supervisory team had met to discuss her skills training, as Prof. Green might then have been made to realize that without a TNA, he might be placing Paula at a disadvantage. Also, Paula needed to make a significant input to the meeting, as she was the only person who knew what skills training she had received in the past and therefore what might be required in the future. The role of the supervisors should be as advisers only and should not be dictatorial. For supervisors like Prof. Green, a possible solution to get them to perform a TNA would be to ask the student to provide one as a mandatory requirement of the transfer process from MPhil to PhD.

Conclusion

With the increasing complexity of admissions procedures, especially in terms of legal requirements, it is particularly important that students with disabilities are handled with care and consideration. It is also worth keeping up-to-date with current guidelines, such as the Academic Technology Approval Scheme.

Ideally, one should try to be more flexible in the nature of the formal academic entry requirements, where traditionally the minimum requirement has been a 2.1 bachelor's degree. Of course, the problem in the current context is that the majority of students reach this basic requirement, so there should be some other way to select the best students for research study. Unfortunately, this is still a neglected area, and national debate should be encouraged to stimulate new ideas as to how this problem might be resolved. An example of where flexibility has been introduced and is broadly welcomed is in the TOEFL test. Although different components of English language competency are tested by different test formats, it does mean that as long as students have access to a computer and ideally the Internet, then TOEFL testing can take place anywhere and at any time.

As greater demands are placed on academic selectors and supervisors, there is a need for more training in this area. For example, it is important that referees, especially from overseas, understand the implications of the Data Protection Act 1998 and that appropriate guidelines are given to them as to the style, format and content of references.

Regarding the difficulties of understanding overseas qualifications, easy access to a database on these and what the institution will accept as equivalent to UK qualifications would certainly be an advantage.

It is also important to re-emphasize the increasing formality of the admissions process, the contractual status of the offer letter and the importance of having robust procedures in place, should decisions be challenged by applicants.

Different pressures on both students and staff have seen an increase in opportunities for students to be employed part-time as teachers. However, quite detailed institutional guidelines are in place to ensure that teaching quality is maintained, while ensuring that students are not exploited.

Finally, since the early 2000s, because of the many demands now placed on students, induction sessions at all levels have been introduced and are essential in giving students a general awareness of the complexities of doctoral study.

Talking points

- How do we identify the best students to undertake a doctorate?
- We are still not able to replace the formal interview (if it is still considered to be important) for international students based in their home country at the time of application. Will podcasting or other technologies help us in this regard?
- With ever increasing demands on doctoral students, on one hand, and increasing pressures on completion times, on the other, is the very nature of a PhD changing and, if so, is it for the better or for worse?

Key text

Farrington, D. and Palfreyman, D. (2006) *The Law of Higher Education*. Oxford: Oxford University Press.

4

Supervision arrangements

Supervisors' skills and knowledge • Supervisors' roles • Institutional structures • Supervisor workload • Conclusion • Talking points • Key text

This chapter addresses the precepts concerning supervision arrangements and describes methods for establishing good practice and resolving issues. These will help supervisors establish specific arrangements and define a minimum standard for their supervision. Similarly, the extent to which that definition is communicated to – or is open to negotiation with – postgraduate students, is for supervisors to decide. This aspect of supervision, although it is addressed in codes of practice and policy statements, is not, therefore, a definitive art; supervisors have discretion in deciding how to play their role.

Consequently, the contents of this chapter may be subjects for supervisor–student discussions. One of the key purposes of such discussions is to develop a student's understanding of the supervisor's role. The fact that their understanding will not remain static provides further argument for ongoing discussion of roles and remits, throughout the research project. For example, the following brief narrative shows how dramatically a student's expectations of the supervisor can change over the course of the doctorate:

During his PhD the student complained in the strongest terms about his supervisor and only just stopped short of making a formal complaint to the university. He later confessed that, when he looked back on his experience a few years later, having taken up an academic post himself, and taken on the role of research supervisor, he found that his views had changed. What he had previously seen as neglect by his supervisor, he now saw as freedom. The freedom his supervisor had given him in the early stages of his PhD had taught him, he said, to be independent, to organize his own time, to use his initiative and to work without close supervision, unlike in industry where he felt he would have been under much closer supervision. He now feels that this freedom and independence are unique and valuable features of the PhD.

Striking a balance between 'freedom' and 'neglect' may be the most difficult task for a supervisor. Getting it right every time, all the time, may be close to impossible. In addition, there may be times when, as in the above narrative, the student feels that the balance has tipped one way, or the other, while the supervisor disagrees. It is essential that supervisors take responsibility for helping students to understand and manage this freedom, monitor students' experience of it and help students to manage any perceived needs. This monitoring requires supervisors to enable students to express their views and concerns, since we know that some students are reticent about doing so: 'The academic is obliged to pay particular attention to aspects of supervision that the student may hesitate to raise or question' (Mackinnon 2004: 404). This suggests that while it is important to have good 'supervision arrangements' in place, their effectiveness may depend on regular discussion of those arrangements.

This chapter also outlines the skills and knowledge that supervisors require, describes the potential roles that they may play and considers institutional structures that support them. Throughout this chapter, student's views, drawn from interviews and focus groups in a number of higher education cultures, emphasize the importance of expectation setting and adjustment.

Supervisors' skills and knowledge

Precept 11
Institutions will appoint supervisors who have the appropriate skills and subject knowledge to support, encourage and monitor research students effectively.

It could be expected that the minimum qualification for a supervisor is having a doctorate, but this is not always the case. New supervisors attend training and/or development sessions, perhaps completing a formal course or module, and they usually co-supervise their first doctoral student, an arrangement that is often a university policy. This arrangement should not be agreed without a genuine mentoring relationship being established to support the first-time supervisor. Mentoring is an important part of new supervisor development, and experienced supervisors may benefit from interactions with new supervisors. At least one of the co-supervisors will be 'research active' – whatever that is taken to mean in the local and/or national context – in the area of the student's research. Workload implications will be considered by both supervisors and mentors and usually agreed with the head of department. Exceptions to these baselines should be discussed with students, and it is even more important to clarify each supervisor's role for the student in cases where a university policy has been put aside for a good reason.

An institution's policy may also specify the acceptable or required forms of supervisor training or development. Experienced supervisors can engage in a range of activities providing ongoing development (described in Chapter 11). At all times, including in the case of supervisor absence or illness, the student should have a point of contact – someone to consult about the research. It is the main supervisor's job to ensure that this arrangement is in place, unless a different arrangement has been agreed, and this too must be understood and agreed by all involved.

The supervisor is responsible for implementing the institution's policy on research supervision. It is therefore essential that supervisors are familiar with the procedures and practices that are required, in addition to any local conventions that have developed in departments. Sourcing these documents is the supervisor's responsibility, and they are generally publicly available.

Supervisor training

Many institutions have a policy that new supervisors will be trained, but the term 'new supervisor' can have many meanings, from first-time supervisors to newly appointed staff with experience of supervising but 'new' to supervision arrangements in a university they have recently joined. This last group may not require the same training or development as first-timers, but information about the specifics of practices in their new place of employment is useful and potentially time-saving.

All those who have responsibility for postgraduate research students in an institution can contribute to the design and delivery of supervisor training, thus new supervisors can learn from administrators, staff developers and, of course, other supervisors in their own and other disciplines, about the essentials of good supervision arrangements. Experienced supervisors can attend updating courses on current developments, such as mechanisms for assessing the quality of research and supervision and recent research and policy on supervision and research training.

A supervisor training and development programme can establish what expertise is needed. While some skills and aptitudes develop over time, it is important to define what these are and actively to manage their development. It is essential that supervisors think this through, taking stock of their knowledge and skills and planning how to improve them. For new supervisors this may be quite straightforward: it will save time and energy if they engage in specific development activities, and these may, in fact, be a requirement in their institutions.

The text box includes potential components of a supervisor development programme. Whether or not new supervisors have access to such a programme, it is reasonable to expect them to have knowledge of these topics and to update their knowledge periodically. This is therefore a checklist for new and experienced supervisors.

What supervisors should know – a checklist

- The place of research students in the department or faculty strategy
- Research student numbers, targets, fees, funding and department strategy
- Submission and completion rates in the department and faculty
- The place of postgraduates in research assessment
- Types of research degree: local structures and descriptors
- Student recruitment and assessment of applications
- Student induction arrangements at department, faculty and university levels
- Definitions of 'originality'
- Codes of Practice (university, department, research council, professional body): precepts or principles and associated practices
- Research planning and monitoring
- Baseline contact
- Progress monitoring, record-keeping arrangements and responsibilities and timescales
- Formal or annual review: criteria and procedures
- Conversion or transfer from MPhil to PhD: criteria and procedures
- Postgraduate committee, research committee, counsellors, tutors and conveners: names, remits, contact details and availability
- Experiences of current and recent postgraduate students in the department
- Research training: department, faculty or other organization
- Student support services: names, remits, contact details and availability
- Health and safety
- Disability legislation
- English as a second language support and courses
- University criteria for the thesis
- Appointment of external examiners
- Library requirements for the thesis format
- Examination: criteria, form(s), conduct, outcomes, grounds for/process of appeal
- Complaints and appeals: procedures, responsibilities and sources of advice
- Intellectual property rights
- Supervisor's personal skills: communicating, motivating etc.
- Case studies and problem-solving.

This broad range of topics includes different types of information, such as straightforward procedural information and the potentially more complex 'human factors' involved in individual cases. For this reason, it makes sense to draw on the experiences and different expertise of all those who are involved with research students, as listed in the text box.

Who contributes to supervisor training and development?

- Person with responsibility for research students in department and faculty, such as postgraduate tutor or dean – knows the system.
- Experienced supervisors – can translate precepts into local practice.
- Staff and educational development unit – may run courses.
- Faculty and institutional administrators – can provide a 'walk through' of the whole postgraduate process, from recruitment to graduation.
- Student support services – may offer specific support, including contributing to new student induction.
- International Office – can advise on range of subjects, e.g. visas for overseas students.
- Students – can mentor each other, form groups, report on their experiences.
- External bodies, such as the UK Council for Graduate Education, Research Councils UK and the Quality Assurance Agency – can be important sources of advice.

Every supervisor has to ensure that they have access to all the information they need; it might be useful if this were regularly brought together in one compilation. Below is no more than a skeleton of a supervisor's 'manual', listing essential documents, but there may be others. Many institutions conveniently put all the information in a pack for supervisors. If there is no such pack, new supervisors will have to compile one and check that they have everything they need:

- Department or faculty handbook
- Postgraduate student handbook
- Code(s) of practice
- University regulations for higher degrees
- Student monitoring forms
- Review forms
- University and department procedures
- Higher degree submission form
- Appointment of external examiner form
- Examiner's report form(s).

These documents outline requirements, regulations and procedures, essential knowledge for supervisors. Pulling together all of them, and checking that the collection is complete, may be straightforward, but they do change over time. Supervisors have a responsibility to check that they – and their students – have the latest version. The consequences of not doing so can be serious, particularly if students become aware of it. The National Postgraduate Committee some time ago drew up a list of questions that prompt students to explore these subjects explicitly with potential supervisors, before deciding where to register for a PhD. (These guidelines are no longer available.) Supervisors can probably anticipate which questions prospective students are likely to ask. QAA (2008a) has produced a list of *Frequently Asked Questions for Students*.

Supervisors' conceptions of supervision will affect their practice. Development courses and other forums can be mechanisms for 'surfacing' underlying beliefs, values and conceptions. For example, a supervisor's conception of 'postgraduate work' will influence his or her conception of supervision. This in turn may influence how he or she helps students to manage the transition to independent postgraduate study:

> Moving from undergraduate or master's courses is a leap of learning behaviours as great at least as that from pre-university to university study. Postgraduate work requires less dependence upon authorities and given information, more long-term independent study, highly coherent methods and planning, risk taking and speculation, problem-solving abilities and strategies.
>
> (Wisker et al. 2003: 93)

Supervisors have a role in delineating the limits of the research project and in helping the student to perceive those limits:

> Sometimes transformational outcomes actually lie realistically outside the bounds of the PhD study altogether. . . . In other cases, the boundaries of the PhD study itself would suggest that further work should be carried out at a later date or by others influenced by the PhD study.
>
> (Wisker et al. 2003: 98)

Precept into Practice – 11

Issue

Dr Beech had recently joined the department as a new lecturer and was keen to take on his first PhD student to help his research get established. Jenny had applied to the same department to start a PhD under the guidance of Prof. Willington, a very experienced supervisor and eminent scientist. As Prof. Willington seemed to be getting more involved on national committees, she suggested that Jenny might want to work under the supervision of Dr Beech, as long as Prof. Willington was still involved in the project as Dr Beech's mentor. Initially, Jenny accepted the proposal and worked hard to establish a good working relationship with Dr Beech, who was excellent in helping Jenny master new analytical techniques. However, when it came to Jenny producing her MPhil/PhD transfer report, Dr Beech was not sure as to how to help her sufficiently, and the report, when it was produced, was ill conceived and lacked appropriate direction. It was a pity that Prof. Willington had not had time to discuss this matter with Dr Beech, as Dr Beech could not bring himself to inform Prof. Willington about his own shortcomings in his supervisory role.

Resolution

As mentor to Dr Beech in his first experience of supervising a PhD student, Prof. Willington needed to play an active role in making sure that Dr Beech was confident and familiar with all his supervisory tasks. However, in this example Prof. Willington was a named mentor on paper only and she failed to provide any practical guidance to Dr Beech. Like a supervisor and student at the start of a research project, needing to discuss their respective roles and responsibilities, a new supervisor and mentor should develop ways of working together to enable a new supervisor to gain the appropriate experience.

Supervising 'effectively'

There is debate about what constitutes 'effective' supervision, and it is important to explore the options. The following points are drawn from discussions of this topic with experienced supervisors and examiners in a range of disciplines:

- An effective supervisor is able to change his or her practice over time, as the research progresses and as the student develops.
- Supervision may be different for each student, and different students may have different expectations. Good practice includes discussing supervision with students; how do they define 'good supervision'? What do they expect? This is not to say that supervisors should ask students how to do their job; instead, it is to acknowledge the value of feedback and, perhaps more importantly, of expectation setting.
- Defining supervision may involve explaining what the supervisor will – and will not – do: 'Any research student is going to require education and training. . . . The supervisors alone will not be able to provide all the necessary education and training' (Universities' and Colleges' Staff Development Unit [USDU] 1994: 29).
- Taking account of individual differences may involve adjusting the style of supervision.
- Providing structure and prompting students to plan are critical tasks for supervisors in the early stages of research.

- Supervision – and learning about supervision – is a reflective process, involving both students and supervisors in reflection on the process.

These supervisors were then asked, how are the knowledge and skills required for effective supervision acquired?

- Many supervisors have learned how to supervise from others, from their own supervision and from observing and hearing about what other supervisors do.
- There has been, traditionally, a certain amount of 'learning on the job', although this can be an unreliable model of learning a complex task.
- Training in supervision is critical, which is why training for new supervisors is now a requirement in many universities.

They were then asked, how can we assess the standard of supervision?

- Observing students' reactions produces cues for further discussion about their experience of supervision and, perhaps, its impact on them.
- Feedback from students, in a formal and anonymized form, can provide generalized or detailed information on the standard of supervision in a large department.
- When milestones or review points are met or missed, this may be an indicator of the quality of supervision.
- Peer observation can provide a useful check on practices and assumptions.
- How students perform in evaluations may reflect the quality of supervision, or it may simply raise questions about supervision as one aspect of the student's educational experience, or about recruitment processes.
- Student completion rates, presentations and publications may be seen as indicators of supervisor effectiveness.

Supervisors' roles

Precept 12
Each research student will have a minimum of one main supervisor. He or she will normally be part of a supervisory team. There must always be one clearly identified point of contact for the student.

While the minimum is one supervisor for each student, this precept recommends that each student have a supervisory team. This team includes an academic with subject expertise, usually designated first supervisor, and a second supervisor, also with relevant expertise, or playing a research management, critical friend or some other defined role. Other members of the team may bring other areas of expertise to the project and may play different roles. At least one member of the team will have experience of doctoral supervision to successful completion.

The first supervisor will explain these different roles to the student at the start of the project. Names and contact details will be given to the student at registration, and any changes in role must be the subject of subsequent supervisor–student discussion. Responsibility for communicating this information to the student, or verifying that it has been communicated, understood and accepted, lies with the supervisor. As in many other settings, simply communicating information is not always sufficient, particularly with the issue of roles, where so much is open to interpretation, with many variations and a degree of flexibility.

The strength of the supervisory team model is that it provides a range of perspectives on which the student may draw. Ideally, it will also facilitate contact with other research students, thus broadening the student's research experience. However, responsibility for effective supervision of the student lies with the main supervisor, unless otherwise specified, formally, to the student, by the department or institution.

Precept into Practice – 12

Issue

Dr Collins was excited about his new PhD student, Michael, starting a new area of research. Dr Collins had explained to Michael that although there would be several academics helping him through his PhD, he was the principal supervisor and would therefore be the first point of contact in all supervision matters. Michael liked Dr Collins and was very happy with the relationship that was developing between them. All was well until Dr Collins failed to return from a four-week walking holiday in the Himalayas. Michael was of course sad to hear that Dr Collins was presently in hospital in Nepal but was frustrated at not knowing what to do next in his PhD studies. It sounded as if Dr Collins would be away for a few more weeks at least, and Michael was concerned that he was losing his way with his PhD. The problem was that Michael really did not know who to speak to in the department about his problems.

Resolution

As an ambitious but relatively junior academic, Dr Collins had been keen to make clear to Michael that he was the principal supervisor. This was helpful to Michael, as he knew his point of contact. However, what Dr Collins had failed to do was to nominate a deputy (ideally from Michael's supervisory team) so that in his absence, such as a long holiday, Michael would have an alternative point of contact. The present situation highlighted the necessity of such an appointment, as Dr Collins' return was unexpectedly delayed, which exacerbated the situation further.

There are many different tasks to be performed by supervisors in the course of supervising a doctorate. These may include student recruitment, applying academic standards, assessing students, taking account of resources (including time, space and financial support) for students, directing, tutoring, providing pastoral care, setting boundaries, developing researchers (including helping students in networking), developing and maintaining a research network and publishing. Not everyone agrees that all of these are roles the supervisors should play – all the more reason to discuss supervision roles with students.

These roles include both administrative and 'teaching' elements. Some of these roles are quite different from others, and may even strike students as contradictory. For example, assessing student's work is a very different role from the informal contact that may occur daily. Effective supervision involves explaining that what might seem to the student like a supervisor's unexpected role change has its purpose and is an essential part of supervision.

This is particularly important if a student is unable or unwilling to voice his or her views or to ask questions. Initially, and possibly at later stages for different reasons, supervisors may not be able to 'read' their students accurately, and they may still be forming a judgement about their students' needs. Even attempting to be generally reassuring can be misinterpreted by students, or may simply not meet their needs at a specific time. Here is one student's view on communicating with supervisors:

> People are not frank. New postgraduates see this and learn not to give mutual criticism. Postgraduates repress their feelings. They could bring things out in the open. They don't make direct statements to their supervisors. For example, when supervisors don't give feedback on your writing it's demotivating. Or when work seems to be taking too long or doesn't seem important, the supervisor should reassure you that you've done enough or that it is useful . . . A friend of mine . . . every few months he goes to the supervisor with something new in the project and the supervisor just says, 'That's fine'. To me, that's not enough. And I know my friend is frustrated by this.

The supervisor needs to find a way to solve – or avoid? – this problem. This can be done in a range of ways: giving feedback on students' academic progress, as well as giving support and encouragement; answering questions raised by the students referred to above (is the work making progress towards a doctorate?); being clear and unequivocal in feedback; enabling students to ask for feedback, and checking that they have processed it accurately; taking time to discuss feedback, rather than expecting students to act on it immediately. Supervision involves learning how each student prefers to receive feedback:

> Whether criticism is best given 'straight' or best tempered to avoid seeming too harsh is also a matter of convention. . . . Those who prefer

criticism given straight are operating on a conventionalized agreement that says, 'This is business; feelings have no part in it'. . . . Those who are used to ways of talking that soften the impact in consideration of the feelings of the person addressed may find it hard to deal with right-between-the-eyes criticism. Both styles have their own logic.

(Tannen 1995: 53)

Both styles of communication have their place in the long learning journey that is the doctorate, but it is the supervisor's responsibility to clarify the stylistic, and other, options and agree a form of feedback that is appropriate. Communication style will not remain fixed for all time, and, like so many other matters, this must be discussed with students. Effective doctoral supervision involves helping students to navigate such adjustments. Here is one student's view of the whole three years of the doctorate:

Problems build upon each other in the second and third years. You turn a corner. The pressure increases. You get to the third and fourth year and you don't know what's going to happen, especially with the viva. If you go in with the knowledge that the viva will be there and will be soon, three years pass very quickly. The last nine to twelve months is a really difficult period. The supervisor should give the student this kind of knowledge and encourage this kind of thinking ahead. And there are other things you need to know – other skills you need to learn. Supervisors don't always tell you about the training you can get. There's no budget for travelling to courses at other universities. Sometimes supervisors see training as irrelevant, even when the student has found it useful. You even have to ask secretaries for small amounts of money.

This student clearly appreciated the value of a particular 'kind of knowledge' and 'thinking ahead', but other students may have different views. Effective supervision therefore involves not only working with students to plan the entire duration of their projects, but also persuading them that this is a sensible approach.

This suggests that supervisors may have to remember that new postgraduates are only beginning to understand the stages involved in research, and may not yet have developed ways of monitoring their work through these stages – learning about these is, after all, one of the purposes of the doctorate. Some of this learning may come from formal courses, and supervisors must find out what training is available, in the department, faculty or elsewhere, and encourage students to do likewise. To support these activities, funds may be available for students travelling to courses and conferences. New supervisors and students may need to do some research on this. This is one of the many areas where supervisors can draw on their own networks.

Basic facilities must also be provided for research students from the start, for example, desk, computer, email, photocopying, inter-library loan and postage.

Supervisors should explain to new students which facilities will and will not be available and what resources are and are not provided. Supervisors then have to ensure that the facilities are in place.

Supervisors can also help students to balance their research with any teaching they take on. Teaching duties can be demanding and even onerous, as students take on the role of 'expert' and perhaps even assessor of students who are not much younger than themselves. Supervisors can help students by inducting them into the literature on teaching and learning in higher education, while passing on 'health warnings' about areas that may be too demanding, beyond their expertise or too time consuming (Morss and Murray 2005). As universities come to rely more and more on postgraduates to teach, there is, or should be, an increased emphasis on developing students' knowledge of teaching and learning in higher education. If the institution does not provide an appropriate course for postgraduates who teach, supervisors may have to offer guidance. While the decision to take on a teaching commitment may be the student's, it is the supervisor's responsibility to check that the student has sufficient knowledge, time and expertise. Research has shown that students do not always receive such support:

> Most PhD students [in this study] were trapped at a particular stage of teaching expertise and because they worked within a culture that emphasized research and had low expectations of them as teachers, they had no obvious incentive or strategy to move forward.
>
> (Harland and Plangger 2004: 82)

Each supervisor has to judge whether or not this situation is appropriate for a specific student, in the specific context of his or her research. Supervisors can also refer students to the type of text that helps them to engage with these issues constructively and, where appropriate, to begin to think about teaching as an element of their careers. For example, a unique feature of *Teaching at University* (Morss and Murray 2005) is a section at the end of each chapter on developing a teaching portfolio, including reading, study and systematic reflection on issues and experiences.

Students' roles

> Individual supervisors can have very different perceptions of their role and these perceptions are not necessarily shared with their students. . . . Students often have to guess their tutors' assumptions as to how to proceed in the relationship. They seem to feel surprisingly powerless if problems arise.
>
> (Thorley and Gregory 1995: 93)

It could be argued that for any supervisor role – such as 'teacher' – there is a complementary student role – such as 'learner' – so that supervisor and student can play very different roles. An alternative view is that many of the responsibilities of managing a research project are shared between supervisors and students. This may seem obvious to some, but it is potentially confusing for students. In addition to managing the research – which may or may not be a shared responsibility – there is also the matter of managing the relationship, which is also a shared responsibility. However, where responsibilities are shared, effective supervision involves taking up the 'default' position, that is responsibility for ensuring that each student knows his or her role at any point in the research, along with the actions, processes and outputs required, lies with the supervisor.

Institutional structures

Precept 13
Institutions will ensure that the responsibilities of all research student supervisors are clearly communicated to supervisors and students through written guidance.

For some time, universities, faculties or departments have had written documents defining supervisors' roles and responsibilities and often aiming to maintain the standard of research supervision. Supervisors are responsible for finding out about these documents and updating their knowledge, as required. Whatever set of principles the institution uses, it is essential that supervisors consider their implications for how they play their role. They should, of course, discuss this with their students. Furthermore, supervisors are responsible for aligning their supervision practices with their institutions' policies. Most if not all institutions will have a code of practice.

A code of good practice can provide a set of guidelines for both the student and the supervisor. It can provide a starting point for negotiating the student: supervisor relationship. . . . It can and should cover:

- rights and responsibilities for all parties in the process, i.e. the student, the supervisor, the department, the faculty, the institution, the examiners.

(Hole 1997: 3)

A supervisor can use the institution's Code of Practice for Postgraduate Education (different institutions may give it other titles) in discussion with students to clarify roles and responsibilities, in terms of 'mutual responsibilities and obligations rather than rights' (Mackinnon 2004: 395). This discussion should clarify for the student that the code of practice is, in a sense, an agenda for more detailed and ongoing discussions about the management of the research project. A code of practice is not generally sufficiently specific to be considered as a 'contract' – although it is sometimes seen as such by students – but the supervisor is responsible for both prompting this discussion and ensuring that students understand the status and relevance of the code of practice for their position as students.

The contents of a code of practice for research supervision may vary from one institution to another, and supervisors should aim to implement the appropriate code in its current edition. Most codes specify the supervisor's responsibilities, often in quite general terms. Importantly, they may purport to set out the 'minimum standard' of supervision, as shown in the text box.

The supervisor's responsibilities

1 Giving guidance, support and advice to the student at a satisfactory level
2 Monitoring direction and progress in the student's research project
3 Maintaining regular contact with the student
4 Assessing the student's development needs
5 Helping the student to solve problems
6 Providing instruction on research methods
7 Giving the student feedback on work and progress
8 Ensuring the student understands and practices ethical research
9 Helping the student to prepare for reports, reviews and assessments
10 Informing the student of institutional sources of guidance and support
11 Helping the student to attend conferences and publish
12 Continuing to develop as a supervisor.

(Extract from a code of practice on research supervision)

The implication of this list for supervisors is that they may have to make each element more specific than it is here and explain its relevance for individual students and their projects. This is likely to be a key part of the process of establishing 'supervision arrangements'.

For example, where the code of practice asserts that the supervisor is responsible for maintaining 'regular contact' with the student (item 3 in the list), there is clearly a need for both parties to agree on definitions of both 'regular' and 'contact'. Moreover, these words will have multiple meanings during the course of a doctorate. In some codes, these words appear in both the supervisor's and the student's roles. Normally, this means that there is shared responsibility to maintain communication and reporting, but once the research is underway, and once challenges appear and different interpretations are formed, there can be confusion and disagreement, and these can take time and energy away from the work of the research. Some students may take 'regular contact' to mean 24-hour access and instant supervisor response; it is the supervisor's responsibility to check the student's understanding and to gain their acceptance of the boundaries. Some institutions specify the minimum frequency of contact, and supervisors are responsible not only for acting on this but also for ensuring that students know what to expect and find it acceptable.

In addition to the quantity of regular contact, supervisors also have to consider its quality. Where there is frequent informal contact, there is also a need for more formal meetings. Here is one student's view on the quantity and quality of supervision:

> My supervisor was in the next room. I could see her at any time. But this became a poor policy. Things were discussed, but not formulated coherently, not in terms of deadlines. She didn't say, 'I expect you in two weeks to be at this point'. It was just a nod of the head. But it wasn't followed through. We had so many informal chats, it was difficult for me to write everything down. I said things to the supervisor directly, because we're so close. Then a year later she said, 'You never said that to me'. And I know full well that I did say it and she disagreed with it. But she doesn't remember it. And I think, well, am I going crazy? You can't go back and say, 'You did say this'.

How can supervisors address this issue? They can start by discussing formal and informal processes with students at the start of the research. They can discuss the risks of relying on informal processes alone. They can debate the pros and cons of being systematic in record-keeping and minute-taking, both in the context of the doctorate and in professional settings. They can survey the range of frameworks for planning and managing the doctorate that are now available. They can work with the student to develop a format that suits. They can agree to review their use of formal and informal processes on a specific date. Perhaps only the last of these options – review and discussion of supervision arrangements – can ensure that the problem is both identified and resolved.

Perhaps a more fundamental question is, how can supervisors find out whether students have such problems? Chapter 7 deals with the topic of student feedback, but in this chapter a real student perspective underlines the need for supervisors not only to define their own practice but also to discuss it with students in order to gauge their understanding and expectations. Student views are incorporated throughout this book in order to set up an interaction between supervisors' roles and students' perspectives. The implication for supervisors is that they should consider how to capture students' perspectives, so that they can help students to adjust their expectations, as appropriate.

Similarly, 'feedback on work and progress' (item 7 on the above list) has to be provided within a reasonable amount of time and should be constructive, critical and effective. While these three criteria seem reasonable and sound, how are they to be gauged? How will a supervisor determine if feedback has been 'effective'? Does this mean that supervisors have to gather feedback on their feedback? Should they take time to determine the relationship between types of feedback they give students, actions taken by the students and progress made with the research? Realistically, there is a limit to the amount of time and energy that supervisors can dedicate to determining the effectiveness of their feedback to students, but they can observe how students respond – while ensuring that students perceive this aspect of supervision – think about what they do and ask students what they think.

Precept into Practice – 13

Issue

Prof. Hughes had decided to take on his last PhD student before he retired. Through Prof. Hughes' Middle Eastern contacts, Abdul, a fully funded overseas student, was accepted to study for a PhD. Of course, Prof. Hughes was a very experienced supervisor who knew the ropes, and every September, when the new university Code of Practice for Research Supervisors and Research Students arrived on his desk, it was immediately filed away, usually without consultation. Abdul was also given a copy of the same document, but did not really have time to read it properly, as he was still in the process of moving into his new accommodation with his wife and family. As was usual, Prof. Hughes liked to give his new students written assignments, so that he could get a feel for what they understood about their chosen research topic. Abdul spent a lot of time producing his first assignment and handed it to Prof. Hughes on time. However, Abdul became increasingly concerned, when, after four weeks, he still had not received any feedback on the assignment from Prof. Hughes. Had Abdul made a mess of this assignment? What was he to do now? Now, every time he saw Prof. Hughes he tried to avoid him, as he was frightened of what he might say.

Resolution

Although Prof. Hughes and Abdul had both received the university's Code of Practice for Research Supervisors and Students, neither had read it. If they had, they would have been aware that a number of changes had been made, especially with regard to student feedback. Prof. Hughes should have provided timely (presumably within four weeks), constructive and effective feedback on Abdul's assignment. It is suggested that, in future, the supervisor should indicate when feedback will be given. It is also highly recommended that both supervisor and student give more than a cursory glance to the university's Code of Practice for Supervisors and Students.

Supervisors have responsibility for putting the code into practice. For example, 'assessing the student's development needs' (item 4 on the above list) may be interpreted as telling the student that there is a gap in their knowledge, or that courses are available, or it could mean that supervisors are expected to take an active role in prompting, supporting and resourcing their students' development. The extent and limits of this active management will not be the same for all students or for all supervisors. The implication for supervisors is therefore that they should discuss their views on this with students.

Often there are several codes of practice operating at the same time. Professional bodies and research councils have codes that potentially add to the above list of responsibilities. This could be confusing for students, who are generally adept at finding such materials, but may not be sure how they apply in universities where they are registered. It is essential that supervisors make sense of this range of codes, both for themselves and for their students. Everyone involved with doctoral students should know what the code(s) of practice involve for supervisors and students in their institution.

This is not to say that a bureaucracy of supervision should be developed; some of the 'discussions' and 'notes' recommended in this section can be very brief. Developing sound 'supervision arrangements' is not about generating paper work for its own sake, or about having an insurance policy in case things go wrong; instead, it is about developing an understanding with new students, including expectation setting and helping them to adjust to what, for most, is a new role. Perhaps more importantly, such discussion gives supervisors insights into students' thinking and expectations throughout the doctorate.

Supervisor workload

Precept 14
Institutions will ensure that the quality of supervision is not put at risk as a result of an excessive volume and range of responsibilities assigned to individual supervisors.

Some institutions specify the maximum number of doctoral and/or master's students that supervisors can take on, and for many supervisors simply applying this limit will be straightforward. However, in some instances the limit is more flexible and potentially more complex. Institutions and supervisors in some institutions – sometimes in different departments or schools in the same institution – have discretion, and workloads may be less formal and even negotiable than the idea of 'limit' implies. This area may be linked to funding and other matters. Such variation is potentially challenging for students and new supervisors alike.

The implication for supervisors is not necessarily that they need to start explaining to students how each student is accounted for in their workloads – although that might help students develop an understanding of academic work. This chapter has shown the range of activities that research supervision encompasses, and new supervisors particularly need to know their institutions' guidelines and ensure that these activities are accounted for in their workloads. There is a case for regular discussions with heads of department about workload allocations, and these are routine in many departments.

The notes on this precept call on institutions to 'find ways of showing their support for supervisors' valuable contribution to the research environment' (p. 17), and a key form of support is providing time. One implication for new supervisors is that recording actual time spent on all the activities involved in supervision might be instructive, both in terms of their time management, but also in terms of making a credible case for time to their heads of department.

Ultimately, supervisors are responsible not only for providing support and guidance to students but also for ensuring that the support and guidance are sufficient, and the notes on Precept 14 conclude by reminding us that there has to be agreement on this for supervision to be effective: 'Supervisors and students *should agree between themselves* the level of interaction required and what constitutes sufficient time, in terms of quality as well as quantity, to devote to the supervisory role' (QAA 2004: 17, our emphasis). This emphasis on discussion and agreement between supervisor and student is a theme both in this book and in the QAA precepts. Discussion and agreement create both the foundation and the test of effective supervision. A typical example follows where an academic put himself into a difficult situation by taking on too many duties without due consideration for his students.

Precept into Practice – 14

Issue

Prof. Sturgess was well liked in the university, and having been made head of department only a couple of years previously, she had been appointed dean of faculty. However, not surprisingly, these appointments now took up most of her working time, and although she always used to have weekly meetings for her research group, these were becoming few and far between. In the university's drive to increase research income, Prof. Sturgess had been successful in a recent grant application, which would pay for two more PhD students, taking her total to six. The problem was that current PhD students in her group were already finding it difficult to hold regular progress meetings with her, and increasing her student load would only make matters worse.

Resolution

Often a major difficulty in this situation is getting someone like Prof. Sturgess to realize that she has a problem and that discussions with senior academic colleagues could be useful. Some academics want to take on more responsibilities, especially in more senior managerial roles, without thinking of the effect this could have on more routine matters, such as supervision of research students. First, it does not seem to be a good idea to take on these two managerial roles, and perhaps this should be an institutional recommendation for supervisors. Second, delegation of certain duties to other members of the supervisory teams may ease some of the pressure on Prof. Sturgess. Third, the institution might wish to consider whether recommendations should be in place to reduce supervisory duties to a minimum when academics have senior managerial roles, and whether generating income to support research students in such a situation might be inappropriate.

Conclusion

There are many sources of guidance about supervision arrangements, and every university has its own policy, procedures and processes, but it is essential that each supervisor establish appropriate arrangements for each project and each student.

The arrangements they develop must be aligned with institutional, perhaps also faculty, departmental and professional, requirements in a way that is visible to the student. However, arrangements may change over time, as the project, the student and the supervisor develop. Supervisors are responsible for actively managing this process, explaining to students which supervision arrangements will change, and in what way, what the purpose of the change is and what actions are required by student and supervisor. In this context, the institutional policy or code can be genuinely useful, if it maintains coherence in supervision arrangements.

This chapter has outlined essential issues to be taken into account in developing supervisory arrangements. This is not simply a process of 'bureaucratizing' supervision; discussing roles and remits is an essential part of postgraduate student induction, the subject of Chapter 6.

Talking points

Perhaps the most disturbing of our findings is the disjunction between what [supervisors] think they are providing and the dissatisfactions of students.

(Becher et al. 1994: 188)

- Student expectations and understanding of the supervisor's role – as illustrated by the narrative at the start of this chapter – show how misconceptions can lead to hostility and suspicion. There is potential tension between 'freedom' and 'neglect' in the doctorate. Students do not always perceive them to be in balance. What can supervisors do about this?

- The type of 'disjunction' identified by Becher et al. (1994) in the quotation above may be inevitable – but supervisors have to help their students deal with it. What are the best ways to do this?

- In interviews with experienced supervisors there was debate about whether or not it is essential to have good personal relationships with students. Some supervisors argued that a personal relationship is not important – the research is what matters. Others felt that establishing a personal relationship is a key part of their role, often leading to lasting friendships. This issue may, therefore, be a matter of personal choice.

- The literature on doctoral supervision has focused on the functional dimension – i.e. project management – but there is more to supervision than that. Lee (2008) identified four other dimensions and combined all five in a conceptual framework for research supervision:

> enculturation – where the student is encouraged to become a member of the disciplinary community; critical thinking where the student is encouraged to question and analyse their work; emancipation – where the student is encouraged to question and develop themselves; and developing a quality relationship – where the student is enthused, inspired and cared for. These can all be mapped onto the doctorate.
>
> (Lee 2008: 267–268)

Key text

Lee, A. (2008) How are doctoral students supervised? Concepts of doctoral research supervision. *Studies in Higher Education*, 33: 267–281.

5

Monitoring and review arrangements

Supervisor meetings • Progress reviews • Meeting log • Conclusion • Talking points • Key text

Mechanisms for monitoring student progress are essential foundations for the quality of the research student experience and can ensure successful completion of a high quality doctoral programme. As the principal funding agencies and research councils step up their requirements for performance indicators to evaluate doctoral programmes, institutions have shown a greater awareness of the need for timely and successful completion of postgraduate research degrees by including within their regulatory frameworks, explicit arrangements for progress review as discussed below. Due to the increasing pressures on both supervisors and students to complete the doctoral research programme within a prescribed period (usually four years for a full-time student), these review arrangements often result in the need to give more support of all kinds to students, including supervision, counselling and computer services. Thus the QAA expectations have led to increasing demands on the supervisor to define, and where possible strengthen, arrangements for meeting their students, in the face of the apocryphal but widespread student criticism that, 'I never see my supervisor'. Equally there is a requirement for the doctoral student to attend progress reviews, whether informal or formal, and to respond to the inputs and agreed actions appropriately – all of which will underpin and strengthen the success of the research programme.

In this chapter we will discuss the many different monitoring and review arrangements for research students, several of which have been introduced over the last few years, and consider how they may help to raise the quality of research degree programmes.

Supervisor meetings

Precept 15
Institutions will put in place and bring to the attention of students and relevant staff clearly defined mechanisms for monitoring and supporting student progress.

At the start of any research degree programme, one of the main responsibilities of a supervisor or supervisory team is to manage the expectations of the student as regards the type and frequency of meetings. The Code of Practice (QAA 2004) makes recommendations about:

- The minimum frequency of scheduled meetings between student and supervisor, or supervisory team, and the purpose of such meetings
- Guidance on the nature and style of the student–supervisor interaction, including discussions about academic and personal progress.

Essentially, meetings fall into three categories: casual, informal and formal.

Casual meetings

Casual meetings usually are brief and often focus on addressing specific questions that will help the student to pursue his or her studies. In some subject areas, such as science or engineering, where students may be working in laboratories, these encounters may occur daily, whereas, for example, in arts-based disciplines, such casual meetings might be quite rare. Realistically, the nature and outcomes of such a meeting will determine whether a record, however brief, should be kept.

Often students feel that there is a power imbalance in student–supervisor relationships, and this can particularly relate to the organization, conduct of meetings and receiving feedback as follows:

> At first I thought that when the supervisor doesn't give you feedback, you can't put pressure on them. You can't give them a deadline. You don't have that power. Later I learned that I could make demands. But students at the start are not aware of this as an option – that they can validly make demands. They shouldn't be frightened. But it doesn't work that way. There's a pecking order. You get frustrated at not being able to get your ideas through. The supervisor gets frustrated too and takes that out on

you. . . . I read a book on assertiveness. I now feel I can establish my rights, rather than have them trickled down to me. And if people don't respond, then fine. You can move on from there. But some supervisors won't accept this.

Informal meetings

Informal meetings, in contrast, are held specifically to monitor student progress. It is to be expected that for many students such meetings would be more frequent early in the first year of the programme than, for example, in the second and later years. It is also known that there are discrete stages in the supervision development process (Anderson 1988), and that these stages and the nature of the supervisor–student relationship change over time (Gurr 2001). Gurr (2001: 86) went one stage further and described a distinct supervisory transition: 'as a student undergoes academic growth during candidature, the supervisory style needs to be adjusted to a more hands-off approach in order to allow competent autonomy to be developed'.

For full-time students informal meetings may occur every four weeks or so, and it is strongly recommended that they be recorded for a variety of reasons, not least being the need to establish an audit trail (see below and Precept 17). Regular informal meetings, unlike casual meetings, usually present an opportunity for in-depth discussion for an hour or more and must be recorded. It is at such meetings that appreciation of good progress can and should be expressed, whereas if there is genuine concern about lack of progress, the appropriate mechanisms can hopefully be put in place early enough to remedy the situation. If after a period of time a student does not make sufficient progress, then it might be appropriate to involve another colleague, for example the departmental graduate tutor and/or head of department, to discuss the issues that are limiting progress. In this regard, it is essential that students are provided with information outlining procedures that the university will follow, if a situation arises where insufficient progress is being made. As noted in the QAA Code of Practice (under Precept 17), it can be strategically very useful if records of these regular informal meetings are drafted initially by the student, and promptly sent by email to the supervisor. The student then develops a sense of ownership for the meeting record, while the supervisor can immediately assess what the student may have understood from the meeting, make appropriate corrections, help with reporting style and promptly return the document to the student for amendment. Moreover, an email record of the meeting serves as a more or less permanent record for audit trail purposes (in the event of an appeal) and, with the agreement of the student, can be used to inform additional members of the supervisory team and others; external sponsors, for example, are often impressed on receiving these regular reports on progress. It is just as important for the student to maintain meeting records, as for the supervision team.

Such informal meetings with part-time students will typically occur less frequently than casual meetings, although communication by telephone and/ or email is considered essential and regular contact should be encouraged. This is especially important for students who are off-campus, overseas or in remote locations (for example, on fieldwork), who do most or all of their research work away from the institution. In these cases, it is especially important to keep accurate records of all contact.

Formal meetings

Formal meetings which deal with a review of a student's progress and forward planning are discussed in Precept 16.

Pastoral care

Although the supervisor and supervisory team have a pastoral role in managing the postgraduate student, increasingly an independent pastoral tutor may be appointed and may even be a member of an expanded supervisory team. The role of the pastoral tutor is to provide personal support and advice and is especially important when difficulties arise in the supervisor–student relationship, or if it is likely to break down. The pastoral tutor can have a particularly important role in the first year, when the student may not have the confidence or experience to know what to do if he or she experiences difficulties in working with a supervisor. Such a situation may require the pastoral tutor to play an active role in improving the supervisor–student relationship. In small departments it may be convenient for the graduate tutor to take on this role, whereas in large departments, pastoral tutors will be selected from a pool of experienced academics. Due to workload demands it may be possible to arrange only one or two informal meetings between a student and pastoral tutor per year. However, once initial contact has been made by the student, pastoral tutors are usually available to provide independent advice at any convenient time outside of the research-review meetings.

Student isolation, as described below, is a typical example where a pastoral tutor may be able to offer guidance:

> I was in a small department. There were five postgrads from different countries, each one from a different country. Then there was a group who were all from the same country and they tended to speak their own language, which is something they like to do. Going through that, you're on your own essentially because they tend to stay apart. You don't benefit from their knowledge, when they've been there three or four years before you. So you don't intermingle socially, on the level where you can talk about the difficulties they've had over the three or four years.

Precept into Practice – 15

Issue

Andrew, a first year MPhil/PhD student, realized he had difficulties understanding what his principal supervisor, Prof. Grenvil, was asking of him in his research project. Moreover, Andrew was a little shy and somewhat afraid of the high-flying Prof. Grenvil and unable to develop a satisfactory working relationship with him. The problem was that as time went on, Prof. Grenvil was beginning to think that Andrew was unable to cope with the demands of the research project and considered him to be a bit of a disappointment.

Resolution

It was a rather depressed Andrew who attended the first annual meeting with his pastoral tutor, Dr Beale, who soon realized early in the discussion that Andrew was unhappy with his lack of progress, primarily caused by his poor relationship with his principal supervisor. Dr Beale also realized that he had to act quickly and let Prof. Grenvil know of Andrew's difficulties. Fortunately, Dr Beale understood that he had to be tactful in his meeting with Prof. Grenvil and that, depending on Prof. Grenvil's reaction, he might have to follow up this first meeting with a second that would include Andrew, so that in the right atmosphere, both supervisor and student could speak honestly about their relationship, but, it was hoped, in a constructive manner.

Progress reviews

Precept 16
Institutions will put in place and bring to the attention of students and relevant staff clearly defined mechanisms for formal reviews of student progress, including explicit review stages.

It is normal practice that each research student prepares at least one progress report per year, including proposals for future work, for review by a formal mechanism. This report forms the focus for a meeting with the supervisory team, with or without a reviewer who is not part of the supervisory team, such as the graduate tutor. In some departments there may be an independent review panel – perhaps with the supervisor(s) there as observer(s), particularly for the transfer review. The supervisor usually prepares an independent report on student progress and states whether it is satisfactory or unsatisfactory. This part of the report is often countersigned by the student. Furthermore, the student may also be asked to report on his or her experience, and this is usually countersigned by the supervisor. The supervisor's recommendation may be assessed by the graduate tutor and/or the relevant research degrees committee (or equivalent) and the outcome communicated to the student by Registry.

Some sponsored students, particularly those supported by an overseas government or by an industrial or other research agency, may be required to report at more frequent intervals – typically six-monthly – and to produce proposals for future work. Usually these reports include a brief statement by the supervisor on his or her view of the student's progress.

In the progress report, the options available to the supervisor include a recommendation that the student proceed to the next stage, or that action be taken by the Graduate School (or equivalent) to address the need to improve progress – which can ultimately (but exceptionally) result in termination of a student's registration. Apart from the MPhil transfer to PhD at the end of the first year of study, which is discussed in some detail below, the other important progress review dates occur at the end of the second and third years of study. At the end of the second year a similar progress report is submitted to the graduate tutor (or research degrees committee or equivalent). Usually only those students whose progress has not been deemed to be satisfactory are considered in detail (with or without an interview), and in these cases remedial action may be advised. For third-year students, in addition to the progress report, details of the thesis plan, the expected submission deadline and comment on any practical constraints on completing the thesis on time should be provided.

Because of the serious nature of progress reviews, the Code of Practice recommends the following be considered and the student informed accordingly:

- The implications of the possible outcomes of review meetings
- The criteria to be used for making decisions about the extension, suspension or termination of a student's registration
- The mechanism(s) by which a student may appeal.

Of course, these issues will be determined by institutional regulations, but it is recommended that this information be made available to students and supervisors in an institutional research student handbook, either as a hard copy and/or as an electronic version.

It should be noted that institutions take these progress reports very seriously, as they are often seen by the graduate tutor, head of department and graduate dean. Overall findings of these reports may also be discussed at faculty and university research committees and may lead to further action, such as policy development, if necessary.

Precept into Practice – 16

Issue

Julie was coming to the end of her second year of study, after having success-fully completed the MPhil/PhD transfer process in the previous year. Her supervisor, Dr Grant, was pleased with Julie's progress and with his own recent successes in obtaining major commercial sponsorship. The latter arose from the findings of Julie's research and, perhaps not surprisingly, Julie's future work would be closely linked to these commercial interests. While pre-paring for her second-year progress talk, Julie began to realize that her presen-tation would be incomplete and plans for the future work vague, as a Materials Transfer Agreement (MTA), signed by all parties to protect confidentiality of the work, was preventing her from discussing her research project in full, and was possibly compromising the review process.

Resolution

Maintaining confidentiality by a signed, legally binding agreement is in some cases necessary and unavoidable. This means that the formal progress review has to be treated as a special case. Julie will still be required to present her work and put forward plans for future experiments, but in a way that maintains confidentiality of the data. Apart from some of the details not being released, the review process can still go ahead. However, as this is a special case, all supervisors, including commercial parties, should meet to review Jane's pro-gress and future research plans and produce a report that will not compromise confidentiality of data and which will be sent to the department or equivalent Graduate Research Committee for their consideration. In the formal review of Julie's work, her routine presentation of findings, together with the special report, should be considered before a final decision and any relevant feedback are communicated.

Transfer from MPhil to PhD

Students who already hold an appropriate master's degree obtained by research may be permitted to register directly for the degree of PhD. Similarly, for example in Ireland, a student who holds an appropriate taught master's degree can register for a PhD directly. However, such students have to success-fully undergo a confirmation procedure (similar to the MPhil to PhD transfer procedure), usually before the second year of research for full-time students. In the majority of UK institutions, students are registered initially for the degree of MPhil (or another master's degree, such as the MRes), with the expectation that, subject to satisfactory progress they will later transfer to the PhD track. Not surprisingly, with increasing pressure on students to complete on time, there is even greater emphasis and importance placed on this crucial academic milestone.

The decision to recommend transfer to a PhD is often taken towards the end of (or just after) the first year for full-time students and towards the end of the second year for part-time students. The decision is usually based on:

- Satisfactory progress, as indicated by the supervisor
- Production of a transfer report (or mini-thesis)
- Satisfactory performance at an independently chaired panel interview (or mini-viva) based on the transfer report and the student's response to questions and issues raised by the panel
- Evidence that the student has participated satisfactorily in the development of generic skills, such as in a Research Training Programme, either with the requisite number of credits or some equivalent measure.

An example of a typical procedure for transfer of registration from MPhil to PhD is shown in Figure 5.1.

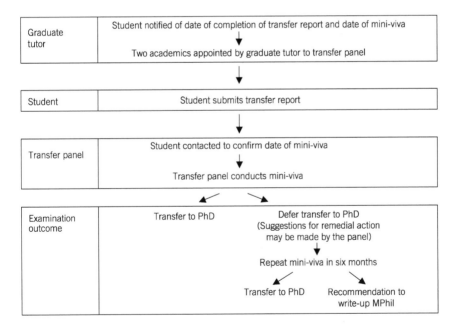

Figure 5.1   Procedure for transfer from MPhil to PhD.
Source: University of Sheffield

Transfer report

Typically, the transfer report will consist of a literature review, which would be written as an introduction to the report, followed by a summary of progress to date. An essential feature is the student's plan for future work and/or a detailed description of the research question. In science-based subjects there would also be a brief description of materials and methods, and the major part of the report would consist of results and their interpretation in a discussion section. In the liberal arts, social sciences, management and humanities, the transfer report may take the form of one or more draft chapters of the thesis, together with a detailed discussion of the research question in the context of the pertinent literature. Submission of a transfer report should normally be made with the agreement and support of the supervisory team.

Mini-viva

Very often the transfer interview equates to a shortened version of the PhD viva. Students are assessed by a transfer panel comprising two (or occasionally more) independent academics appointed by the graduate tutor (or equivalent), with or without the members of the supervisory team (depending on the institution) as observers. The purpose of the 'mini-viva' is for the transfer panel to review a short presentation by the student of the report (often using PowerPoint or equivalent), to clarify any ambiguities within the report, to discuss the research issues arising from the report and to establish that the student's knowledge of the field and plans for future progress are of a standard appropriate for transfer to PhD. It is essential therefore, that the members of the transfer panel are familiar with the student's research field.

The interview is conducted under the chairmanship of a senior academic in a similar way to the PhD oral examination; it normally lasts for about an hour. Both the transfer report and the mini-viva are assessed separately, as for a PhD thesis and the viva, with details of the assessments inserted on a transfer recommendation form (for a typical example, see Figure 5.2). Recommendations, made in absence of the supervisor(s) (if present in the first place), are signed by the panel members, and sent with other relevant documentation to the Registry or the Graduate School (or equivalent) for approval, following consultation, as appropriate, with the supervisory team. A key feature of the transfer recommendation form is that it provides excellent formative feedback to students on their progress. A number of outcomes are possible after the mini-viva, as was outlined in Figure 5.1.

Name of student:...

Name of supervisor:...

Transfer/upgrade report
Does the report provide evidence that the student is capable of developing their area of research to meet the standard required for PhD or MD in terms of: (1) research methods; (2) writing abilities; (3) original ideas; (4) familiarity with the literature and (5) presentational skills?

Viva Voce
Was the student's performance satisfactory?

Recommendation for transfer/upgrade to PhD or MD (please tick one)

YES	*REFER TO COMMITTEE

Please continue below or overleaf if required.

Signature:..   **Date:**.....................................
Senior examiner

Co-examiner...

The student's progress will be evaluated by a panel of the School Graduate Research Committee.   If appropriate, the examiners (above) may also advise a re-write of the report which will be considered by the committee.   The assessment will also include progress in the RTPs, Laboratory books, supervisor statements, etc.

Figure 5.2   MPhil to PhD/MD transfer report form.

Source: University of Sheffield

Meeting log

Precept 17
Institutions will provide guidance to students, supervisors and others involved in progress monitoring and review processes about the importance of keeping appropriate records of the outcomes of meetings and related activities.

A meeting log is a useful tool for recording the outcome of regular informal meetings. Copies of logs can be kept by student and supervisor. As noted above, a helpful stratagem widely used for this purpose is to arrange for the student to first-author the report on a meeting. These reports have a number of potential uses:

• Record of student progress (including an indication of the level of progress

attained), which is now sometimes required as part of the overall progress review
- Clarity over joint ownership of (*or*: 'jointly agreed') current and future research objectives
- Documentary evidence showing proof of meetings (especially when both parties exchange by email, or in some institutions, jointly sign) in cases of student complaints of inadequate supervision or on other grounds (for example, lack of facilities, access to conferences etc.)
- Identification of problems in the research programme and/or supervisory or other problems (for example, pastoral issues affecting the student's work).

There are a number of ways that a log can be kept. First, there are hard copies (Figure 5.3), which are completed and jointly signed off by supervisor and student.

Research student: .... Supervisor: ....

Date of last meeting: .... Date of this meeting: ....

Duration of meeting: ....

	Supervisor	Student
On a scale of 1 to 5, where 1 is very poor and 5 is excellent, how would you rate the progress of the project since the last meeting? If appropriate please comment below.		

Achievements since last meeting and other comments (continue overleaf if necessary)

	Supervisor		Student	
	Yes	No	Yes	No
Has the student made sufficient progress since the last meeting?				
Are the supervisor and student clear about current objectives?				
Have any specific problems associated with the work or the supervision been identified? If appropriate, please comment below.				
Are the supervisor and student clear about the work to be done before the next meeting?				

Goals for the next 4–6 weeks and other comments (continue overleaf if necessary).

Student signature:..

Supervisor signature: ....

It is suggested that a supervisory meeting is held at least every month. The supervisor should retain the reports as a record of the student's progress and copies should be held by the student. First year students are required to submit six completed reports prior to transfer of registration.

Figure 5.3 Supervisory meeting report.

Source: University of Sheffield

Second, there are electronic copies, which can be completed by student, supervisor or both, and then signed off by both. Third, students might like to use meeting logs (which can still be copied to and signed by a supervisor) as part of their personal and professional development plan (PPDP), which may be hosted on a personal digital assistant (PDA) device or in a reserved and protected area of the institution's web space. PPDPs are widely seen as a useful tool for the student to privately review and reflect upon their performance in a context wider than research progress alone – and also to plan for the future. These are mentioned in Chapter 2 and discussed in more detail in Chapter 6. Issues concerning confidentiality need to be recognized and resolved at the start of the doctoral research programme, in order to establish a mutually beneficial basis of trust from the outset.

Meeting logs are now widely used, as they are often easy and quick to complete and provide an excellent record of progress, which is relevant to both parties. They are particularly useful for starting discussions in a formal meeting and formulating clear objectives for the next meeting.

Precept into Practice – 17

Issue

Jeremy was now in his fourth year of a part-time PhD with Prof. Singleton. In the first three years, Jeremy's work had been outstanding, and Prof. Singleton had no concerns about him completing his PhD on time. However, at the beginning of his fourth year, Jeremy had encountered serious personal and work problems, and his research project had been inactive for several months. In the first three years of the PhD, neither Jeremy nor Prof. Singleton had concerned themselves with the formality of completing meeting logs on a regular basis. However, in this difficult fourth year, Jeremy got out of the habit of having meetings with Prof. Singleton, as there was no research progress to report and, of course, meeting logs were not completed. In any case, he had too many other things to worry about. Unfortunately, months had elapsed without any informal or formal contacts between the two parties.

Resolution

Early on in the PhD both Jeremy and Prof. Singleton should have been encouraged and/or pressurized to complete meeting logs on a regular basis. Perhaps ideally, it should be the student who produces the log and asks the supervisor to approve it. In this case, the difficulties seem to be those of the student. Ideally, the student should still be meeting Prof. Singleton on a regular basis and completing meeting logs, even if little or no progress is being made. Arguably, it is in this type of situation, when difficulties have arisen, that meetings and/or meeting logs are most useful. If a part-time student, in particular, becomes inactive research-wise, and if the supervisor is busy with many other commitments, contact can be lost for a considerable time before anything is done about it. In this situation, Prof. Singleton should encourage Jeremy to arrange some meetings, and in this case take the initiative to complete the meeting logs, and ask Jeremy to approve and sign them. If and when Jeremy's difficulties have diminished and he can continue with his research project, he should then take responsibility for completing a meeting log on a regular basis.

Conclusion

At the outset the supervisor is responsible for clarifying with the student, the type and frequency of meetings. These arrangements can then change by mutual consent as the research programme progresses. At the same time it is important that regular informal meetings are recorded, using, for example, email exchange or a meeting log, which can be shared by supervisor and student.

The pastoral tutor, possibly as part of a supervisory team, can identify and help with personal and other issues that sometimes, but not exclusively, arise early on, in order to help avoid a breakdown in the student–supervisor relationship.

Formal review of progress reports submitted at least annually by the student, with appropriate comments from the supervisory team, are essential for encouraging and documenting satisfactory progress, and in addressing what further action needs to be taken in the case of unsatisfactory progress. Similarly, in order to ensure that students are able to meet the challenge of completing the doctoral programme successfully (or to ensure that, where appropriate, students are directed early onto a master's exit route), a transfer panel from MPhil to PhD is widely used as a formal assessment process, involving submission of a transfer report by the student, followed by a mini-viva. Phillips (1992) found that there was a wide variety of practice in the way that the MPhil to PhD transfer was handled. Some departments have extremely formal procedures in operation while others are less structured and informal. However, in the light of the QAA (2004) guidelines, the process is generally becoming more formal.

Finally, the development of the student's PPDP, hosted on a PDA or on reserved, confidential computer space at the institution, is proving to be a valuable tool for developing the student's capacity for reflection on progress and for encouraging effective planning for the future.

Talking points

- Unlike the MPhil to PhD transfer process, judging progress at later stages of the PhD can be problematic.
- Both pastoral care and progress monitoring can be difficult with part-time students.
- How long can it take before a student runs out of time to transfer from MPhil to PhD – in other words is there an upper time limit when transfer must have taken place?
- Asking for copies of meeting logs as a requirement for the transfer process ensures that progress meetings have taken place.
- Whose responsibility is it to arrange a meeting when contact between supervisor and student has lapsed?
- Should novice supervisors be taught about supervisory management styles in order to help develop their own styles and to understand different supervisor–student relationships?

Key text

Gurr, G. M. (2001) Negotiating the 'Rackety Bridge': a dynamic model for aligning supervisory style with research student development. *Higher Education Research and Development*, 20: 81–92.

6

Induction and training in research and generic skills

Research and other skills • Personal and professional development • Defining and reviewing development needs • Induction • Developing 'communication and other skills': the case of writing • Recording progress • Conclusion • Talking points • Key texts

> The training of postgraduate research students within the structure of a research degree programme is a controversial and difficult issue for many academics and for the institutions within which they work. So it should be ... because when colleagues grapple with the issue of research training, they are compelled to think about what it means to do a PhD.
>
> (Roberts 2007: ix)

Induction is important because it sets the student up for the whole educational experience of the doctorate, but any induction will be predicated on a definition of what it means to do a doctorate. What are the 'training' elements? What are 'research skills'? What are 'generic' skills? What is essential, and what is optional? How much depends on the student's needs? To what extent is providing 'research training' the supervisor's responsibility? What standard should such training meet, and how can supervisors assess it? How much of this will supervisors provide, and how much relies on others' expertise? How can the 'silent majority' of part-time students access training – and do they, as has been argued, have different needs (McCulloch and Stokes 2008)?

This chapter explores what is often called the 'training agenda' or the 'skills' agenda, addressed in Precepts 18–20 (and in Appendix 3). These precepts raise questions about what supervisors can do to support this agenda, and this chapter shows how these precepts can be embedded in supervision.

Research and other skills

New students arrive with some skills, but other skills will be learned or developed during the research. The first step for supervisors is to conduct a training needs analysis at the start of the first year; thereafter, the student is encouraged to 'become an increasingly autonomous learner' (Gough and Denicolo 2007: 3), but supervisors will still monitor skills development and other training.

Seeing the doctorate as a training or learning process is common sense to some, but contentious to others. Whatever position supervisors – and students – take in this debate, there is a range of modes for training students: self-directed learning; departmental courses; workshops; presenting at seminars and conferences; training courses; formal, assessed courses; informal learning, networking and, of course, supervisor direction, feedback and mentoring (adapted from QAA Code of Practice, 'Appendix 3: Skills training requirements for research students' [QAA 2004: 33–35] and originally developed from Research Councils UK [2001] as the *Joint Statement of Skills*).

How much of this 'required' skills development can supervisors provide? How much will be 'sourced' from elsewhere? Can supervisors rely on students to find training opportunities to meet their needs? Is funding available for students to attend training courses elsewhere? Have student and supervisor agreed what the training needs are? An essential starting point is to review the skills students already have.

While the subject of skills learned during a doctorate will also be the subject of debate, sooner or later student and supervisor have to decide on a training programme. Reviewing a list of skills, whether generated by the discipline or the specific research project, is as good a way as any of defining training needs. For example, the QAA (2004) list (Appendix 3) has two full pages of skills groupings:

(A) Research skills and techniques
(B) Research environment
(C) Research management
(D) Personal effectiveness
(E) Communication skills

(F) Networking and teamworking
(G) Career management.

(QAA 2004: 34–35)

For each of these, there are definitions in Appendix 3 of what students should be 'able to do' after training. To some supervisors, these will seem relevant to all doctorates; others will argue that the terms, as they stand, are too generic. However, supervisors can ensure that each is defined, in terms of what each means for a specific doctorate and a specific student. Taken together, these skills are integral to research, and it can be assumed that they are included in the precepts, because focusing on these skills has benefit for the research project and contributes to the student's education.

A key question that supervisors face is how far to go in the 'programme' direction – in what sense can a doctorate be considered as a 'programme of study'?

> The notion of a 'PhD programme' takes on a more pertinent meaning . . . whereby the notion of a programme implies a series of specific and managed events . . . this points to a modularized approach where students can receive the best training appropriate to their needs, while, simultaneously, the responsibility for the PhD as an experience and outcome becomes more heterogeneous and dispersed.

(Reeves 2007: 158)

A key feature of this definition of a doctoral 'programme' appears to be relevant not only to the research but also to the researcher. What does this mean for the supervisor's role? Those who fear that this approach dilutes the doctorate will have legitimate reservations about this approach and an understandable reluctance to adopt it. However, supervisors may find that they have little room to manoeuvre and that their resistance is stigmatized: 'The problem with skills training is . . . the supervisor' (Reeves 2007: 152). Reeves presents four ways in which supervisors can be seen to undermine their students' skills development:

(1) sabotage, when supervisors refer to skills training as 'a complete waste of time';
(2) indifference, when supervisors fail to support the training element, holding and expressing the view that 'non-academic staff [providing skills training] have nothing to offer the PhD';
(3) apparent support for the training agenda, but conveying to students that it is an external imposition – 'if we don't go along with the training agenda, the institution will lose money';
(4) hypocrisy, when supervisors praise the training but actively undermine it locally.

(Reeves 2007: 152–153)

Supervisors' views are, of course, highly influential for students, and supervisors' attitudes towards training can directly influence students' approaches to it, thus influencing its potential benefit.

Each supervisor will have his or her own view on training, and that may, of course, be influenced by its content, quality and providers. This chapter is not intended to promote all forms of training; instead, it is intended to prompt supervisors to consider the training element in doctorates they supervise. If that training is not up to scratch, or does not meet students' needs, supervisors surely have a responsibility to help students find other forms of training, perhaps elsewhere. This is a matter of urgency when training elements are needed for progress in the doctorate. As time passes, lack of training can lead to other problems. Nor will everyone agree about what training should occur when. For example, while Race's (2007: 141) schematic of postgraduate training places training for the viva in year three, Trafford and Leshem (2008) argue that it should begin at the start of the doctorate.

Whenever skills training is offered, whatever content or mode is used and whoever delivers it, the word 'requirements' in the QAA precepts not only conveys the importance of the skills agenda, but also means that it is less a matter for debate and more a matter for implementation. For example, there will be conferences that students should attend; there will be journals that are suited to their work – either 'entry level' or high impact journals – a choice, supervisors can help students to make. In other words, supervisors can ensure that the 'other' skills that students develop during a doctorate are those that help them to complete their research.

Personal and professional development

Precept 18
Institutions will provide research students with appropriate opportunities for personal and professional development.

The notes provided on this precept raise several questions. What can supervisors do to 'enhance their [students'] employability? What does 'assist their [students'] career progress' mean (QAA 2004: 20) in practice? As for the balance of 'wider employment-related skills' and the 'core objective' of a doctorate, that too will be calculated and agreed – by supervisor and student – at an early stage and reviewed at key points throughout the doctoral process. Student themselves can be active participants in defining their learning needs, and this in itself is seen as an important aspect of research and professional practice: 'Research students are encouraged to recognize the value of transferable skills in enabling them to take ownership and responsibility for their own learning, during and after their programme of study' (QAA 2004: 20). This language will not necessarily be meaningful to all students; the implication is that supervisors might have to explain what this means in the context of their university, the student's project and the resources available for skills development. One such conversation might not be enough; there may be further discussions, redefinitions and, ultimately, even discussion of competing definitions.

This may be the subject of debate with students who simply want to get started on their research, without all this definition of skills etc. This raises the issue of 'timeliness' (QAA 2004: 20) – what is the appropriate time for students to receive each element of their training? Perhaps a more important question is how much training is needed at the start of the doctorate, before students start their research? Which elements can be considered mandatory, for a specific project, at this stage? For example, what training or support is needed for postgraduates who teach (Morss and Murray 2005)? Should this be offered before they start teaching, or can it be provided as they go along? Will there be further training needs analyses at later stages in the doctorate?

Precept into Practice – 18

Issue

Rachel was in the second year of her PhD, which was funded by industry, and was having a frustrating time in the laboratory after spending months trying to get a crucial experiment to work. Despite the efforts of her supervisory team, Rachel just was not making much progress, which was dampening her enthusiasm. It did not help that she was the only PhD student in the department doing this type of work.

Resolution

Fortunately, her institution ran a Local GRADschool that was provided free to all local doctoral researchers, irrespective of funding source, and this was useful, as the National GRADschool is provided free only to Research Council funded students. GRADschools are a major provider of personal skills training and advice through courses that normally last between three and five days. Rachel found that the Local GRADschool gave her new insights into her PhD programme, better perspectives on her achievements and skills, and best of all, increased her motivation to get her experiment to work.

One implication for institutions is that training provision should be reviewed regularly. Perhaps it will be accredited, as is the case for the Research Training Programme at the University of Sheffield. Does the supervisor have a role in designing a curriculum, or for evaluating the quality of research training, even when it is provided by others? Perhaps not, if the training is provided by other departments or at other institutions, and if those departments or institutions evaluate its quality and communicate that evaluation to supervisors. Perhaps yes, if its impact on the student's personal or professional development is limited. In other words, supervisors will inevitably make some form of evaluation – informally, if not formally – of the impact of research training on their students. They are likely to evaluate the quality of training in terms of whether or not student have learned what they need to know or do. However, informal evaluation in this instance has potential attendant risks: it might seem more subjective and it might be less systematic. A further complication is that the benefits of some forms of training are not recognized till later, perhaps even after completion of the doctorate.

Defining and reviewing development needs

Precept 19
Each student's development needs will be identified and agreed jointly by the student and appropriate academic staff, initially during the student's induction period; they will be regularly reviewed during the research programme and amended as appropriate.

Experienced supervisors can quickly draw up checklists of skills their students need and are likely to be adept at aligning these with, for example, research council requirements, particularly if funding has been provided for training. Defining what students should 'be able to do/demonstrate' after training is one way of preparing to assess students' skills after training, and, as for any other course of study, these can be explicitly defined and agreed.

Precept into Practice – 19

Issue

Dr Eagle was a relatively new supervisor but had worked hard at the institution's compulsory Certificate in Learning and Teaching for new academic staff and was very supportive of the requirement for a training needs analysis (TNA) for new PhD students. He had organized a TNA with his PhD student, Laura, soon after she had arrived, and all training needs had been planned for the duration of the PhD. However, as often happens in a PhD programme, Laura's research had moved in a different direction during her second year and was likely to continue to deviate from the original research plans in the third and final year. The problem now was that the original TNA and current needs were becoming incompatible and were beginning to disturb Laura, as she was getting towards the end of her second year, and Dr Eagle did not seem to be aware of the current mismatch of planned and current needs.

> **_Resolution_**
>
> It is naive for the supervisor and student to consider that once a TNA has been carried out early in the first year, that is the end of the matter. As is shown in this example, it is important to monitor annually that the original TNA is still relevant. Of course, if the research project has changed substantially, then it should be a matter of some urgency that the TNA is closely examined and reconfigured.

There would be no harm in having a development plan, in tandem with the plan of work for the research project. In fact, mapping training over the lifetime of the project is one way of spelling out the learning stages involved in the doctorate. Some argue that there should be a doctoral 'curriculum' (Mullen 2001).

Evaluating training requires a review of its impact on the student: did the student find it useful? Is the relevance of the training to the research, or the researcher, clear? Should the issue of relevance be addressed in student–supervisor discussion? What further training needs were identified?

While supervisors are not responsible for the quality of training courses, they can gather information about them and, perhaps more reasonably, check that such information is being gathered: participants' feedback, participants' learning, behaviour change, application of skills learned and impact of these changes on the research and the researcher (Lewis and Hall 2007: 105).

Induction

Here is one student's view of the first three months of the doctorate:

> In the initial three months there's a lot you can do to maintain the relationship with the supervisor. . . . Also, if you're unaware there could be a problem you walk right into it. The first year's strange. Everything's unknown. Most students feel they do not know what is expected of them. The student's got to remember it's their project. It goes where they want it to go . . . essentially, it's yours and you should put it to the supervisor, 'This is what I want to do'. If he or she agrees, that's fine. So you've got to establish quickly the structure of your project, the three years.

This student articulates what he saw as a common problem in the early stages of the doctorate. Although it is difficult to know how widespread it is, he was convinced that his experience was typical. While the problem seems simple, there are several potential interpretations of this account: it could be that the student was unable to take responsibility in the early stages because he knew very little about the PhD and about his supervisor; the student might have had a dilemma – wanting to be responsible, but afraid of making mistakes or of being seen as a weak student; or with the best of intentions, the supervisor might have been alternating between giving direction and asking the student to take more initiative; or it could be that there was insufficient planning in the first three months, with inadequate goal setting, leaving the student feeling that goals had not been achieved; or it might be that planning and discussion had taken place, but had not been recorded in writing, and had been forgotten, or was remembered differently by supervisor and student.

When asked to consider this problem, students produce a wide range of views on what should be done in this situation:

- 'All students should read *How to Get a PhD* (Phillips and Pugh 2005), and the department should bulk buy copies of this book for all students.'
- 'Supervisors should encourage students to ask questions about what they do not know, even "silly" questions; students should find out about the whole structure of the PhD, what to expect at each stage, all the way through to the viva, even how to use the library.'
- 'Students should take responsibility, for example, for calling meetings right at the start, and take minutes, otherwise the supervisor forgets.'
- 'Supervisors should make time for students every week in the first three months.'

What are the implications of these interpretations and proposed solutions for supervisors? What would be a reasonable response from a supervisor to the problem posed – how can it be resolved, or can it be avoided altogether? As with the student responses, discussions with supervisors produced a range of options:

- 'Encourage students, during the first three months, to find out about the PhD process and take time (two days was suggested) to explore the library.'
- 'Encourage students, at this early stage, to attend a thesis writing course, if available, or to find information in other forms.'
- 'Begin to work with students on sketching their doctoral programme and their research project over the whole three or four years (or more, for part-time students).'
- 'Prompt the student to put this sketch in writing/diagram display and return to it regularly at supervision meetings to revise deadlines for writing and research tasks.'

Whatever our interpretation of this situation, and whatever our proposed solution, it is clear that this case raises questions about the induction process experienced by the student in this case. It appears that some of the essential elements were missing.

Essential elements of postgraduate induction

The essential elements of induction include the following:

- Introduction to the doctoral process, including review and assessment
- Library resources and literature search skills
- Communication skills: presentations, reports, abstracts and thesis writing
- Research methods training
- University code of practice on higher degrees or supervision
- Professional body's and/or institution's code of practice
- Ethics: definitions, procedures and approval
- Plan of work, e.g. Gantt chart, parallel tasks and deadlines (A Gantt chart is a planning tool that displays sets of tasks over time in a linear graphic. It is useful for showing parallel tasks, i.e. a range of tasks that have to be performed at the same time. They are therefore useful for research students who have several different tasks to do in the course of a doctorate. In addition, a Gantt chart shows whether tasks are to be done in sequence or simultaneously or where they overlap, and this supports students' planning.)
- Other forms of support, contact names, email addresses
- Project management
- Seminars, presentations and conferences (including deadlines for abstracts)
- Training and/or support for teaching, if required
- Discussion of all of the above, to check student understanding and identify any remaining questions or issues.

'Induction' does not simply mean introducing the student to the institutional and disciplinary conventions and courses; induction is also a time when supervisors assess students' potential and calculate what type of supervision role they will be required to play. Anderson (1988) identified four styles of supervision:

(i)   direct active, characterised by initiating, criticising, telling and directing;
(ii) indirect active, characterised by asking for opinions and suggestions, accepting and expanding supervisee's ideas, or asking for explanations and justifications of supervisee's statements;
(iii) indirect passive, characterised by listening and waiting for supervisees to process ideas and problem solve; and,
(iv) passive, characterised by having no input and not responding to supervisee's input.

(Anderson 1988, quoted in Gurr 2001: 86)

Supervisor style can be adapted not only to suit the needs of different students but also to meet students' needs at different stages in the doctoral process (Gurr 2001). This dynamic model of supervision has advantages, although it is possible to imagine that some of these changes could be unsettling for students if they were not discussed and agreed. Above all, what is useful about using a specific model of supervision is that areas of both matching and potential conflict between students' and supervisors' models can be identified and discrepancies can be addressed (Lee 2008). Used this way, induction can function as an introduction to the supervisory relationship.

Developing 'communication and other skills': the case of writing

There are many 'other skills' that can be developed in different ways during a doctorate (Cryer 1998; Gough and Denicolo 2007). This section explores the idea that supervisors can help students develop such skills, illustrating the point by focusing on one communication skill – writing – and exploring how development of this skill can be embedded in supervision.

The implication for supervisors is that they can develop their knowledge of academic writing by accessing the literature on the subject, and can extend their knowledge of other skills in the same way. This is not to suggest that supervisors know nothing about academic writing – clearly, they will have considerable knowledge and experience of successful writing and publication – but that they can add to their knowledge by accessing literature beyond their disciplines. In addition, or alternatively, they can draw on others' expertise in these areas.

Starting with a literature search on 'academic writing', supervisors generally find that very little has been published in their disciplines. However, material can be accessed in the higher education literature, which exhibits an array of conceptual and practical approaches. While it is not useful to review them all here, selected approaches are suggested, particularly those that have already been adapted for doctoral students (Murray 2006a). References and directions for further reading are provided for supervisors to follow up. The purpose is to indicate the wealth of material out there that can be used to help researchers develop their writing skills in ways that will be relevant to their future careers, while helping them to complete a thesis on time.

Doctoral students have to learn to write to the highest standard in several forms, depending on the discipline: they need to acquire skills for writing a thesis, journal articles, conference abstracts, various forms of report – for annual review, progress reports, reports to funders, etc. – and research proposals. Many of these writing skills are transferable to other research settings, other types of professional work and other audiences. The implication for supervisors is that they have to help students develop an understanding of the requirements of each form of writing and, crucially, the stages involved in producing each one.

The word 'writing' – and the instruction to 'write' – can have many different meanings:

- Getting something down on paper
- Drafting
- Putting initial thoughts in writing
- Producing a specific form of writing, e.g. chapter, paper or report
- Revising
- Outlining.

The act of writing may involve all of these, but the instruction to 'write' does not define the requirements. The implication is that when students and supervisors talk about 'writing', it can be helpful to define and agree the scale and scope of a specific writing task, as well as the criteria that will be used to evaluate it, whenever that is relevant.

Similarly, for any act of communication – oral or written – key considerations are audience and purpose. The audience for a student's writing is surely the supervisor, but what role is the supervisor intending to play, when reading a specific piece of writing? Given that the supervisor's roles range from developer to assessor, knowing the specific role they play at any time is helpful to doctoral writers. In addition, the audience for doctoral writing includes the internal and external examiners and transfer panel, who will apply specific criteria. This is a complex context, and, for new researchers, it can complicate the apparently straightforward process of writing for an audience. In addition, other audiences come into play when students write for publication (Murray 2006b).

The same question applies to purpose: what is the main purpose of a piece of doctoral writing? This too can range widely, from demonstrating growing knowledge of the literature to making a case for methodology, for example. The purpose of writing during doctoral education is not just to document learning; some writing processes, and some of the writing tasks that supervisors set, are intended to stimulate learning. This means that students often write in uncertainty – or creativity? – and this may require writing without a sense of the criteria for evaluation of writing. This is different from writing in undergraduate courses.

An effective strategy for writing in this way is freewriting (Elbow 1973), a well-established approach, but not one with which supervisors are generally familiar. It involves writing continuously, without stopping, for five or ten minutes about any aspect of the research, or about any subject all, without concern for continuity or other aspects of academic writing. This produces writing that is for the student's use only; it is generally not for supervisors to read. The purpose of this approach is to allow students to concentrate on developing their ideas in writing, rather than focusing on technical aspects of writing. Supervisors who encourage their students to use freewriting say that they do so because it can help students to draft a complex section of their thesis, for example, or process new ideas or think creatively. Practised regularly, freewriting can help students to develop the writing habit. Discussions of this type of strategy are also useful for revealing practice issues, i.e. for exploring the processes whereby excellent academic writing is produced.

In addition to the general skills of advanced academic writing, there are also discipline-specific writing skills and conventions, and part of the doctoral process is learning them. Similarly, the question of the relationship between writing and other research processes may be seen as determined by discipline: reading, data collection and analysis, for example, all involve potentially different forms of writing, with further differences appearing as the research progresses and as the student's knowledge grows.

This raises the question of time: are there appropriate early, middle and late writing tasks in the production of a thesis? Does this too depend on the discipline in which the study is conducted? Is it also dictated by the student's progress? Whatever the supervisor's views on these questions, students need some idea of the stages in their writing process. As their research progresses, the question of the extent to which their writing meets doctoral criteria becomes more and more urgent for them. With so many definitions of and views on academic writing, it may be useful to think in terms of 'developing a common language for talking about writing' (Murray 2006a: 82).

For example, students attending courses on thesis writing, or academic writing, are likely to return to their departments with a new set of concepts, perhaps some new strategies and even new writing behaviours. They may use terms to discuss their writing that have not come up in previous discussions of their writing with their supervisors, such as freewriting, defined above. This can create a form of temporary language barrier, and even conflict between supervisor and student. In addition, students' expectations of feedback may have changed as a result of attending a course – in fact, during the doctorate there are likely to be many such changes, as students grow in understanding and confidence. Participation in a writing course may bring these changes to the surface. For supervisors, this presents a challenge in balancing responses to these changes while remaining consistent, as far as is appropriate, in their feedback on a student's writing.

Writing a thesis includes a number of different writing tasks. Some of these reflect the student's learning process, others reflect the research process and some combine the two. Each student has to learn to write in several different ways, and each supervisor has to find out how much the student already knows and decide, often in collaboration with the student, which of these tasks is relevant to the study:

- Writing a literature review (Hart 1998)
- Constructing academic arguments
- Using modes and conventions from the academic discipline
- Writing for other audiences (Murray 2006b)
- Writing for publication (Murray 2009b).

Another way of thinking about thesis writing is to define the steps in the process – getting started, constructing a thesis argument, serial revising, establishing a contribution to the field – and these can be mapped over the time allocated for the doctorate, in parallel with the research plan.

For each of these steps, different writing activities can be used, such as freewriting, generative writing, writing to prompts, outlining, developing productive writing practices, work-in-progress writing, incremental writing, creating closure, revising, writing for publication and post-viva revisions (Murray 2006a). The relevance of these strategies to academic writing contexts generally and doctoral students specifically is well established (Caffarella and Barnett 2000; Elbow 1973; Krashen 2002; Lee and Boud 2003; McGrail et al. 2006; McVeigh et al. 2002; Murray 2006a, 2009b; Pololi et al. 2004; Torrance et al. 1993). What might pull these activities together is a pedagogy for 'helping doctoral students to write' (Kamler and Thomson 2006).

Given this variation, students may need a bit more than a general invitation to write, such as 'write a draft of your literature review by the end of next month'. In this context, defining the writing task means giving it a specific scale and scope, including length and level of detail. In addition, it might be useful, at least in the early stages of the doctorate, to help the student to plan the stages in producing a draft chapter. Even highly intelligent, qualified and motivated students benefit from guidance in the performance of what is, after all, a series of new writing tasks in a new genre. In fact, some of the brightest students may be the ones who seek out explanations from their supervisors on what exactly is expected in their writing.

Writing issues

The following issues are important for defining each writing task:

- Defining writing tasks: making expectations and criteria explicit
- Or leaving them implicit or open
- Helping your student to select an appropriate form of writing
- Defining its scope and scale, from appropriate options
- Defining what is acceptable for early drafts of chapters and papers
- Defining 'good' and 'bad' writing at different stages in the doctorate
- Defining requirements for each revision
- Specifying what/how much structure is expected in early/mid/late writing.

Writing activities can be developed and used to help students move through stages of the doctorate: e.g. writing a summary of the thesis, outlining the stages in the argument and making explicit how each chapter supports the claim to 'contribution'. This prompts students to construct their contribution, prior to revision of the complete first draft, or prior to producing a first draft. They can work on introductions for each chapter that match up to this summary. They then check for internal coherence within the whole thesis and within each chapter. This is just one way of defining the task of moving into the final phase of the thesis-writing process, but these tasks can be done earlier. It depends on the field, the subject, the project, the student and the supervisor. This contingency can be confusing, even infuriating for students, but if rationales are provided, and processes articulated, they can see the value of each writing task and revision iteration that their supervisors request.

Perhaps the most important factor in a doctoral student's writing development is supervisor feedback. It sends strong signals to students about standards, progression and criteria. Supervisors may or may not have a 'typology' of comments (Murray 2006a: 214) that they use in feedback, but it is a good idea to discuss with students the intended meanings – perhaps including potential learning points and proposed revision actions – of the terms they use. Giving students time to discuss their interpretations of feedback and, if appropriate, to articulate responses to it, can be an important step in their development, allowing them to rehearse arguments and debate counterarguments. These are important 'other' skills for their future careers. In addition, research has shown that giving and receiving feedback on writing, in peer review sessions with other students, is considered by students to be one of the most effective ways of developing academic writing (Caffarella and Barnett 2000: 39). These activities may also prepare students for peer review.

Some areas may lie beyond the supervisor's expertise, such as English language support (Paltridge and Starfield 2007), or beyond what the supervisor sees as his or her role, such as proofreading. In these cases, it is even more important that these student needs are defined at an early stage and support found to meet them.

This section has explored the case of writing. This is one area where supervisors can play a major role in students' skills development. The case is made here that this role can be strengthened by supervisors' knowledge of the literature on academic writing, along with definition of the many different writing tasks and types of writing involved in the thesis-writing process.

Moreover, it could be argued that supervisors should access literature on a range of skills, not just on writing. Some of the literature may be found in their disciplines, or, more likely, in higher education research journals (e.g. *Studies in Higher Education, Higher Education Research and Development, Journal of Further and Higher Education*). There are also sources of information in higher education virtual or real centres for the study of their disciplines. In addition, a growing number of textbooks for students provide information that may also be useful to supervisors.

Other topics that are available in higher education and/or disciplinary literatures, that come under the heading of skills training, and could be of use to supervisors, include oral presentation skills, including preparing for the viva (Murray 2009a), motivational strategies (Bandura 1977), project management, time management, self-directed learning, emotional intelligence, teaching and learning in higher education (Morss and Murray 2005), mentoring, group work, goal setting, preparing a curriculum vitae, English as a second language (Paltridge and Starfield 2007) and interviewing. This is not to say that supervisors will want to research all of these areas for themselves; they may access expertise elsewhere in the institution, research council or some other body. However, making clear that there is an expertise base in these areas that is worth getting to know is a message to send to students at appropriate moments in the doctoral process. Supervisors may decide that students can research some of these areas, but the division of responsibility will have to be clear to all involved, and it may vary from student to student.

Whatever their level of knowledge of writing, supervisors can reveal their own writing skills and strategies – which often remain tacit – to students. Students are often fascinated when supervisors describe their actual academic writing practices and experiences. This provides a form of instruction in advanced academic writing skills, so that modelling writing practices can be an element of supervision. Beyond their own knowledge and practice, supervisors probably need a repertoire of strategies for helping students to develop their writing skills. This does not mean that supervisors become 'writing teachers', but it does mean that they can access literature for sound principles and tried and tested practices to implement the precepts.

Recording progress

Precept 20
Institutions will provide opportunities for research students to maintain a record of personal progress, which includes reference to the development of research and other skills.

In Precept 20 the expression 'Institutions will provide opportunities for' is open to a number of interpretations, one of which is that supervisors have a responsibility to ensure that students know about, use and benefit from such 'opportunities'. Many institutions already have personal development planning processes in place, so supervisors may not have to reinvent the wheel. However, for students who have never experienced this type of system, supervisors do have an explicitly defined responsibility: to provide 'additional guidance and support' (Precept 20, QAA 2004: 22). For supervisors who have never used this type of system, there should be some development and/or support, which they may have to seek out.

For many, this will be a perfectly adequate way of acknowledging skills development; for others, it will appear to produce an artificial separation of research and 'other' skills. It depends how personal development planning is used. This takes us back to the question at the start of this chapter – what does it mean to do a PhD? If it means training in both research and other skills, then the award of the PhD recognizes those skills. If it means completing a research project, with less emphasis on skills, then supervisors and students may begin to call for an additional form of recognition of those skills, in the form of a certificate, for example.

With all this attention to training, learning and development in research and 'other skills' – with 'milestones' in students' performance – it makes sense to have some way of managing it all, recording what the student has done and recording training and evidencing its impact for future employers. Taking stock can also be used to consolidate learning. Even if it is managed by students, supervisors may have an active role in this process (Gough and Denicolo 2007: 5).

In addition, it is probably not adequate simply to plan a student's development; it is reasonable to expect that there should be some way for students to incorporate their development – in a range of activities – into a coherent statement of what they have done and what they have learned during the doctorate. Writing this 'statement' may be easier said than done, and, since it is yet another new genre of writing, supervisors may have a role in supporting students in writing it.

Precept into Practice – 20

Issue

There is no doubt that recent developments in graduate education have placed increasing pressures on students to develop their personal and academic skills. Of course, these developments should result in a number of lifelong benefits. However, Ian who was in his first year of his PhD was finding it difficult to keep abreast of the many demands on his time and all the tasks he was supposed to be engaged in. Despite the efforts of his supervisory team, at times Ian found his situation overwhelming, and he was desperate for some sort of order and reflection in his academic life.

Resolution

In these circumstances the production of a personal and professional development plan (PPDP) might have been useful to Ian. Most institutions now provide this type of support for doctoral students, in the same way that undergraduates have benefited from the development of their personal and academic skills through a PPDP. A PPDP can be flexible, in that students can create and access their own record of development either online or by a permanent paper record. Although it is up to students to decide how they wish to use the plan, it is generally envisaged that it will be student led, with opportunities for discussions between supervisor and student, as required. Many students find that a PPDP is a useful tool for reviewing and reflecting on performance and for planning career development.

While there are learning opportunities with PPDPs, there are also challenges:

> The challenge for us, as educators, is to bring to the experience of activity-based course tasks a sense of intellectual challenge. . . . We can do this by encouraging colleagues to view reflection on their own learning as worthwhile practice and as an instance of higher level thinking. . . . With an extended programme of PDP, LNA [Learning Needs Analysis] and other activities followed by appropriate tasks, having an assessment dimension makes the learning experience more rounded, allowing the learning to be absorbed more deeply.
>
> (Gough and Denicolo 2007: 6)

The prospect of skills development being more formally recognized or assessed raises the more serious – for students – question of whether or not these skills will come up in the viva examination. It is not uncommon for questions to be asked at the viva about training and skills development. A personal development plan would be a useful resource for students preparing for such questions.

Conclusion

Assessing students' skills is an important initial step in supervision. Training needs analysis can be seen as an established element of student induction. Clearly, this assessment continues throughout the research project, informally and/or formally.

There is a limit to the skills training that supervisors themselves can provide. Perhaps it would be helpful for everyone involved for supervisors to do a diagnostic assessment not only of their students, but also of themselves. This would have two benefits for supervisors and students. First, it would help supervisors to be realistic and open about areas where they can and cannot support students. Second, it would identify areas where supervisors could increase their knowledge. For example, the section on academic writing in this chapter sampled literature that is available for supervisors to use, and there are similarly developed literatures on other skills relevant to the doctorate. Accessing these literatures could then have benefits for both supervisors and students.

Talking points

On the subject of skills training for doctoral students, Craswell (2007) raises many potential talking points:

- 'The employability discourse is an essentially reductive discourse that presents no solid evidence to justify erection of a *deficit* model now being used to push workplace skills training for [Higher Degree Research] students' (Craswell 2007: 388).
- How do supervisors reconcile the skills-for-work agenda with the research-specific skills that are developed during the doctorate?
- Is there a bias in current skills training requirements towards the perceived skills needs of doctoral students in the sciences, or are these skills equally relevant for students in other disciplines?
- Surely doctoral graduates will develop their skills further after graduation, whatever professions they enter? If this is so, to what extent, or level, should doctoral programmes prepare students for different workplaces?
- How do supervisors decide which research and other skills students need? Do they use aggregated data on large numbers of students? Or do they use local information about cohorts of research students and their individual development needs? Or do they consider each student individually?
- How should supervisors evaluate the quality of training provided by others?

Key texts

Gough, M. and Denicolo, P. (2007) *Research Supervisors and the Skills Agenda: Learning Needs Analysis and Personal Development Profiling.* London: Society for Research into Higher Education.

Murray, R. (2006a) *How to Write a Thesis*, 2nd edition. Maidenhead: Open University Press.

7

Feedback mechanisms

The purpose of feedback • Forms, forums and formats • Feedback models • Who are the stakeholders? • Student feedback to faculty or department • Responding to feedback • Involving postgraduates in the institutional audit process • Feedback from external examiners' reports • Conclusion • Talking points • Key texts

Precept 21
Institutions will put in place mechanisms to collect, review and, where appropriate, respond to feedback from all concerned with postgraduate research programmes. They will make arrangements for feedback to be considered openly and constructively and for the results to be communicated appropriately.

The purpose of feedback

The purpose of feedback in this context is to gauge the quality of supervision, and feedback can form part of the quality assurance process. Alternatively, the purpose of feedback may be to assess the quality of the whole doctoral programme. It may involve identifying strengths and weaknesses. Or it may be to measure a specific programme in relation to some benchmark. Given this range of purposes, it is to be expected that there will be different models, different ways of implementing them and different views on their appropriateness.

Forms, forums and formats

Everyone involved in research degrees should provide feedback:

- Current students
- Those who recently completed research degrees
- Supervisors
- Review panels
- Internal examiners
- Research administrators
- External examiners
- Research sponsors
- Collaborating organizations
- Employers
- Alumni.

As with several of the precepts, there is a link between Precept 21 and Precept 4, where a list of specific factors recommends that information on the following is collected annually:

- Submission and completion times and rates
- Pass, referral and failure rates
- Withdrawal rates
- Number of appeals and complaints, reasons and outcomes
- Analysis of examiners' comments
- Recruitment profiles
- Feedback from research students, employers, sponsors and external funders
- Information on employment, destinations and career paths of graduates.

Clearly, supervisors will hold much of this information about the students they supervise and will usually be asked to forward it to the person with relevant departmental, faculty or institutional responsibility at regular intervals, but at least annually. The implication for supervisors is that they will keep records of a range of types of information for every student they supervise. This implies that it would help to know, in advance, what types of information will be gathered by their faculty and/or department and at what times in the academic year and/or in the student's course of study.

Other formal features of the feedback process include providing separate arrangements for individual and collective feedback, for example in a student forum. In addition, there should be arrangements for students to give confidential feedback, if they wish. The implication for supervisors is that they will check that the students they supervise know of these arrangements, understand how they work and use them, without putting them under pressure to reveal any aspect of their feedback. For some students, this is all easier said than done, since cultural and other factors may inhibit their use of such processes.

Feedback will have little value – and will be seen to have little value by students and supervisors – if no action is taken in response to it, or if any action that is taken in response to feedback is not communicated to everyone involved in research degrees. In addition, feedback has an important role in the quality assurance process, as part of regular review of standards, i.e. at least annually. For a feedback system to have real impact, information about action taken in response to feedback will be promptly available to all involved, i.e. to all of those listed at the start of this chapter. Otherwise, if there is no response to feedback, or if there is a delay in the response, people very quickly get the message that this is just 'going through the motions'.

Feedback models

The previous section outlined a collection of feedback factors and participants, but each institution, and each supervisor, may have a specific goal in mind, and may therefore adopt a specific model. The literature shows that there are many models for assessing the quality of doctoral programmes and provides more details on how feedback systems can be managed. Feedback models, in this context, fall into four main types.

First, one model involves rating doctoral programmes, departments or disciplines according to the reputations of researchers who supervise doctoral students, taking into account their publications, research grants and awards. These ratings can be based on perceptions of academics and/or ratings of their outputs, and there is an increasing number of quantitative measures for this. While these measures tell us much about the quality of supervisors' research, they tell us less about the quality of the student experience and education. While many will assume that there is a direct connection between supervisor achievement and the quality of doctoral education, it is surely important to evidence this presumed connection.

Second, one feedback model involves assessing doctoral programmes on the basis of students' reported experiences and their achievements after graduation, including their 'career trajectories' (Golde et al. 2006: 55). Surveys of students can identify, for example, perceived gaps in preparation for different careers, in terms of research and other skills. However, relying on student perceptions alone has limitations.

Third, quantitative measures can be developed, including thesis submission, programme completion, attrition and graduation rates. It is also possible to count postgraduate student publications in many disciplines. However, where there are small numbers of students, there can be wide variation, making it difficult to draw sensible conclusions from aggregate data. While these might seem, to some, to be purely bureaucratic processes, there are some indicators that supervisors are more likely to know about than others in the institution, such as a student's career destination after graduation, although this will not, of course, be true for every supervisor. However, these measures are unlikely to be seen as direct indicators of the quality of either postgraduate student learning or supervision, and many supervisors will have limited access to this quantitative information.

Fourth, there are external reviews, which can be conducted at department level, or may be part of periodic or regular, rolling institutional review. However, these may be limited to certain measures and, since the stakes may be high, there is a potential to modulate any critique, thus removing many learning points and increasing understandable cynicism about such exercises. It is difficult for departments and supervisors genuinely to learn where they need to improve, if external reviews are conducted in this spirit. This is not to say that external reviews are a sham – far from it; instead, it is to raise the question of whether competitive forces can influence outcomes. Moreover, this review of modes of feedback shows the particular aims that each can achieve. Given their strengths and weaknesses, it could be that the best model lies in mixed methods. For example, collecting student feedback, perhaps the most commonly used source of information, may have limited value, since it only provides student views at one point in time. By contrast, a longitudinal study records postgraduates' views at several points in their programme and provides insights into their developing understanding and skills (Nyquist et al. 1999). The purpose of such studies is not to assess doctoral programmes, but to provide information about students' experiences. A limitation is that they are time consuming, which may be one reason why they are not the norm. However, where longitudinal studies have been conducted, they are instructive.

The right model is the one that relates to both an agreed vision for the department and a clear goal for improvement. A convincing model of feedback on doctoral supervision will be one that provides evidence of the whole educational experience. To achieve this, it must be holistic, taking into account different dimensions of that experience. In order to work and be workable, it must address questions supervisors actually want answered. An example of a holistic process is the Carnegie Initiative on the Doctorate (Golde et al. 2006: 59–71), whose central concept of graduate education was developing students as stewards of the disciplines. Over three years, this project asked supervisors and students three sets of questions:

1 What is the *purpose* of the doctoral program? What does it mean to develop students as stewards of the discipline? What are the desired outcomes of the program?
2 What is the *rationale and educational purpose of each element* of the doctoral program? Which elements of the program should be retained and affirmed? Which elements could usefully be changed or eliminated?

3 How do you know? What *evidence* aids in answering those questions? What evidence can be collected to determine whether changes serve the desired outcomes?

(Golde et al. 2006: 60)

Since answers to these questions will be based on judgement, it was argued, they should be answered collectively. This suggests that while the questions are useful for individual supervisors to ponder, they are even more useful when considered by departments. However, it was found that barriers stood in the way of this process: difficulty in defining the goals of a doctoral programme, many academics' unfamiliarity with research techniques in education, academics' attitudes towards evaluation, the process of incrementally growing a desire for change and the culture of academic autonomy and privacy (Golde et al. 2006: 62). Each challenge was addressed in this project (www.carnegiefoundation.org.cid).

While these models may be seen as addressing issues beyond the one-to-one supervision relationship, or perhaps going beyond the remit and control of supervisors, they do relate to the student experience. While supervisors – especially those who are new to the role – may not see themselves as having a place in these processes, it is their responsibility to participate in some form of programme review. If no such review exists, it might be in the best interest of all involved if supervisors took it upon themselves to raise the issue at least, drawing on established, published examples in the higher education literature. If, however, review mechanisms are in place, it is certainly the supervisor's responsibility to respond to them and to make students aware of them.

Who are the stakeholders?

The decision about which model or form of feedback to use can be influenced, or even driven, by those who have a vested interest in the quality and improvement of research supervision. The precepts used in this book refer to 'all concerned with postgraduate research programmes', but clearly some have more influence than others:

Many parties have a vested interest in the evaluation of doctoral programs, and the stakes are high. . . . Judgments about program quality affect resource allocation within the university and may also affect grant funding and other external resource decisions. Unfortunately, important decisions about doctoral-level programs are often based on informal, anecdotal appraisals. Formal, systematic, evidence-based assessment of the quality of a doctoral program is an important challenge for universities.

(Golde et al. 2006: 53)

This is not to say that feedback should be designed around the vested interests of a particular constituency. Identifying the needs of key stakeholders, that is those with a vested interest in postgraduate education, is one way of focusing the process of gathering feedback. This raises the question of the specific form that feedback to such stakeholders should take. Likewise, there is the question of frequency. Are the stakeholders those who employ doctoral graduates, those who fund doctoral studentships or doctoral students themselves? Or are they all stakeholders, perhaps in different senses? The answers to these questions will shape the form(s) that feedback will take: should it be formal, systematic, evidence based and regular? What roles will supervisors play in these forms of feedback? Will they be involved in designing and implementing it?

Student feedback to faculty or department

Faculties and departments may collect postgraduate feedback regularly. This may be anonymous or individualized. In some departments generalized feedback is discussed by the whole department. New supervisors need some way of finding out whether or not their practice is perceived by students as effective. What are the criteria? Is an evaluation form useful? Is one already in use? Is it meaningful to students and supervisors? Is it an exit form, sent to recent graduates? What about ongoing feedback, administered while there is still time for supervisors to take action on problems that are identified in feedback? Should this be discussed with senior colleagues? In what forums will feedback be discussed? A supervisor who sets out to gather feedback in any form will, of course, have to think about whether or not – and how – to align their feedback system with the department's, for example, and avoid duplication.

Student feedback, expressed in frank and free terms, is not always easy reading. Here is one student's view on feedback:

> Universities and industry are worlds apart. The university is not professional, especially when it comes to postgraduates. This is due to the fact that problems aren't recognized, principally by supervisors. But students take their problems away with them. Many of them never tell anyone about the problems they've had with their PhD. So the department can't learn.

This student's feedback was given in a series of confidential interviews. This extract is a direct quotation, representative of the students interviewed, at the students' request, by an academic from another department. Two students demanded that their interview be recorded, and wanted their comments to be shown at all supervisor training courses. While it was decided, partly in the students' own interest, not to use the recording in this way, the setting is described here in order to convey the strength of these students' feelings. More importantly, if this interview had not taken place, the department would not have known these students' views. Alternatively, the students' strong feelings might have led them to make a complaint. Perhaps more worryingly, there was no feedback to the students after these interviews, ensuring that they potentially remained dissatisfied with 'universities' in general and 'the university' in particular.

In addition, there is the question of how to interpret the student's words:

- The student quoted above, perhaps on the basis of industrial experience, has identified real weaknesses in the management of the PhD, *or*
- Supervisors do not read the material available on improving the management of the PhD, which includes recommendations about collecting student feedback, *or*
- The supervisors that this student refers to think, perhaps wrongly, that they receive adequate feedback already, directly from their students, *or*
- Supervision has not been evaluated through student feedback.

Solutions proposed by the students merit consideration. This does not constitute a list of action points, but a collection of insights into where these students were coming from, what their expectations were and what they understood by 'feedback':

- Students should get a chance to put their views on paper.
- Departments should learn from student feedback.
- Departments should acknowledge that without a feedback system they cannot know all the problems postgraduate students have.
- We want to record our views in some way before we leave this place.

Whatever we think of these proposals, there should probably be some response to them. This response might be one of the ways in which students learn what they can – and cannot – expect from supervision.

The short extract from the student interview quoted above opens up a range of issues and interpretations, not all of these would be considered on every occasion by every supervisor, but there are issues about how we interpret feedback and the extent to which we can realistically respond to their requests. It might be helpful if these issues were communicated to students. Inactions, as well as actions, can be communicated to students, along with reasons for them.

What can a supervisor do in the situation that these students described? How can supervisors know that this situation exists? They can develop a feedback questionnaire, sent to students after graduation. Where research student numbers are small, the faculty can protect student and supervisor anonymity by developing a faculty-based system, thereby including greater numbers of responses. A supervisor can propose these initiatives at faculty level and see them through the committee system. There will be debate about the management of feedback systems, perhaps over several meetings: who should collect the forms? Should aggregate data only be presented? In what forum? Who should be responsible for ensuring that feedback is acted on? A department can involve experts in the design and management of a questionnaire and can conduct a few exit interviews in order to gather ideas about what should be included in the questionnaire. Choosing to adopt none of these practices increases the likelihood that students will feel that their voices are not being heard.

The following example of a questionnaire given out to students resulted from some of the steps described in the previous paragraph, i.e. the supervisor worked with colleagues in the department to develop the questionnaire and championed it through departmental meetings at which pros and cons were debated and amendments made. At the time of writing, this form has been in use in that department for more than ten years.

While the idea of a student questionnaire was discussed in Chapter 2, there is a different focus to each discussion. In Chapter 2, the focus was on institutional processes, while in this chapter the focus is on supervision. This form (Table 7.1) provides the type of feedback that perhaps sits more squarely within the supervisor's locus.

In the case of this feedback form, in order to protect students' anonymity,

Table 7.1 Postgraduate appraisal form

Please give a rating of **1** (poor) to **5** (excellent) on each of the following aspects of your postgraduate training and the educational provision offered to date. Circle the number which you feel is most appropriate in your case. Additional comments are welcomed and should be made in the space provided (and continued on a separate sheet if required). Special consideration should be given here to any area of your training or Departmental/University provision which you feel could be improved.

On submission of your 9/21-Month Report complete this form and send it to the Departmental Office. Since this is an entirely confidential appraisal **do not** enter your name or the name of your supervisor.

1 Accessibility of your research supervisor

1	2	3	4	5

2 The time devoted by your research supervisor to discussing aspects of your project with you

1	2	3	4	5

3 Your supervisor's level of interest in your research topic

1	2	3	4	5

4 The level of expertise available to you on your research topic

1	2	3	4	5

5 The organization and planning of your project

1	2	3	4	5

(Continued overleaf)

Table 7.1 continued

6 The overall quality of supervision you have received

1	2	3	4	5

7 The tasks being set for you within the overall postgraduate programme

1	2	3	4	5

8 The materials, laboratory equipment and support facilities available to you within the Department

1	2	3	4	5

9 The materials, equipment and support facilities available to you within the University

1	2	3	4	5

Comments

Source: University of Strathclyde

none of the feedback is individualized for supervisors. Even in a large department, where student numbers might protect student anonymity, the decision was made not to include supervisors' names. Feedback is collated and considered by the department as a whole. In this system students' comments provide food for thought for all supervisors.

Not everyone will agree with this approach to the issue of confidentiality. Some will argue that where there is bad practice the department needs to know and should take action to improve the student experience. If a supervisor's completion rates are poor, this statistic will not, in any case, be private, since completion rates are discussed in a range of forums. However, if there is negative student feedback about a named supervisor, in many instances supervisors will guess who the student is, rightly or wrongly. Many students would feel uncomfortable about this. Some would feel that it presented a risk not only to their courses of study but also to their careers. The supervisor might feel equally exposed, and probably would not have a 'right to reply'. While in principle, therefore, openness is desirable, there may be too many risks to everyone involved. The key factor in the effectiveness of such systems will be how departments and supervisors learn from and act on anonymous feedback.

If questionnaire response rates are low, a financial incentive can be offered to students, as in the following case, from the University of Sheffield Medical School.

Both hard copy and electronic questionnaires were given to postgraduate research students annually in order to obtain feedback on supervision and institutional resources, such as the library etc. Despite several reminders to students, feedback was usually never greater than about 20 per cent. After two or three years, the School Graduate Research Committee tried to increase feedback by offering financial incentives. Although the questionnaire continued to be anonymous, at submission the student's university number was separated from the main questionnaire, and each was placed in a separate file. The file that contained the student numbers was then emptied into a receptacle, and a chosen academic colleague (not the faculty officer who would be assessing the questionnaires) pulled three names out. The first name was given £50, the second £30 and the third £20 (all in book tokens from the School Postgraduate Research budget). The questionnaire return rate increased by about 10–15 per cent, but never reached 40 per cent, in spite of reminders and the cash incentive. A more recent development has been to hold a social occasion for postgraduate research students at about the same time as the questionnaire feedback is required and to get students to complete the questionnaire there and then, without letting them take it away. On the whole, this has been quite successful, but it is dependent on the students coming along. If you get a poor turnout, then your questionnaire return will be poor too.

Student feedback is sometimes elicited informally, as when prospective students discuss their plans with current or former students. Supervision may be discussed in this context, as illustrated in the precept into practice for Precept 21.

Precept into Practice – 21

Issue

Mary was very pleased to have discovered Dr Simons, who was working in the field she wished to explore for her PhD. Dr Simons was also working at a highly rated university, so Mary was fairly confident that should she be accepted to work with Dr Simons, she would obtain a worthwhile doctorate. Mary therefore decided to go ahead and make a formal application, citing Dr Simons as the preferred supervisor. After a short while, following submission of the application, Mary was contacted by Dr Simons to invite her to attend an informal meeting to discuss the PhD project. Mary duly went along and had a good chat with Dr Simons, whom she found a little aloof but very knowledgeable. During the conversation, Mary asked Dr Simons how experienced he was in PhD supervision. Strangely, she thought, he seemed unable to give her a satisfactory answer. She decided not to push the subject, but when Dr Simons later offered her the position, she asked for time to consider a number of options. In reality she wanted to reflect on how she felt about the prospect of working with Dr Simons as her supervisor.

Resolution

There is no doubt that when a student chooses a supervisor (and vice versa), both parties have to consider seriously whether or not they can work together for a minimum of three years' full-time study. As we know, the student–supervisor relationship can be one of the most important factors in determining how successful a PhD student is, so any doubts at the interview stage should be clarified immediately before any commitment is made. In this case, Mary spoke to the head of department and was able to obtain the contact details of a few previous doctoral students of Dr Simons. Interestingly, she discovered that out of four previous students only one had been successful in obtaining a PhD, and that the others had all found Dr Simons to be a difficult man to work with. This information enabled Mary to make the right decision for her.

This case is not about finding fault with Dr Simons; rather, it illustrates the gap that can open up between a supervisor's self-perception and a student's perception of his or her supervisor:

> While supervisors may be able to demonstrate a range of approaches, they may also have a dominant or default position which is most powerfully experienced by their students ... while a supervisor might exemplify a range of conceptual approaches, the student experiences one or two predominant approaches.
>
> (Lee 2008: 277)

The discussion of this case, along with the discussion of the student perspectives quoted above, illustrates the type of 'open' and 'constructive' consideration of student feedback recommended in Precept 21.

Responding to feedback

The precept reminds us that not only should institutions gather and discuss feedback, but also they should respond to it. The questions that then come to mind are when, in what forum and for what purpose? 'Responses' can be considered in individual or aggregate terms. For example, an individual supervisor's response to feedback might be to engage in some form of further development. However, it is not known whether or not this type of 'response' is regularly communicated to students. Departmental responses to feedback are generally more public. This distinction between private and public may be one of the purposes of including the word 'appropriately' in Precept 21.

The question is how to communicate actions taken in response to feedback to students and other stakeholders: should there be a generic response to the student cohort as a whole, or can there be more specific actions, as required, by the department? Since the example of the feedback form above asks questions about a range of issues, it might be appropriate to respond to student feedback on, for example, research facilities. However, even in such a large department, one student's comments on equipment, for example, might be identifiable, and this takes us back to the question about whether all students would be prepared to say what they think about what they perceive to be problems. This is not to criticize this feedback form, since supervisors in that department have debated these issues before agreeing to use it and presumably continue to use it because they find it has value; instead, this discussion raises questions that other departments may want to think through as they develop their own feedback mechanisms.

The subject of continuing development for supervisors is covered in Chapter 11, where there is more detail on development strategies, but it is relevant to the subject of acting on feedback. Responding to feedback can and should shape a supervisor's development plan. This is not to say that student feedback – to take one type of feedback – is the only influence, since there will be many, but to emphasize the importance of feedback for supervisor development.

In a series of interviews, experienced supervisors were asked two questions that are relevant here: first, 'Is it possible to be a better supervisor?' and second, 'How would you improve your supervision?' Their answers illustrate how student feedback, along with other influences and interactions, can contribute to a supervisor's continuing development:

- Some supervisors take the approach that they are always learning about supervision – and about themselves as supervisors; others feel that there comes a point where they have learned all they need to know. This form of self-assessment can be complemented by student feedback.
- It is important to keep track of current developments in the PhD in our own subject areas.
- Discussing supervision with peers and experts can help. Peer observation and feedback can provide new insights and affirm good practice. This can also provide a check on any deliberate changes in supervision practice.

More specifically, how did they define continuous development for supervisors?

- Further training can reinforce existing good practice. It can also provide additional strategies for supervision, for trouble-shooting and problem-solving. It may be an opportunity to learn from the experiences of other supervisors, including those in other disciplines who may face similar challenges.

- Updating is important, so that we are aware of new developments in quality assurance, the changing nature of the doctorate, the emergence of a doctoral curriculum, the growing emphasis on both research skills training and 'other skills' training, the various ways in which these are being delivered – and funded – in our disciplines and changes, if there are any, in the role of the external examiner. All of these potentially affect us in some way.
- Discussion with more experienced peers can be very useful, even those in other disciplines, particularly if these peers are knowledgeable about new developments, new 'drivers' and their implications for your discipline.
- Learning from mistakes is one way – this requires the acknowledgement of a 'mistake', along with further definition, some dialogue, a supportive context that will neither expose nor exploit the mistake, and perhaps consolidating the supervisor's learning, perhaps including a change in some aspect of practice or thinking and, of course, monitoring the impact of that change.

The supervisors quoted here had the opportunity of an interview to make explicit their beliefs and practices, and, in most cases, their ongoing development. It would be interesting to hear students' views on these points. These supervisors demonstrate that responding to feedback is just one feature of a model of continuing development.

Involving postgraduates in the institutional audit process

[S]tudents should feel free to provide whatever information they feel is appropriate (providing that information is relevant to the focuses of the audit) and to organize it as they choose.

(National Postgraduate Committee 2005a: 1)

The National Postgraduate Committee (NPC) provides an interesting commentary on selected points from the Quality Assurance Agency's (2006) guide for student representatives, clarifying what might and might not be appropriate responses to it, in terms of postgraduates:

For example, some submissions have included aspects of social life and also other institutional services not in the context of the student's learning experience. These points are inappropriate to submit to the audit since they are beyond the scope of what QAA exists to monitor. It is important that the main focus of the audit is considered carefully from the student perspective and that it looks at the institution's practices on a general level.

(National Postgraduate Committee 2005a: 1)

This approach emphasizes the 'student's learning experience'. Presumably, this means 'learning' in specific ways, as defined, to some extent, by the department, perhaps also by the research project and surely also by and/or for the individual student? Whatever the origins of the definition, it is clear that this policy not only places emphasis on 'the student perspective', but also puts it at the centre of audit. The fact that this is the subject of an NPC paper suggests that this is not always the case. For supervisors working in departments or institutions where students are central in this way, this will be unproblematic; for those in institutions where this is not the case, there may be issues to be resolved. Student participation can be one such issue, as even when institutions put students at the centre of their processes, the students themselves do not always respond positively or avail themselves of this opportunity. Unfortunately, low response rates and low levels of participation can undermine the validity of the evidence that is garnered from student feedback. Instances where postgraduate students have not been included in audit should be specified, along with, one suspects, reasons for this.

Having established these principles, the NPC paper goes through all the QAA precepts, considering their implications for involving postgraduates in audit. For Precept 21 there is the following guidance:

> Postgraduate representation is important, and especially for postgraduates as NPC has always promoted. This code supports that all the more and it should enforce institutions to help in the process, whereby there are effective feedback mechanisms, both local and central through which appropriate action can be taken on issues raised by postgraduate research students. This is another area where student representative bodies have a responsibility to take part and avail themselves to postgraduates as an independent body that can extend its remit to postgraduates. Therefore it should be questioned how effective feedback systems are and if there is open opportunity and support for a representative group of postgraduates to be involved in representing collective issues.
>
> (National Postgraduate Committee 2005a: 1)

In contrast to the feedback form that is completed by individual students, this approach emphasizes the role of the postgraduate 'group' in raising 'collective' issues. There are also six more specific 'tips' for achieving this, including the following two:

- Is there a specific postgraduate committee and is their role sufficiently involved in the [audit] process to directly represent the interests of postgraduates to the running of the information gathering? Such factors are of vital importance.
- How would you communicate to postgraduates? This is not as straight forward as it may be for undergraduates via posters, student events and other things that are largely used by undergraduates. Postgraduates are in

fragmented pockets of an institution, with few central places that they congregate, so information in the NPC resources folder will assist here.

The 'folder' referred to includes the following resources:

- How do we involve postgraduates? – The answers
- Representing postgraduates in small institutions
- Communicating to postgraduates
- Representation of part-time postgraduates.

It would be interesting to see how these issues are addressed in different institutions, and supervisors should probably know how they are managed in their own institutions.

Feedback from external examiners' reports

This is an area where access to feedback may be restricted, making it difficult for students, supervisors and institutions to learn from it. For example, a survey of the 125 universities (response rate of 72.58 per cent) who are members of the UK Council for Graduate Education focused on regulations and procedures for access to doctoral examiners' reports, and found that 'access may be restricted to certain post-holders within institutions and to the members of the examining panel, with candidates and/or supervisors gaining access only under limited circumstances' (Powell and Brown 2007: 6). Whether students have a right of access to this material via the Freedom of Information Act 2000 is a good question. In most institutions, the examiners were not informed of the procedures for access to reports. In some institutions, the small number of requests to see examiners' reports were from appeal candidates only. In the three institutions where examiners' reports were made available to supervisors – but not to students – the purpose was to assist the supervisor in preparing the student for the viva. There was evidence of reluctance to open preliminary reports to wider readership, since these reports were often revised in light of discussion at the viva: 'comments in those reports are made without the benefit of interrogation and therefore do not necessarily reflect the true quality of the work or the likely outcome in terms of an award' (Powell and Brown 2007: 14).

This appears to contrast with the guidance – or requirement? – of the Higher Education Funding Council for England (HEFCE): 'Examiners' reports to be made available to the student after the viva' (Pearce 2005: 20). The provision of training for external examiners – by institutions – is also recommended, but this generally meets with some reluctance. This is perhaps because academics are aware that by inviting a colleague to be an external examiner they are asking a great favour and do not want to impose an additional burden. Or there might be reluctance to ask a senior colleague to attend training, thereby implying that the colleague needs such training. Or there might be an assumption that experienced examiners do not require training.

Whatever the reason, external examining is an academic role that has historically been performed without training. Again, HEFCE prompts a rethink: 'Training for examiners to be available as part of the institution's staff development' (Pearce 2005: 20). Since this item is part of the 'standards' agenda, and since HEFCE is a major 'stakeholder' in higher education, it is timely to review the grounds for reluctance to adopt these practices, although it is not clear who has responsibility for carrying them out: there is ambiguity

> about under whose auspices this staff development should take place – i.e. should institutions train their own staff to be higher degree examiners, or is it a responsibility of the institutions doing the hiring . . .? The latter has already become standard practice for the external examiners of undergraduate degree schemes or taught Masters programme.
>
> (Pearce 2005: 21)

This suggests that effective supervisors might search out such training, attend courses for doctoral examiners that will soon be the norm and/or check that potential examiners have attended training.

The findings of the UKCGE survey question the inclusion of examiners' reports on the list of feedback sources. They also raise questions about the transparency of results, although it was noted in the report that 'transparency is something that universities have recently come to take more seriously' (Powell and Brown 2007: 16). The survey appears to have prompted some institutions to review their procedures, and there appears to be a simultaneous move towards openness in procedures.

The survey reveals a residual tension between the drive to openness, on the one hand, and the desire to protect confidentiality, on the other. Institutions are concerned to defend themselves against appeals, but, at the same time, want to learn from external feedback. A helpful strategy might be to clarify the purposes of different kinds of reports: some are part of the assessment process, others are for providing feedback to candidates and supervisors on the assessment of the work and a third type could be for monitoring the quality of research degrees, in terms of the standard of the work produced, the conduct of the course of study, or of the examination or both. Institutional procedures concerning access to these reports are shaped by their purposes. The question is, 'do regulations achieve what is intended in terms of these kinds of dimensions?' (Powell and Brown 2007: 17).

Finally, there is a potentially tricky issue for supervisors who do have access to examiners' reports:

Where access to reports is given then some uniformity of practice for the sector might usefully be developed regarding who gets access and at what point in the examination process. (The existing practice of granting access to students in some cases and supervisors in others militates against equality of treatment.)

(Powell and Brown 2007: 18)

Supervisors are generally not in a position to establish 'uniformity of practice' – or are they? Could they be seen, by some students perhaps, as part of a system that 'militates against equality of treatment'?

Conclusion

Although this process sounds simple, at first, department members found it difficult to suspend scepticism about the value of taking time to discuss things taken for granted. Over time, however, this deliberative process proved liberating and intellectually exciting.

(Golde et al. 2006: 60)

This chapter raises three main points for supervisors: first, there is the point about collecting different types of data on the doctoral programme – not just on supervision – and second, there is the point about ensuring that some of this feedback is not just considered 'openly' within the supervisor's institution, but is also available to external stakeholders, including prospective students. Third, there is the issue of supervisors demonstrating that they have taken feedback on board, and have acted on it, such as for example, dissemination of results and discussion of an action plan at some form of staff–student meeting and ongoing dialogue with students via a representative body. This might in turn also enhance and encourage greater student involvement in feedback processes (via questionnaires, forums and student representatives). Otherwise, there will be little point to the feedback, or there will be a perception that feedback has neither purpose nor impact, and people will very quickly disengage from the process. On a more positive note, given a level of collaboration, feedback can be an intellectually challenging and stimulating process. Perhaps more importantly, there is satisfaction in improving doctoral programmes, which is surely in the best interests of everyone involved.

Talking points

- Should student feedback be anonymous, or should it name supervisors, so that feedback goes directly to the person who can act on it? How should this be done?
- In your experience – or according to other sources – how are supervisors likely to respond to generalized, anonymous student feedback?
- How should responses to feedback – in any form – be communicated to stakeholders? (And who can be considered as 'stakeholders'?) By supervisors directly? By supervisors feeding back to the department?
- What can be done if students do not use a questionnaire about supervision, or if the response rate is 30 per cent or less? What can supervisors do? What can departments or schools do to gather feedback? What other feedback mechanisms can they use?
- How should supervisors keep track of their development needs and activities?

Key texts

Golde, C. M., Jones, L., Bueschel, A. C. and Walker, G. E. (2006) The challenges of doctoral program assessment: lessons from the Carnegie Initiative on the doctorate. In P. L. Maki and N. A. Borkowski (eds) *The Assessment of Doctoral Education: Emerging Criteria and New Models for Improving Outcomes*. Sterling, VA: Stylus.

Maki, P. L. and Borkowski, N. A. (eds) (2006) *The Assessment of Doctoral Education: Emerging Criteria and New Models for Improving Outcomes*. Sterling, VA: Stylus.

8

Good examination practice

Criteria • Assessment procedures • Communication • Preparing students for the viva • Supporting students during thesis revision • Complaints and appeals • Conclusion • Talking points • Key texts

The award of a doctorate generally depends on satisfactory performance in an oral examination – the 'viva' or doctoral 'defence' – usually lasting two to three hours. In the UK the student, or 'candidate', usually defends the thesis in response to questions from two people, an external examiner and an internal examiner. In other countries, a thesis committee of four or more act as internal examiners, with one or more external examiners, and other students may be present. In the UK the viva has traditionally been conducted behind closed doors. In other countries it is a public event, to the extent that other people in the department may attend – sometimes at the discretion of the candidate – or, in some countries, that literally anyone can attend. For the 'closed doors' model, since the mid 2000s, one development has been to record the viva, to provide the university with a record of what occurred. This record is generally not made public, but is kept by the university and consulted if there is an appeal.

However, this – and other aspects of doctoral examinations – may change. The implication for supervisors is that they need to keep up-to-date with current policy and procedures in relation to the examination – both locally, in their institutions, and nationally, as well as internationally – as for all other aspects of doctoral education (Walker et al. 2008).

Supervisors may attend their students' vivas, though in most universities this is up to the students. The supervisor usually has no formal role in the viva and does not participate in the discussion, although students are not always aware of this beforehand. Students have been known to ask if their supervisors will help them if they get into difficulty during the viva (Murray 2003a).

This aspect of viva procedure will be self-evident to those with experience of vivas and of supervising or examining theses, but the point of including it here is to show that students seem to draw on myth, legend or hearsay as much as regulations and procedures, when it comes to understanding the viva. Some students never see anything in writing about the viva at their universities. Others do, but without fully understanding it. This means that supervisors have a responsibility to explain what the viva involves and, crucially, to create opportunities for students to practise the skills they need to perform well.

In the absence of information, students often ask fundamental questions about their vivas: who will be there? Can I take my thesis in with me? How long will it last? What are they likely to ask? What do I do if I can't answer a question? Such questions suggest that students recognize that the viva is unlike other examinations and interviews, and therefore merits investigation in these deceptively simple terms. For most students the viva is a new type of communication event, and as such requires careful definition and analysis before planning and preparation can begin.

A growing body of research on the doctoral examination asks similarly fundamental questions about the doctoral examination and about the purpose of the doctorate itself, since the two are inextricably linked (Johnston 1997; Murray 2009a; Walker et al. 2008). Researchers have established that there is variation in viva practice not only between but also within institutions (Jackson and Tinkler 2007; Tinkler and Jackson 2004). By contrast, others have identified commonalities, such as questions that recur in vivas across the disciplines (Trafford and Leshem 2002). Alongside recent developments in quality assurance, it has to be said that there is still evidence of unfairness and institutionalized discrimination (Loumansky and Jackson 2004), suggesting that the QAA precepts, and other similar codes, have an important role to play. This chapter draws on the precepts, on research and on students' views in order to identify key issues that the viva presents for supervisors.

Criteria

Precept 22
Institutions will use criteria for assessing research degrees that enable them to define the academic standards of different research programmes and the achievements of their graduates. The criteria used to assess research degrees must be clear and readily available to students, staff and external examiners.

It has been argued that the three 'most common criteria' (Burnham 1994: 32) used at vivas are, has the candidate, first, 'clearly laid out the problem to be addressed'?, second, 'consistently developed this theme throughout the chapters'?, and third, 'skilfully stated the relevance of the conclusion for the discipline?'.

In addition, each university will have criteria for the doctoral examination. Generally these combine evaluation of the thesis and of the student's performance during the examination. While the criteria of 'originality' and 'contribution' will probably be applied in all doctoral examinations, the specific formulation of the criteria to be used in an institution will most likely be written on the examiners' report form. The implication for supervisors is that they should ensure that each student knows the specific criteria that will be used in his or her examination. These criteria can be explained, discussed and used in viva preparation sessions. It therefore makes sense for supervisors to initiate this discussion well before the viva, when students are starting their research, so that they begin to develop an understanding of what is expected right from the start.

This discussion might raise useful questions about the stages along the way: for example, to what extent will students meet criteria in years one and two of full- or part-time doctoral study? Or will these criteria only be applied in year three, or even later for part-time students? These issues also apply, of course, to criteria for assessment of professional doctorates (Scott et al. 2004), for which some, not all, institutions require a viva, in addition to other forms of assessment (Pearce 2005: 17). In this instance, the implication for supervisors is that they should ensure that students understand the relative weight of different forms of assessment during the doctorate and how criteria are applied in each case.

Many students report that they have neither seen nor heard of the examiner's report form. While most are aware of the criteria of 'originality' and 'contribution' for the doctorate, students do not routinely see exactly how these are articulated in their institution. Where there is also a thesis report form, in addition to a viva report form, students – if they see them – begin to understand what is expected of them. Clearly, while simply 'seeing' the criteria used on these forms is instructive, it is much more helpful if supervisors take responsibility for discussing criteria with students, particularly when supervisors relate such discussions to students' ongoing work, that is throughout the doctorate. Otherwise, there is a risk that criteria remain abstract, and their relevance to a specific research project remains unclear – a situation that supervisors can prevent.

Familiarity with the specific form and wording of criteria that will be used at their examinations is an important part of examiners' and students' preparation:

• The thesis makes a distinct contribution to knowledge.
• The candidate possesses a good general knowledge of the field.

- The thesis is a record of original research.
- The literary style and presentation of the thesis are satisfactory.
- The thesis is in part or in whole worthy of publication.
- The oral examination was satisfactory.

Some disciplines, like art and design and practice-oriented research, use different criteria:

> The role of written to practical work within practice-led research does not fall neatly into two categories: information versus data for example. The two represent different aspects of a complex evolving process. . . . The viva therefore takes on a more significant role than just the opportunity to ensure the identity of the researcher. It may be the first real opportunity for the researcher to demonstrate fully the connections between practice and research, the effect of research on practice, and the embodiment of research within practice.
>
> (Swift and Douglas 1997: 20–21)

Swift and Douglas (1997) have produced a set of guidelines for students in art and design, which could, to some extent, be a model for others who are not doing the 'traditional' PhD.

Precept into Practice – 22

Issue

It was the most nerve-wracking day of his life when Steve had his viva. He had experienced quite a difficult time over the course of his studies, which had not been helped by a forced change in supervisor. To be honest, his new supervisor was not particularly interested in the topic of Steve's research, which he thought was a little outdated. Nevertheless, he had looked at the draft thesis chapters and given whatever help and advice he could. On the day of the viva Steve did not feel very confident, but thought he had done enough to scrape a pass, as he had been working on this project for the past four years. However, Steve quickly realized, from the nature of the examiners' questions and the fact that the viva ran for over four hours, that things were not going too well. At the end of the viva, after the examiners had conferred, Steve was stunned to discover that the examiners considered that he should not be awarded the degree of PhD, recommending that an MPhil degree be awarded instead.

Resolution

We are aware that there might have been some supervisory issues with Steve's PhD, and we do not know if Steve had been consulted regarding the selection of examiners. However, one important factor that is often neglected is the understanding – by both supervisor and student – of the criteria for

> assessment of research degrees. When examiners are appointed they are routinely sent comprehensive guidelines on the assessment criteria. However, unless the supervisor takes responsibility for making the student aware of them, the criteria are often neglected, so that the student does not know exactly what should be in the thesis and how to behave in a viva in order to achieve a successful outcome. It is recommended, therefore, that criteria for assessment of research degrees should be made available to both supervisor and student at the beginning of the research degree programme, and that these criteria should be consulted on a regular basis.

In addition to applying specific criteria for thesis and performance, the viva may have a range of implicit or explicit purposes, and these too should be discussed with students well in advance of the viva. In general terms, the purpose of the viva is to allow the university not only to check the standard of the work but also to verify that the student did the work:

- Did the student do the work?
- Did the student write the thesis?
- Can the student do research independently?
- Does the student have a good general knowledge of the field?
- Does the student understand the limits of his or her contribution?
- Can the student defend the work and the thesis in discussion with experts?

While these purposes may be self-evident to supervisors, students are not always aware of them as potential lines of questioning in the viva. This suggests that it is worth discussing the viva's purposes as part of the student's preparation.

Moreover, it is worth restating that while supervisors may be fluent in the terms used in doctoral criteria, students are unlikely to be as familiar or comfortable with them. Furthermore, it would be an oversimplification to assert that some of these terms had only one meaning, or that their meanings remain constant:

> Standards are ensured by having peer examiners who are *assumed* to know the thresholds, but there is little (if anything) to determine whether this is actually the case, and practically nothing is known about what goes on inside the private domain of the PhD viva voce examination. . . . there are real issues about who determines what is meant by clarity, equity, reliability or consistency.
>
> (Loumansky and Jackson 2004: 24)

Even if candidates and supervisors agree definitions of 'clarity' and 'consistency', examiners bring their own meanings to the table, and examiners' definitions are likely to carry more weight on the day. It has been argued that this is one way in which power and privilege are protected, while discrimination is perpetuated. This power dynamic is another potential student–supervisor talking point. For example, students may be encouraged to talk with 'authority' about their work at their vivas, but this runs counter to students' awareness of the greater authority – in many senses – of the external examiner. The implication for supervisors is that they should help students to prepare to debate terms like clarity, consistency and contribution and to illustrate them with reference to their research and their theses.

Assessment procedures

Precept 23
Research degree assessment procedures must be clear; they must be operated rigorously, fairly and consistently; include input from an external examiner; and carried out to a reasonable timescale.

The examiners' judgements about the extent to which a candidate meets the criteria are recorded on one or more reports. Depending on the institution's procedures, the external examiner may write a report on the thesis prior to the viva, and at this point a decision can be taken not to progress to viva if the thesis is judged to be weak, or if it is so good that the external examiner deems the examination unnecessary. In other institutions, once the thesis has been submitted for examination, the examination process (comprising independent considerations of the thesis by the internal and external examiners, followed by the viva voce examination) must be seen through to completion.

At the viva, the external examiner examines the thesis by asking the student questions. At the end of the viva, the examiners write a joint report, giving their decision – pass, pass with corrections, pass with minor revisions (to be completed by a certain date, to the satisfaction of the internal examiner), further research to be conducted (to be completed by a certain date, to the satisfaction of the external examiner), second viva required, degree not awarded, MPhil awarded. They write the reasons for their decision on the examiners' report form and mark the criteria for the doctoral award, listed on the form, that the student has met.

The implication of this general outline for supervisors is that they should know their institution's specific regulations and procedures:

- Appointment of external examiners – what is the process?
- Examiners' preparation – what materials are they sent?
- Examiners' training – what is provided?

In addition, a general publication provides guidance for external examiners in higher education, although it is not widely available (Partington et al. 1993). This external examiners' handbook is perhaps most useful for lists of questions that examiners can ask about different sections of a thesis:

- In the literature review, has the candidate slipped into 'Here is all I know about this subject'?
- Does the candidate make explicit links between the review and the design of the study?
- Is the candidate aware of the limits to the reliability, validity, confidence or generalizability of the study methods?
- Have the main points to emerge from the results/analysis been picked up in the discussion?

(adapted from Partington et al. 1993)

When this section is drawn to their attention, students find it very useful in preparing potential questions and answers for their vivas, but, realistically, it is unlikely that they will come across this material and, even if they do, they might not notice this section of the handbook. The implication for supervisors is that they can introduce these questions – or other examples – to students and use or adapt them for practice sessions and mock vivas. These questions are also thought-provoking for students earlier in the doctoral process.

More comprehensive, and more widely available than the examiners' handbook, is Pearce (2005), which covers in detail the procedures for examining a thesis (adapted from Mullins and Kiley 2002), prior to the viva (see text box).

Examining the thesis

- Checking university's criteria
- Speed-reading and scanning the thesis
- Reading abstract, table of contents, introduction, conclusions
- Close reading – allowing three hours per day per chapter and taking notes
- Second reading (if there is time) – allowing minimum of eight hours
- Editing and proofreading: listing typos and corrections
- Checking references for knowledge of the field
- Identifying key sources to consult in order to judge the thesis
- Summarizing impressions of each chapter for pre-viva report (1000–2000 words)
- Noting controversial points – drafting possible viva questions
- Spot-checking references for accuracy
- Considering how the thesis could be revised or improved
- Listing key points or problems with each chapter
- Evaluating hypothesis and argument

- Evaluating methodology – theory and practice
- Evaluating extent to which aims were achieved
- Considering alternatives
- Assessing stated contribution to the field
- Evaluating what new information, evidence or technique the research produced
- Evaluating evidence used to support claims
- Weighing strengths and weaknesses
- Noting how or where the thesis meets university's criteria.

Further details on each of these tasks – and suggestions for others – are provided by Pearce (2005), and there will be local variations in guidance for examiners. For the thesis report, universities provide guidelines on contents, some quite general, others very specific. Some universities specify the contents of the joint report that examiners write after the viva, as in the following extract from Oxford's (2001) guidelines:

> The joint report should include . . . a statement of what the thesis purports to do, and an account of what it actually covers. Evaluative comments should be as full as possible and should include an indication of the strengths as well as the limitations, weaknesses and lacunae. The candidate's performance in the oral examination should receive comment. Candidates' explanations for any deficiencies in the thesis should receive appropriate mention.
>
> (quoted in Pearce 2005: 61)

If examiners disagree in their pre-viva reports, this should be spotted by someone in Registry, who will then refer the matter to the senior academic with responsibility for graduate students or research degrees. There should then be some form of 'mediation' (Pearce 2005: 69), in order to see if the viva can go ahead. If this discussion does not happen, and the external is aware of a strong difference of views, he or she can take it up with Registry and thus ensure that the issue is recorded.

Differences of views among academics are inevitable, but expressing them may have implications: 'New or inexperienced examiners should also be alert to the fact that this is another of those moments in the examining process where domination or outright bullying may occur' (Pearce 2005: 70). Examiners and supervisors may feel that they are balancing concerns for their own profiles with their desire to support candidates and, of course, implementing university procedures properly.

Examiners' reporting is another aspect of the process that students often wonder about. Many are curious to know what exactly goes on before and after the viva, and will recognize that all of the steps listed above affect the assessment of their work. The implication for supervisors is that they should explain the whole examination process – not just viva arrangements – to students in advance, and it could be argued that students should know precisely how their work will be assessed right from the start of their doctorates. Supervisors can also read up on the literature on examiners' reports, in order to get a broader view and to explore potential issues (Johnston 1997; Mullins and Kiley 2002; Powell and Brown 2007).

Nearer the time of the viva, a further implication for supervisors is that they should check that specified arrangements are in place. This can help to prevent unnecessary delays and reduce uncertainty for everyone involved in the examination.

Precept into Practice – 23

Issue

Dr James has travelled halfway across the country to be external examiner for Judy's viva. Although Dr James had been pleased to be chosen to examine one of the eminent Prof. Greenwood's PhD students, on the day of the viva he was a little hassled, as his train had been delayed because of snow, and he was concerned about whether he would be able to get home that evening. So, to save time, the booked examiners' lunch was replaced by a sandwich, which meant that the start of the viva was delayed by only a few minutes. Judy had written a good thesis, and Dr James realized early on in the viva that she was a bright student, so he was determined to show her that he was also an authority in this field. Unfortunately, neither of the examiners was keeping an eye on the time, and both student and examiners were enjoying themselves during the viva, until Dr James glanced at this watch and suddenly realized that he had only 50 minutes till his return train departed. So the viva had to be brought to an abrupt end, and Judy was told that she had passed her PhD just as the taxi arrived to take Dr James back to the station. Unfortunately, the joint examiners' report was not completed that day.

Resolution

It is a pity that after a minimum of three years' full-time study, so little time and effort should be given to producing the joint examiners' report on the thesis and viva. However, this is not uncommon, as the report is often treated as an afterthought. It is almost as if the business of the day is completed once the viva is finished and the recommendation has been given verbally to the student. As the student has the right to see at least a summary of the report (in cases where there are appeals), it should be given more importance. Ideally, the best time to produce the joint examiners' report is just after the viva. Otherwise, allocating sufficient time for completing this report should be part of the planning process, including allowing time for completing the report when organizing the external examiner's travel arrangements.

The viva is chaired in different ways at different universities: it may be chaired by the internal examiner, or there may be an independent chair, someone who has not been involved in the research project being examined. More and more institutions are introducing an independent chair to the viva. Their role is to ensure that both standards of conduct and academic standards are maintained. However, we recently heard of an independent chair who began by explaining his role and then proceeded to mark a set of exam scripts during the viva. The implication for supervisors is that, if this behaviour is not good enough – and it is not – they should find a way to feed that back into the system to ensure that it does not happen again. Otherwise, it probably will, and the claim that the independent chair has an important role will seem hollow to visiting examiners and will ring false to students. Even where supervisors have no formal role in the doctoral examination, therefore, they can influence practice.

Communication

Precept 24
Institutions will communicate their assessment procedures clearly to all parties involved, i.e. the students, the supervisor(s) and the examiners.

This precept gives responsibility to institutions, but the implications for supervisors are, first, that they should actively seek the information they need and, second, communicate it to students. This communication should include most, if not all, of the information covered in the previous section on procedures.

How institutions communicate the outcome of doctoral examinations varies:

There is generally much less formality associated with the post-viva report than the pre-viva one, and it is less common for candidates and supervisors to be sent a copy (although data protection laws now mean that they can request one if they so wish).

(Pearce 2005: 98)

This means that supervisors will not have access to all the information about how judgements were made about their students' work and performance. The implication for supervisors is that they should know their institutions' formal and informal systems, and that they should check that students understand the nature, intention and format of procedures. This may seem straightforward, but there is potential for confusion if the supervisor expects the 'institution' to communicate to students all that they need to know.

Precept into Practice – 24

Issue

Nawal had been looking forward to her viva date, as she hoped that she would be able to return to her family overseas soon after. During the viva all went reasonably well, she defended her thesis admirably, and she thought that the examiners had been fairly impressed with her work. When the examiners had conferred after the viva and invited Nawal to hear their verdict, she was disappointed, as the PhD was not to be awarded immediately. A revised thesis had to be submitted, fortunately without another viva. She went away feeling unsure as to what had gone wrong and wondering how much longer she would have to wait before returning to her family.

Resolution

An issue here is that there are differences between institutions as to what constitutes minor amendments to a thesis. Is it the amount of work that has to be done and/or within a certain timescale? An example from one institution is that a case for minor amendments means that they can be completed within a period of three calendar months. As well as disparities between institutions, another problem is that there may be significant disagreement as to what can be achieved within a certain time period. It is important, therefore, not only to know the relevant regulations but also to thoroughly understand them. For many students, there can be a significant difference between minor amendments and resubmission, especially when the latter attracts a significant financial penalty.

Preparing students for the viva

On the day a robust performance is required but be careful to avoid dogmatism. Examiners are impressed by thoughtful, reflective candidates who give consideration to constructive criticism and are able to modify their arguments accordingly.

(Burnham 1994: 30)

Preparing the student for this 'performance' is one of the supervisor's most important responsibilities. Preparation can take the form of mini-vivas, a short form of viva that takes place at the end of the first and second years, for example. Some departments make mini-vivas part of the annual review process or part of the MPhil–PhD transfer process. Students who have experienced this system say that it helped them prepare for the 'real thing': 'You really have to understand what you've written about in your report'. Alternatively, or in addition, practice can take the form of mock vivas, which simulate the conduct of the real viva.

The case for practising for the viva is perhaps self-evident: the student's performance during the examination can theoretically influence the examiners' decision. The argument against viva practice has also been made: a mock viva could make students more apprehensive. While this shows sympathy for the student, it fails to acknowledge the fear that lack of practice might instil.

For supervisors trying to decide on what is best for their students, another factor may be institutional requirements: many universities, and other bodies, see the mock viva not as an option but as a requirement. The implications of this for supervisors are that they have to organize viva practice sessions. One practice session may not be enough – and how would 'enough' be judged? Students may benefit from a range of different types of session, designed to give them different types of practice, in a 'graduated' way, from informal and straightforward to complex and contested. Practice sessions can have increasing levels of difficulty and perhaps different kinds of difficulty. More detail on this idea of graduated practice – including examples of specific activities to use – is provided in Murray (2009a).

Supervisors and students can write questions to use in these practice sessions. Writing different types of question – easy, difficult, challenging, coming from a different subdiscipline, abstract and specific – is a good exercise for students. This approach can help the student to identify strengths and weaknesses in the thesis, and to develop ways of describing and/or debating them. Examples of what students might consider either easy or difficult general questions are shown in the text box.

General questions: easy and difficult

- How did you come to be working in this area?
- How did you develop your interest in this subject?
- Please summarize your thesis for us.
- Who would you say are the main researchers in your field today?
- Would you say that your thesis has any weaknesses?
- Surely it would have been better to use a different approach, such as . . .?
- How do you see research on this topic developing in the future?

Students and supervisors can develop a range of follow-up questions for each of these and can practise different ways of answering them.

Research has shown that there are recurring viva questions, suggesting that students should probably practise with these, perhaps also making them more specific to their own studies, although there is, of course, no guarantee that their examiners will ask these questions. The following are frequently recurring viva questions:

- What led you to select these methods?
- What are the theoretical components of your framework?
- How did you decide on the variables to include in your conceptual framework?
- How did concepts assist you to visualize and explain what you intended to investigate?
- How did you use your conceptual framework to design your research and analyse your findings?

(Trafford and Leshem 2002)

It is also possible to practise more negative questioning styles, where the examiner interrupts the student or continually challenges what the student says. This is not to condone aggressive behaviour by the examiner, but to raise the student's awareness that there will be debate. Probing the student's work, thinking and findings is a legitimate part of the doctoral examination. Students can find it intimidating to debate their work, at length and in detail, with senior scholars, and it is surely one of the supervisor's roles to prepare them for what is, for most, a new task.

There is also a range of verbal strategies that students can develop for discussing their work in a viva (Murray 2009a). The following is a selection, but experienced supervisors and examiners often have their own collection and their personal favourites:

- *Speaking in the past tense*: avoiding overgeneralizing or overstating the claim to the contribution that can be made on the basis of the study's findings.
- *Being specific*: showing in-depth knowledge of key features of the research – names of key researchers, dates of publication of key works in the field and specific steps in the research process, however routine – and key features of the thesis, for example page numbers for key strengths and weaknesses, key illustrations or turning points in the thesis argument.
- *Linking generalizations to specifics*: getting into the verbal habit of moving from a general statement to a specific instance, example or piece of evidence in the study and in the thesis.
- *Starting with the thesis*: planning answers to examiner's questions with reference to specific points in the thesis, putting exactly what is in the thesis into oral discussion, because the focus of this examination is, after all, the thesis.
- *Speaking in the first person, saying 'I'*: indicating that the student being examined did the work – 'I decided to . . . I considered . . . I carried out the . . .' –

and wrote the thesis. This is a major stylistic shift from the impersonal style in which a thesis is written in some disciplines.

- *'Define-defend'*: responding to a challenging question – e.g. 'Why did you not use the . . . methodology?' – not by going straight to a defence of the methodology used, but starting with a definition of the methodology, then justifying it, then giving reasons for rejecting alternatives. This can prevent students becoming, feeling or sounding defensive.
- *Discussing pros and cons*: presenting or reviewing options – e.g. for methods or interpretations – in terms of their constituents and purposes, so as to demonstrate wider understanding.
- *Answering the question*: remembering that this is a key task in the viva, as in any examination.

Some of these strategies will seem obvious to supervisors, but discussions in viva workshops at many universities over the years reveal that they are not obvious to all students. The implication for supervisors is that these strategies – and/or others – should be built into viva practice sessions. The strategies are not particularly difficult to understand, but they do take some practice.

The aim of all practice sessions is to develop the student's ability to respond to examiners' questions in an appropriate, professional manner, whatever the question, whatever the examiner's tone. With this type of practice, not only do students perform to the best of their ability, but some even enjoy their vivas (Murray 1998).

Supporting students during thesis revision

For some supervisors, their work is done when the student leaves the viva, but for others, their students may still need their support. Supervisors can support students with corrections or revisions to do by helping them to define precisely what still has to be done – what each revision should involve, for example. This may mean deciding on the scale and scope of revisions, perhaps making examiners' comments more specific. Interpretation of comments can be checked with the internal examiner. The supervisor can also provide feedback on draft revisions.

If the student has a sense of anti-climax after the viva, the supervisor may have a role to play in helping the student find motivation to complete revisions. If the student mistakenly sees the requirement for revisions as a failure, the supervisor can build confidence by correcting this misconception. If the student secures a job or another research contract or in any sense 'moves on', the supervisor can follow up and check the student's progress with their corrections or resubmission. Some students have reported that they were demoralized by the thought that they would have to do 'more writing' after the viva because they thought that they would be free of writing after the viva. This is a point that supervisors can make to students much earlier in the thesis writing process, so that students see post-viva revisions as part of the thesis-writing process.

Complaints and appeals

Precept 25
Institutions will put in place and publicise procedures for dealing with student representations that are fair, clear to all concerned, robust and applied consistently. Such procedures will allow all students access to relevant information and an opportunity to present their case.

As with many of the precepts, this guidance for 'institutions' surely has implications for supervisors. They are best placed to check that students understand 'representations', or whatever they are called at their institutions. They can also check that students know and understand that there are formal and informal 'representations', and that there is a difference between complaints, 'representations about general matters (including conduct)' and appeals, 'against specific outcomes or decisions' (QAA 2004: 26).

With complaints, there are generally informal processes, and supervisors should check that students know what these are. When students have a problem that they have not been able to resolve with their supervisors, they need to have someone else to consult. It should be clear to all students who that person is, and the implication for supervisors is that they should check that students know this. This is not to say that all students will understand the difference between 'formal' and 'informal' in this context, since many will fear that they are formalizing the issue even by simply consulting another person in the department. Supervisors have a role in assuring students that this process can be helpful to all involved, themselves included.

When should supervisors communicate the appeals process to students? At an early stage, students need to know and understand the possible grounds for appeal in relation to the doctoral examination: procedural irregularities in the conduct of the examination; circumstances (perhaps specified by the institution) affecting the student's performance of which examiners were not aware when they made their decision; inadequacies, bias or prejudice demonstrated by the examiners during the examination. Disagreement with the academic judgement of examiners is generally not considered grounds for appeal. Only once a case has been through a university's appeals process can a student take it to the Independent Adjudicator (England and Wales) or the Scottish Public Service Ombudsman (Scotland) – supervisors can check that students know this (see Chapter 9).

The student complaints included throughout this book, along with the large number of complaints received by, for example, John Wakeford, who provided the real cases included in Appendix 2, and has published many others in occasional pieces for the *Guardian* newspaper, suggest that these apparently common sense principles are not, in fact, in operation across the board. They also indicate that students who have bad experiences – and some of them have been treated very badly indeed – are going to speak out, and some will take legal action – all the more reason for supervisors to work with students on 'resolving problems at an early stage' (QAA 2004: 26). An example of a student who was unhappy about the way he was being treated by his supervisor is outlined in the precept into practice for Precept 25.

Precept into Practice – 25

Issue

At the previous research meeting when Kevin, a first-year student, had reported on his most recent findings, he had been severely criticized by Prof. Peters once again. Kevin accepted that Prof. Peters would want to give him important feedback on his work, but when this was done in an abusive manner, Kevin felt humiliated. Kevin just could not understand why Prof. Peters behaved in such a way, and the constant verbal abuse was getting him down. What could Kevin do about it? He wanted to discuss his problems with another academic but he was not sure who would be best to talk to.

Resolution

All institutions should have clear guidelines in their Code of Practice for Research Supervisors and Research Students or equivalent, for students who wish to consult academic staff about any problem that may concern them. Ideally, if the guidelines are clear and the relevant personnel can be consulted, this may help prevent problems at an early stage from developing into a potentially more damaging complaint. In this instance, the institutional guidelines on abuse would need to be referenced. It might also be in Kevin's interest to see whether a replacement supervisor could be found.

Conclusion

Of late there has been some debate concerning the long-term future of the viva voce in the UK. Some opinion suggests that the only sensible use of the process is where there is genuine doubt over the quality or integrity of the written dissertation or other public form of work. In this argument, if internal assessment and external opinion agrees [*sic*] that the work is obviously of the standard required, then the role of the viva becomes redundant. The remaining purpose – proving ownership by the candidate can be validated by the supervisors and/or other internal personnel . . . the argument against the 'traditional' use of the viva is that in some cases it is more a form of ritualised behaviour than a necessary requirement. In a case where all concerned are perfectly content with the work submitted, one would have to ask for whose benefit the viva was being held.

(Swift and Douglas 1997: 19)

This raises interesting questions about the purpose of the viva. As long as the viva is used in the doctoral examination we have to acknowledge that it does have a number of these purposes, and that its purpose may vary from institution to institution and even, it could be argued – if each doctoral research project is deemed to be unique – from one student to another. However, each university's regulations and procedures should bring coherence to examination practices, and supervisors, along with examiners, are the agents of these procedures.

This chapter places responsibility for implementing procedures with supervisors, but students can also take an active role in seeking out information and discussing its meaning. The implication for supervisors, since they are in the strongest position to influence students, is that they should encourage this, but that does not mean responsibility shifts to students:

The current climate of lifelong learning in the academy suggests that students should take responsibility for their own learning. Such individualism enables advice to research students to continue to be that it is for them to face the horrors of the viva and try to deal with them (Murray, 2003[b]). Such advice takes no heed of patterns of inequality, nor does it call institutions to account. And yet the academy is currently imbued within a culture of accountability and quality assurance. It seems inevitable that in the end the PhD viva voce examination will fall prey to this. However, 'quality assurance', without challenging the power structures inherent in 'quality', is not enough.

(Loumansky and Jackson 2004: 31)

This chapter sought to help supervisors find a way to reconcile the individual and the institutional. While Murray (2009a) looks at what students can do to prepare for their vivas – material that will also be of use and/or interest to supervisors and examiners – this book focuses on what supervisors can do. One of their key roles is to empower and enable students to understand procedures and the values that underpin them, to know what they have to do to progress and to develop their own position in these debates.

Talking points

- What can a supervisor do about bad practice in a doctoral examination? What should a supervisor do when an external examiner fails to follow the institution's procedures? What can supervisors do about aggressive examiners?
- What can be done to solve the problem faced by small departments in appointing internal examiners, from a small number of staff?
- What can academics do about the problem of the increasing pressure to recruit more postgraduate students, when there are not enough staff to supervise them?
- Should postgraduates have a say in the selection or appointment of their examiners?
- With an increasing demand for external examiners to have credibility and experience of examining at doctoral level, when can an inexperienced external examiner be appointed?
- Who reads or monitors external examiners' reports? What are possible outcomes of that monitoring?
- Should student training courses that are part of the Research Training Programme be discussed at vivas? Is accumulating a specified number of credits for such courses a condition of the award of the doctorate (e.g. 45 credits at Sheffield University, at the time of writing)? If so, how many credits are required? If not, should they be? What are the pros and cons of this model for acknowledging research student training?
- How is published work examined in the viva?
- Is student feedback sought during the viva? If so, what happens to that feedback? What happens if the feedback on supervision is negative or critical?

Key texts

Murray, R. (2009a) *How to Survive your Viva: Defending a Thesis in an Oral Examination*, 2nd edn. Maidenhead: Open University Press.

Pearce, L. (2005) *How to Examine a Thesis*. Maidenhead: Open University Press.

9

Complaints and appeals procedures

Complaints • Appeals • Conclusion • Talking points • Key text

Universities are witnessing a rise in the number of complaints and appeals made by students. Although as a proportion of the total, postgraduate research students do not make that many complaints, supervisors need to know their university's procedures in this area and be aware of common reasons for complaints and appeals, so that they can preferably be avoided from the outset.

First, a significant issue is that across institutions there may be differences in procedures for complaints and appeals, so it is wise to have a thorough knowledge of those relevant to your institution. Second, it is worth remembering that if a complaint or appeal is not upheld at an institution, depending on where one's institution is in the UK will determine which independent body the grievance can be taken to. In a changing society, it appears that litigation is generally becoming more popular, and today's students are more likely to take complaints and appeals through the legal process. Third, it is especially worth remembering that of those students who now routinely take out legal expenses insurance, the vast majority are postgraduates.

In this chapter, we will discuss in some detail the institutional procedures for making complaints and appeals and the potential involvement of the Office of the Independent Adjudicator, with relevant case studies.

Complaints

Precept 26
Independent and formal procedures will exist to resolve effectively complaints from research students about the quality of the institution's learning and support provision.

Definition of a complaint

To avoid confusion, the National Postgraduate Committee (see www.npc. org.uk) in the UK has come up with the following definition:

> A complaint is a case where a student is dissatisfied with the academic support or services made available, which may have had some consequences on the student's academic progress. This could include sub standard academic facilities, supervision or poor quality of support or extreme difficulties faced with an individual in the institution. There are many reasons why a student, former student or prospective student may wish to lodge a complaint with different ways in which the complaint is handled. The outcome of a complaint cannot change the outcome of an examination. At the very best, a student could be awarded damages due to an unsuccessful outcome being a result of bad service from the higher education institution.

It should be made quite clear that a complaint cannot be made against a matter of academic judgement.

Although there would normally be greater flexibility time-wise for making a complaint than an appeal, in some institutions a complaint is unlikely to be considered from a former student who has not been registered for the research degree for a period of six months or more at the time of making the complaint. An example of a complaint would be a case of inadequate supervision. Whenever the student realizes that there is a problem a complaint can be made and the earlier one is made, the better for all parties. Unusually, a complaint of inadequate supervision can still be made at the viva stage, as in some instances it is only then that the student realizes that their supervision has been inadequate. However, an earlier complaint would probably have been more successful in resolving the issue, and as some institutions do not allow a student to complain about inadequate supervision once the thesis is submitted, earlier is therefore advisable.

It is worth remembering that a student has a right of independent representation, which may well come from the local Union of Students, and such a body may provide considerable expertise and assistance to the student. It is very important that supervisors keep appropriate records of meetings with students in order to clarify any issues which may arise and have been high-lighted in Precept 17 (Chapter 5). It is also possible that the case review stage is invoked following an unsuccessful academic appeal (for example, see Case 1 below) on the grounds that the case was dealt with incorrectly. Rarely, a complaint can be made following a successful viva outcome but where the student experience, possibly through a procedural irregularity, was unfavourable.

As described below, both complaints and appeals procedures involve several stages, and appropriate guidelines can be found in institutional booklets such as the Code of Practice for Postgraduate Research Students and/or websites. Details are also usually found in the institution's students' charter.

More detailed information on academic appeals and student complaints can be found in the QAA (2007a) Code of Practice Section 5: *Academic Appeals and Student Complaints on Academic Matters*. This Code of Practice identifies general principles and a comprehensive series of system-wide expectations relating to the management of academic quality and standards in higher education.

Example of a complaints procedure

Students are always advised to seek advice from their supervisor in the first instance and preferably at an early stage. This can often resolve issues before they progress further. However, in the case of inadequate supervision, it might be a difficult topic to discuss with a supervisor, and another possibility could be for the student to talk to their pastoral tutor or another member of the supervisory team. An alternative strategy would be for the student to talk to the departmental graduate tutor and/or head of department. If a complaint has still not been resolved and possible remedies put in place, then it is at this point that the complaint moves to the formal stage. Each institution will have its own formal procedures for dealing with complaints of an academic nature. For example, a complaints form may be completed by the student and sent to the registrar and secretary. Complaints involving postgraduate research students will then be directed to the relevant administrative office which will arrange for a faculty officer (such as a dean) to consider the case and make a decision. Some universities have appointed specialist staff, often with legal expertise, to deal with complaints and appeals from students. More often than not, the administrative and advisory role in respect of consideration of such cases from postgraduate research students will be undertaken by someone in the Graduate School office (or equivalent). The process itself may involve seeking further information from the relevant department by correspondence. The decision could be that the complaint is upheld and some form of remedial action is proposed – which may include a formal apology on behalf of the institution and in extreme cases, some form of compensation. Alternatively, the complaint may not be upheld – in which case the student should be provided with a brief explanation of reasons. If the student is still not satisfied with the faculty officer's decision, then they can usually have their case considered further by a higher authority within the university – for example, via a case review procedure. In this example, the student is required to complete a case review form giving reasons why they are not satisfied with the decision taken in respect of their original complaint and stating what would be their desired outcome. The case is then sent to the relevant university officer (pro-vice chancellor) who makes a decision as to whether or not the complaint should be taken to a case review panel. If a panel is convened, the student has the choice either to appear in person before the panel, with or without representation by a friend or adviser, or for the panel to deal with the case by written submissions only. If a member of staff has been named in the complaint, they will be invited to the meeting and have the option to bring along a colleague or adviser. Once the panel has made its decision, the student is informed of it in writing, together with reference to the Office of the Independent Adjudicator (OIA), which acts as an external student complaints arbiter, should the student wish to take the matter further, and if their case is eligible to be considered under the scheme. Even if the student is unhappy with the verdict of the OIA there is still the possibility to take the matter further through litigation. A number of legal firms now specialize in the higher education sector, and among other services will attempt to bring challenges against the decisions of the OIA by way of judicial review or civil claims in both the County Court and the High Court. A flowchart of the various procedures is shown in Figure 9.1.

It is important when dealing with both complaints and appeals that all procedures, as described in institutional literature, should be carefully adhered to, and that the student should be kept informed of progress with the case at all times.

Office of the Independent Adjudicator

In 1997 the National Committee of Inquiry into Higher Education, chaired by Sir Ron Dearing, identified a need for institutions to review the way in which they handle complaints by students. The committee recommended that institutions should change their complaints handling procedures to ensure that they:

- reflect the principles of natural justice
- are transparent and timely
- include procedures for reconciliation and arbitration
- include an independent external element
- are managed by a senior member of staff.

Following consultations, the OIA was established in 2003 and commenced a student complaints scheme in 2004. The Higher Education Act 2004 provides for the appointment of a designated operator (OIA) of a student complaints scheme in England and Wales, and all higher education institutions in England and Wales are required to comply with the rules of the scheme. Students in

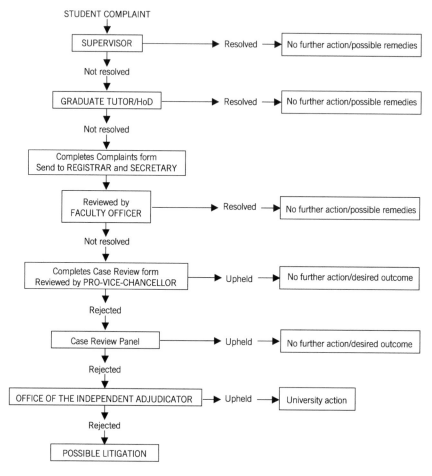

Figure 9.1   Complaints procedure.

Scotland are able to complain to the Scottish Public Service Ombudsman, which was set up in 2002. In Northern Ireland, at the time of writing, universities were still using the Visitor system (the system used in the UK before the OIA was set up) and even though a similar OIA scheme had been rejected, proposals have been made to consider an Ombudsman scheme similar to the one used in Scotland.

The OIA describes its procedures as informal, and a decision is generally made based on information provided by both parties. There is normally no provision for face-to-face meetings or hearings. If the OIA finds that the complaint has been justified, the OIA can recommend to the institution that it does one of the following:

- Take steps to assist the student in some way
- Ask the complaint to be looked at afresh because the internal procedures of the institution had not been properly followed
- Recommend that the institution change the way it handles complaints, or change its internal procedures
- Recommend that compensation is payable.

Apart from the OIA not being able to consider cases that relate to academic judgement, it cannot look at a complaint if it is or has been the subject of court proceedings. Moreover, the OIA can take on a case only when all institutional procedures have been exhausted and when the student has been given a 'completion of procedures letter' by the institution.

If an institution failed to comply with recommendations made by the OIA, it would be treated in a serious matter and publicized in the annual report of the OIA, for example, 'named and shamed'.

OIA statistics for 2006 and 2007 indicate that it receives about 600–700 application forms from undergraduate and postgraduate students a year, and that of these, approximately two-thirds fall into the academic appeal category. About 65 per cent of complaints are from students over 25 years of age. Interestingly only 5 per cent of cases are from postgraduate research students. Total compensation paid out in 2006 and 2007 was £32,857 and £173,000 respectively.

In a review of the first three years of the OIA, the adjudicator noted an element of 'ambulance chasing' creeping into the advertising of some law firms looking for student business and raising unreal expectations in terms of possible outcomes (Deech 2007).

Recent decisions by the OIA from its website (with permission)

Rather than create a fictional case, we considered it more useful to include details of several real case studies which were dealt with by the OIA and which have been reproduced with its permission.

Case 1

L was a graduate doctoral student at the University of PP. She was found to have plagiarized parts of her thesis but, having regard to mitigating circumstances, was allowed to resubmit it. On resubmission, the thesis was failed. L appealed against this finding, and both internal and external reviewers appointed by the University found that there had been inadequate supervision. The University proposed no further action on the grounds that that there was insufficient evidence about the lack of supervision. L complained to the OIA on two grounds: first, that having followed the guidance of her supervisors, the failure must be due to unfair examination or inadequate supervision and second, that no remedy was offered by the University after an appeal that had taken a year and found in her favour. The OIA found the complaints **justified.** The reasons were that the available evidence supported the view that there had been inadequate supervision, and there had been an internal finding to that effect; therefore it was unreasonable of the University to offer no compensation or other remedy to resolve L's complaint. Moreover, the University's internal investigation of the complaint was protracted, lacked transparency and failed to keep L informed. The OIA **recommended** that the University pay L £2500 by way of compensation.

Case 2

Y was registered as a doctoral student at the University of CC. She submitted her thesis for examination. The examiners' decision was that she had not satisfied the requirements for the award of a PhD but that she could resubmit the revised thesis for the degree of MPhil. Y sought the opportunity to resubmit a revised thesis and be re-examined for the degree of PhD. In her complaint she alleged maladministration, in that the examiners lacked impartiality, experience and discrimination, in that an examiner had been aggressive and patronizing towards her in the oral examination; and unfair practices, namely, failure to respect her freedom of thought and dignity and that medical evidence affecting her performance had not been properly dealt with. The OIA found the complaint **not justified** for the following reason: the conduct of the oral examination fell within the range of reasonable practice and the appointment of examiners was within the general scope of the regulations. Their suitability was a question of academic judgement over which the OIA has no remit. The appeal procedures had been properly followed.

Case 3

Student A was registered as a doctoral student for 7 years. After 2 years he transferred from MPhil to PhD status. After 8 extensions to the deadline for his submission he withdrew voluntarily from the course and complained to the University about his supervision. He sought compensation of £250,000; the University identified defects in the University's procedures and offered £500. A complained to the OIA about his supervisor's failure to warn him that his work was not of the required standard; that he did not receive annual appraisals; and that he was not given appropriate support and communication by the University. The OIA found the complaint **justified** on the grounds that there should have been earlier warnings about the failure to progress and the failure to submit written work. Although A did not complain about his supervision during the 7 years nor did he complete a single chapter of his thesis, firmer control should have been exercised by the supervisor, who should not have repeatedly supported requests for extensions. The student also bore responsibility and should have taken steps to ensure that his difficulties were being addressed. The OIA **recommended** that the University offer £1000 compensation, improve its appraisal and upgrade procedures and show how it would monitor those procedures to ensure compliance in the future.

Case 4

Student X was registered as a full time doctoral student in October; her research proposal was submitted in May and was deemed inadequate. In October of the next year a revised proposal was also found not to demonstrate the required doctoral ability. In the following February X's registration at the University was terminated. X complained to the University and subsequently to the OIA about the unsatisfactory nature of the annual review and about her supervision, on the ground that it cannot have been good because her proposal failed. The OIA found the complaint to be **not justified**. There was no procedural irregularity in the annual review or in the University's internal procedures. The standard of X's work was an issue of academic judgement and outside the remit of the OIA scheme. The University had reached its decision after very careful consideration and it held the opinion, reasonably, that to allow X to continue her studies would have been unfair and irresponsible. X objected to references by the University to the circumstances that had hampered her progress with her work, but these were held to be an unobjectionable record of the reasons for her difficulties.

Appeals

Precept 27
Institutions will put in place formal procedures to deal with any appeals made by research students. The acceptable grounds for appeals will be clearly defined.

Definition of an appeal

The National Postgraduate Committee of the UK defines an appeal as follows:

An appeal is a case where a student wishes to challenge the outcome of an assessment or an examination and it was felt it was conducted unfairly. This could include cases where a student failed an exam through no fault of their own, they were not happy with the marking of the dissertation, they felt that the transfer viva from MPhil to PhD was unfair, that the viva was failed unfairly or that they were withdrawn from the course due to circumstances which were felt not to be fair. Whatever the circumstances are, they have to affect the outcome of the assessment or examination such that they do not reflect a true level of attainment. In such instances there are normally three cases where there are grounds for appeal, which are, a) procedural irregularity in assessment, b) lack of experience of the examiners or in some cases, c) bias of the examiners. The institution will set grounds for an appeal based on these factors and reject any appeals that do not meet one or more of these possible criteria, where they may then advise of the option of making a formal complaint. A further point to note is that a successful appeal would not normally change the result, but normally ask that the assessment is repeated, often with re-submission and re-examination, with any unfair circumstances appropriately resolved.

(www.npc.org.uk/postgraduatefactsandissues/aboutpostgraduates/
complaintsandappealsforpostgraduates)

Unusually, the examination could be declared void and a fresh examination would have to be conducted.

An example of an appeal could be a situation where a student had undergone a viva examination and was deemed to have failed. The student could then make an appeal on the grounds that the conduct of the viva was not appropriate, and that this was responsible for the failure.

It has been said that too frequently, students, and sometimes supervisors, are unaware of their institutional appeals and complaints procedures (Morley et al. 2002: 263), although it is hoped that increasingly this is not the case. However, interestingly, the precise grounds for appeal may vary between institutions.

Example of an academic appeals procedure

An appeal normally has to be submitted within a specified time-frame. A student needs to complete an academic appeals report form within 28 days of publication (notification) of the exam result. The case is then considered by the faculty officer who has to decide whether a prima facie case has been made. Although the faculty officer has the power to uphold a complaint, if the case is deemed worthy of further investigation, they may recommend that it be considered by an academic appeals committee, where it can be dealt with on written submissions or at an oral hearing. If the student is not satisfied with the outcome of this committee then the nature of the appeal can be dealt with under the complaints procedure with completion of a case review form which is considered by the appropriate senior academic such as a pro-vice-chancellor or equivalent. If the matter is still not resolved, then it can be taken to the OIA who consider if the case is eligible under its rules. As above, if the student is not happy with the outcome of the OIA review then they have the option of taking it to litigation. A flowchart of a typical appeals procedure is shown in Figure 9.2.

Conclusion

In an era of a growing complaints and compensation culture, supervisors need to be fully aware of their institutional complaints and appeals procedures and the possible consequences, should a complaint or an appeal be upheld. The positive side of legal firms wanting to move into the higher education sector and the development of the OIA is that it has driven institutions to treat complaints and appeals more seriously. This has meant that both complaints and appeals procedures in institutions are more readily accessible and that designated staff, who can then develop expertise in this area, are assigned to manage these activities.

As a newer idea, Buckton (2008: 11) has highlighted the potential benefit of internal mediation or arbitration in complaints cases and suggests that they be considered if an institution is wanting to make revisions to its complaints procedures. For example, the University of Bristol has adopted mediation to help resolve some of the misunderstandings that can surround a complaint.

With an increasing number of complaints and appeals in institutions and possible serious consequences, many of the precepts in the QAA (2004) Code of Practice that are highlighted in this book take on a special relevance, as they not only attempt to enhance quality of the postgraduate student experience but also try to reduce the opportunities for complaints to be made against supervisors.

Although the OIA appears to have achieved its objectives in dealing with complaints against institutions in England and Wales, it is a pity that the scheme has not been adopted in Scotland or Northern Ireland, as without uniformity there is greater opportunity for students to receive different treatment.

Talking points

- If a supervisory complaint is made, is it the supervisor or the institution who pays costs if the case goes to court?
- A student who is making a complaint can receive Union of Students and/or legal representation. Can a supervisor obtain legal advice and if so, is this provided by the institution?

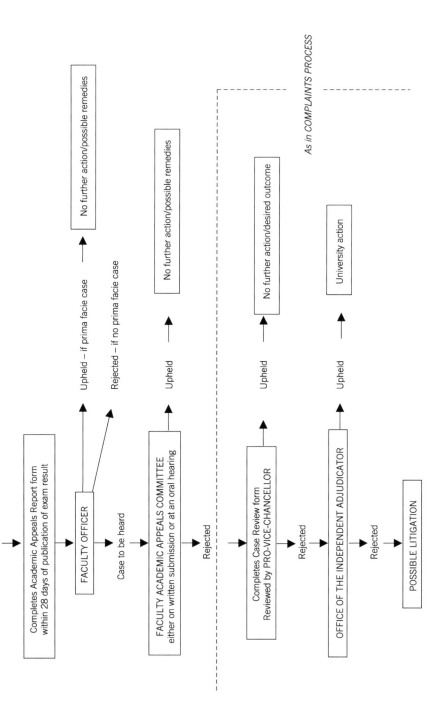

Figure 9.2 Appeals procedure.

- With an increase in more formal procedures as to how complaints are handled and a greater chance of legal action if things go wrong, what impact will all of this have on the nature of the supervisor–student relationship?
- With a greater focus on students' rights, such as the right of appeal for a student, if academic staff are unhappy with the outcome of an appeal, should there be a right of appeal for the university?
- Currently, the levels of compensation paid to students have been low. However, if students started to win large amounts of damages it might be interesting to see how universities would react.

Key text

Buckton, L. (2008) Student complaints and appeals: the practitioner's view. *Perspectives: Policy and Practice in Higher Education*, 12: 11–14.

10

Features of other research degrees

Other types of research degrees – master's • Other types of research degrees – doctorates • Institutional environment • Selection and admission of students • Supervision arrangements • Monitoring and review arrangements • Induction and training in research and generic skills • Feedback mechanisms • Good examination practice • Processes for complaints and appeals • Conclusion • Talking points • Key text

The QAA (2004) Code of Practice *Section 1: Postgraduate Research Programmes* is considered particularly relevant to MPhil/PhD students, as they are the largest cohort of research students. However, the Code of Practice states that it relates to the many different types of research students undertaking research programmes in the UK, but that not all precepts will be equally applicable. The Code then makes specific reference to research master's degrees and all forms of taught or professional doctorate (see Table 1.2) which have been steadily increasing in popularity in the UK since the early 2000s.

The aim of this chapter is to consider research degree programmes other than the MPhil/PhD, in some detail, paying attention to the discussions of the precepts in Chapters 2 to 9 and how they impact on these other programmes.

Other types of research degrees – master's

Typically an MPhil is seen as a research degree in which a thesis is produced of about 40,000 words (word limits vary from institution to institution). In contrast a PhD has more depth, is usually larger and is often of greater originality than an MPhil. For a PhD thesis, a word limit of approximately 70,000 words is typical. Even with the introduction of skills training, possibly as part of a Research Training Programme, both these degrees are almost entirely research focused.

Traditionally, the other type of master's degree such as an MA or MSc is classed as a taught degree, where at least 50 per cent of the credits earned would often be non-research based, with a requirement for a relatively short research-based dissertation.

A more recent development has been the introduction of so-called research master's degrees, such as the MRes. The latter is usually a one-year full-time master's degree with an emphasis on qualitative and quantitative research skills, often through taught research methods modules, for students who are planning to become academic researchers and who use it to prepare for their PhD studies. Similar research programmes, some with the name MA (by research) in place of the MRes, have also been created to meet the requirements of the one plus three Economic and Social Research Council (ESRC) scheme (one year of training in research methods followed by three years of supervised research).

A different type of research master's relates to creative work such as, for example, the MMus where a student has to choose two modules out of those on performance, composition, a dissertation and a folio. A dissertation, therefore, is not obligatory in this case, which is very different from other research master's degrees.

Other types of research degrees – doctorates

A conventional full-time PhD in the UK normally takes three to four years to complete and is the most common doctorate studied. However, in an attempt to improve flexibility of study which is often appealing to overseas students, Joint PhD programmes have emerged whereby international students can spend some or most of their research study time in their home country. Another trend has been the increasing number of institutions in the UK awarding PhDs by publication (Powell 2004), although historically the idea goes back to what happened in Germany in the nineteenth century.

In an attempt more closely to mimic the North American model of a PhD, the period since the mid 2000s has seen the introduction of the New Route PhD, or better described, PhD with Integrated Studies or Integrated PhD. Typically this is a four-year programme, which often (but not always) includes a master's degree together with research skills training. However, although there has been some interest in this new model of PhD programme, the biggest growth in the market has concerned professional doctorates (Powell and Long 2005). The UK Council for Graduate Education (2002) defines the professional doctorate as follows:

> the professional doctorate is a further development of the taught doctorate . . . but the field of study is a professional discipline, rather than academic enquiry and scholarship . . . most professional doctorates are designed to meet the particular professional need . . . the research element of a professional doctorate is focussed on professional practice . . . it is possible for the work to make an original contribution to the way in which theory is applied, or to the nature of practice within a profession.
> (UK Council for Graduate Education 2002: 7)

Professional doctorates such as the Doctor of Education (EdD) appear to have a number of elements in common, as described by Scott et al. (2004): taught courses, specification of learning outcomes often in the form of employment related skills, cohort-based pedagogies, and usually a reduced thesis length in comparison with the PhD thesis, but with the same requirement for originality. An EdD, for example, might comprise two parts: the first consisting of six taught modules each assessed by 6000-word assignments and the second part, a 50,000-word dissertation. Within the professions, most of the professional doctorates fall within engineering, education and business. One of the drivers for the professional doctorate is dissatisfaction with the PhD as a qualification appropriate for advanced professional work outside of academia (Green and Powell 2005).

Institutional environment

One of the obvious differences for any research degree with a taught component is the consideration of the formal teaching element. This has implications for programme approval, delivery and monitoring or quality assurance, including student feedback. At the degree approval stage, the appropriate learning and teaching committee is normally responsible for approving the taught modules and for the standards of any such formal teaching. Of course, this would be in addition to any approval of the research element, which would be dealt with by a graduate research student committee or equivalent. This would also mean that any course or programme review would have to be considered by both committees, which could potentially delay any decision-making.

What we have to remember in evaluation is that we should not think exclusively in terms of MPhil/PhD programmes as the problem with obtaining meaningful feedback lies in the current diversity of research students, and it is clear that it is probably not possible to use one model of questionnaire to fit all student groups. For example, many of these students would have taught components that are generally not considered by such a questionnaire. Even more extreme is the case of the MMus as mentioned above, where such a student may not even be submitting a dissertation. Do we also take into account that students studying for a Joint PhD may probably be out of the UK when the questionnaire is supposed to be returned? Moreover, a number of questions about supervision would probably not be relevant for a PhD by publication. Furthermore, in Part 1 of an EdD as also described above, such a questionnaire would be irrelevant, as this part is not related to the research dissertation. It is clear, therefore, that to achieve meaningful feedback from such a wide array of research students will demand that different questionnaires and/or different methods of feedback are required.

The typical Graduate School will most likely produce a number of helpful publications for research students, such as an Institutional Code of Practice for Research Students, but in reality they will probably be of most relevance to MPhil/PhD students. They will probably be of little relevance to MRes, professional doctorates (in the early stages) and research degrees by performance and/or publication. It is therefore incumbent on the relevant departments to tailor their procedures to take account of the range of their research degree programmes and to provide sufficient relevant advice to specifically cater for these different types of research students. This also raises the question of how inclusive the Graduate School can and should be in an era of a growing number and diversity of research degree programmes.

In general, one of the markers for assessing the performance of an institution in its production of successful postgraduate degrees is the completion rate. When there were mostly MPhil/PhD students, it was easier to get a grip on what the situation was. Now that there are different types of research degrees with, theoretically, different completion times, the situation has become a great deal more complicated and necessitates that the different degrees and formats be looked at individually. Like the PhD, should we be looking at completion rates of research master's degrees and professional doctorates, although as there is a large taught element in the latter it would not necessarily reflect research performance?

Selection and admission of students

Special needs issues may not be important for students wishing to submit a PhD by publication as actual time spent at the institution might be quite small, unless the student is going to produce papers based on the work they undertake at the institution, although access to the library might still be an issue. For Joint PhD students who will spend a lot of their research time in their home country, presumably responsibility for accessing research facilities will depend on what is feasible in the home institution, although it is up to the awarding institution to agree to the arrangements and ensure their suitability.

As mentioned in some detail in Chapter 3, the normal academic criterion for admission to a research degree is a 2.1 bachelor's degree. It is clear that this may not be wholly appropriate for professional doctorates, as a professional qualification and/or professional experience are essential criteria for entry (Neumann 2005: 178). From the very nature of this type of degree, there would need to be much greater flexibility in the decision-making process. An issue here, however, is that with less rigid guidelines, they could potentially lead to inappropriate decisions being made, unless parity in the decision-making process could be maintained. With more rigid guidelines for MPhil/PhD admission, it is easier for admissions tutors to make appropriate decisions than for professional doctorates. It would appear, therefore, that selected personnel (in other words those with professional experience) might be useful in the admissions process for applicants to professional doctorates, together with some training on the different requirements of research degrees, for academic admissions staff in general.

One of the potential benefits for research students is the opportunity to be employed by the institution as a part-time teacher. This would probably not be appropriate for research master's students, but is often made available for doctoral students. Unfortunately, many professional doctorate students are part-time, including most EdD students in the UK (Scott et al. 2004: 32), and because of this, the opportunities for teaching would be more limited. However, this is probably true for all part-time doctoral students.

With increasing demands on MPhil/PhD students since the early 2000s, there has been a growing trend for comprehensive induction provision. Unfortunately, this seems to be mostly true for this cohort of students only. Of course, other research students, such as those undertaking a research master's degree, would presumably receive specific induction material through departmental based activities, as the structure and nature of the courses are quite different. The same is true for professional doctorates, as often in the first stage of the programme there would often be no research activity undertaken, so that a general research student induction session would be wholly inappropriate for these students. A potential group of students who may miss out on induction are those undertaking a Joint PhD, as they may not be at the institution at the time of the induction sessions. It is clear, therefore, that alternative arrangements need to be made for certain groups of research students, and that just running induction sessions for MPhil/PhD students is not good enough.

What can also be an oversight is the consideration of research ethics or governance and health and safety for Joint PhD students undertaking their research in another country. This can be a complicated and difficult issue, but as the students involved are registered with a UK institution, it is the responsibility of that institution to make sure that the research is carried out according to appropriate standards, and that the students are not at risk.

Supervision arrangements

The supervisor–student relationship is all important, no matter which research degree is being studied. However, by the nature of the different research degrees, the relationship will also be different. For a typical PhD, the supervisor is trying to develop the student into an independent researcher, but there will not be time to achieve this for a research master's student, and for a professional doctorate student, this aim may just not be appropriate. Although for the latter, potentially there could be an advantage in that for the EdD, for example, both supervisor and student are involved in education and therefore share a professional interest in, for instance, learning, teaching and assessment (Scott et al. 2004: 106). However, the situation may be quite different for a student wishing to submit a PhD by publication, as the research itself may already have been done elsehwere, and in this case the supervisor may just need to offer academic advice on presentation and coherence of the material. This means that supervisors will need to think carefully about how they develop the most beneficial relationship with the different types of research student.

It is now accepted that most PhD supervisors will themselves have a PhD and usually will be research active. However, it is unlikely that the majority will also possess other types of research degree. Does this automatically mean that a supervisor who does not possess the particular degree that a student is studying for, will be unable to offer good supervision? Of course not, but it does mean that supervisors need to be aware of the different requirements of students taking different research degrees and it is hoped have a good understanding of their structure and content. It is also possible that a potential supervisor may not have the professional expertise or experience required for a professional doctorate dissertation and may seek a suitable co-supervisor in this situation.

For PhDs it is now expected that supervisors will undergo some sort of professional development or training to have a greater awareness of what is required for good PhD supervision and for general updating on local and national guidelines. Unfortunately, such provision is patchy, and for many academics has still not been widely accepted. So where does that leave us with other research degrees? To the best of our knowledge we think that it would be unlikely that supervisors of other research degrees have specific training of relevance to the type of research degree that they are supervising. Perhaps the best solution would be for the institution to hold sessions for supervisors of research master's students and supervisors of professional doctorates. For degrees such as PhD by publication, which tend to be undertaken by relatively few students each year, a short booklet offering advice might be useful. It would appear that a good starting point is to recognize the different supervisory requirements for the many research degrees that could be offered and to consider how best to support these supervisory needs.

Precept 12 recommends that each research student will have a minimum of one main supervisor, but that normally he or she will be part of a supervisory team. Usually for a research master's student a main supervisor is typical, but the student will often have access to a pastoral tutor, course leader and module tutors, which in total constitute a supervisory team. The major difference is that for a PhD the emphasis of all supervisors, with the possible exception of the pastoral tutor, is the research project. Co-supervisors are commonly appointed to research students for a number of reasons, mostly for subject expertise, but they could also be appointed for mentoring purposes of the trainee supervisor. The downside to having a number of supervisors is that they might have quite different opinions as to which direction the research should be pursued. This can be a very significant issue and can be problematic for students, although the assistance of the graduate tutor or head of department might help, but if the situation becomes very problematic, a change in co-supervisor is always an option. The situation is somewhat different, however, in the case of the Joint PhD, where often the co-supervisors may not know each other or meet throughout the duration of the research programme. This could lead to very serious problems for the student and has to be a potential disadvantage of this type of research degree. Therefore, it is important to encourage those involved in co-supervision to get to know and understand each other through whatever means are available, as effective collaboration is based on mutual trust and understanding, which is fostered by regular contact.

It is also considered appropriate that at least one member of the supervisory team for a PhD will have experience of doctoral supervision to successful completion. A relevant question here is whether prior supervision of a PhD is sufficient experience for supervision of a professional doctorate dissertation? One would imagine that as long as the supervisor has appropriate knowledge of the subject, it would be satisfactory. However, in some professional doctorates, portfolios have replaced a traditional dissertation, which are quite different in content and structure from a thesis. In this situation the answer is probably not quite as clear. While this is an issue for all of those responsible for the delivery of professional doctorate programmes, it is one that should have been addressed during the design and approval stage.

Interestingly, although in a 2004 study, about 80 per cent of institutions appointed at least one supervisor for PhDs by publication, that still means that a significant number of these students had no supervisor (Powell 2004). Back in 1996, it was considered that a supervisor was important and it was stated that:

> the appointment of an academic to guide the candidate through the submission and examination processes is one of the means by which the academic standards by which the award of a PhD by the conventional and published work routes can be harmonised. Ideally, the regulations for the award via the published work route should make reference to the duties of the appointed person and in principle it would be possible to formulate a code of practice for the appointee to parallel those which exist for supervisors of conventional PhD students.
>
> (UK Council for Graduate Education 1996: 13)

If a supervisor is appointed, the type of supervisor required will depend on whether the supervisor is needed for their subject skills, or whether it is just to advise on university protocols and requirements for submission of the work.

For a PhD based on creative research, Wisker (2005: 252) suggests that the role of the supervisor expands from that of more standard research, as there is a need to work alongside students to help them release creative energies and develop creative engagement.

From the above it is obvious that there are many, and in some cases, different demands made of a supervisor depending on which type of research degree needs to be supervised. Clearly, one type of supervisor is unlikely to fill all these roles, and a number of considerations need to be made before any supervisor appointment is made.

Increasingly, the graduate tutor has been playing an important role in helping supervisors manage the PhD process. Have they and/or should they play any role in the management of other research students? For research master's students (and with professional doctorates) the answer is probably no, as these students already have a comprehensive supervisory team including that of course leader. Presumably, the graduate tutor would be responsible for the PhD with Integrated Studies, as this is just a variant of the conventional PhD. The Joint PhD would also probably be included, although their role is made more difficult by the overseas co-supervisor. Whether they have a role with students doing a PhD by publication is more difficult to answer, especially as some students do not have even have a supervisor.

One of the PhD supervisor's principal roles is to discuss the student's progress at meetings with the student. Often the arrangements for these meetings can be quite formal and the frequency determined by the needs of the student. The same principle should still apply to other research students but with a number of considerations. First, the frequency of meetings might need to be increased for research master's students as the timescale for the research and thesis preparation are significantly reduced when compared to a conventional PhD student. Second, frequency of meetings for a student wishing to submit a PhD by publication will partly depend on whether the supervisor is required for subject knowledge or not. Thirdly, alternative arrangements for reporting progress need to be made for Joint PhD students, especially those who rarely visit the UK institution.

Monitoring and review arrangements

Although student progress has been briefly mentioned above, the more formal monitoring and review arrangements need to be considered in some detail. For MRes students, two major differences from PhD students are the reduced time-scale of the degree and the fact that there is no transfer to a doctorate. This means that once the research project is underway there is little time for a formal written report. Instead, there would be greater emphasis on verbal reports either to a supervisor and/or a research group. However, more recently, there has been a tightening up on overall monitoring of these students, as they are now more likely to have pastoral tutors whom they have to meet formally, and record the outcome, at least once during the year. After this introduction to the tutor, the latter is then usually available for consultation throughout the year.

Perhaps the biggest difference lies with professional doctorates. Of course, there are variations between programmes and institutions, but in general these students are expected to write a series of progress reports, including a substantial transfer report (Wisker 2001: 257). An obvious difference with this degree lies in the fact that there are usually two parts (the taught part followed by the research part), and that within the research part there may be different stages. Unlike the PhD, these reviews do not necessarily, and will not in some instances, focus on research. Other types of monitoring are therefore used to enable appropriate transfer to the next part and/or stage whatever that may be. Recording of meetings through meetings logs would still be desirable. However, a difference would be in the format of the log, as in the earlier phases of the professional doctorate, questions about research progress would be inappropriate. Either a more flexible log format or different versions of the log during the two parts of the doctorate might then be a solution. It should also be remembered that with a professional doctorate, a portfolio of several smaller research projects can be submitted instead of a dissertation. Again, this highlights an obvious difference in assessment of research progress when comparing shorter research projects to a single in-depth study.

If a supervisor has been appointed for a student wishing to submit a PhD by publication, the situation is very different. As the most required from such a supervisor is assistance in the production of a supporting document to go with the publications, it is unlikely that any such monitoring and review arrangements would be necessary.

This would certainly not be the case for a Joint PhD. In this very different situation, where the student and overseas supervisor are probably not familiar with the detailed requirements for monitoring and review, they may well require instructions on how to follow the institutional guidelines that they will have to have easy access to. Emphasis will also need to be placed on the importance of completing such arrangements in good time.

Although supervisors are now familiar with the more recent requirements for monitoring and review of PhD students, it is clear that although the principles can be shared by other research degree programmes, the actual desired requirements may be very different.

Induction and training in research and generic skills

To an extent these general topics will apply to almost all research degrees, except perhaps doctorates by publication or, for example, by performance. The MPhil, PhD, Joint PhD and PhD with Integrated Studies will probably be considered similar, with respect to induction and training needs. Where differences will emerge are with the MRes and professional doctorate.

The major reason for a difference with MRes students is that usually the course only lasts for one year, and there is a constraint on time due to the need to cover taught components as well as those relating to research. However, in many cases – particularly in the arts, humanities and social sciences – one of the major aims of an MRes is to provide intending PhD students with the qualitative and quantitative research skills they will need in order to undertake their research. Therefore, although MRes students may not cover these research skills to the same depth as, for example, doctoral students, they should be provided with a good grounding. Indeed, some of the taught modules cover topics related to research methods.

For professional doctorates the situation is similar to the MRes, in that there may be no formal requirement for the Research Training Programme, and, although the course is longer than the MRes, it comprises more taught courses in the specialist subject area. Nevertheless, these doctorates will often include taught modules on an introduction to research, on research methods and techniques, and on research design and management. So these doctoral students will also have an introduction to these topics, bearing in mind that usually a series of shorter research projects will be undertaken, rather than a large research project, as with PhD students.

For personal and professional development, such as attendance at conferences, there would probably be less direct benefit to MRes students who are really only just starting out on their research journey than, for example, PhD students. As professional doctorate students are usually more mature and are often part-time, they would be more likely to already have a professional network, and therefore encouragement to attend conferences would probably be unnecessary. Another difference with professional doctorates is that there is not one principal supervisor but more likely several supervisors, and other course staff, including the course director, who would be managing this type of activity.

A similar difference is seen with any skill development plan, in that this would probably be more likely managed overall by the course leader than by a single supervisor. In any case, as mentioned above there would not be the same demand for such a plan by professional doctoral or MRes students.

In the development of specific skills, such as writing, MRes students would have less time, although this would probably be of greater benefit to professional doctoral students. Again with more than one supervisor, this need might be less easy to recognize and manage.

Finally, PPDPs are routinely used by a large proportion of undergraduate students and they would most probably be routinely continued by MRes students, although as professional doctoral students are often mature and may not have had prior experience of such a plan, they might need to be introduced to the concept.

Feedback mechanisms

Student feedback on the quality of their MPhil/PhD experience tends to be collected on at least an annual basis, although with issues for individual students, such as those undertaking a one-year MRes, this timescale would be too long. Also similar to the early stages of a PhD with Integrated Studies and professional doctorate, questions in the questionnaire relating purely to research would be inappropriate, as these three types of degree have a significant teaching element.

As professional doctoral students often have to do more than one research project, any questionnaire that asks about research progress and supervision should allow for multiple responses to be given, in contrast to a PhD.

Even if student feedback is anonymous, which it often is, it can be culturally quite difficult for many overseas students to be critical, and this can lead to an artificially positive bias. How one obtains honest information from these students, especially when they are new to the university, is an ongoing dilemma.

Of course, a problem with anonymity is that any issues including supervision cannot be specifically identified. This means that other ways need to be found for supervisors to become aware of problems if they are to respond and try to improve themselves.

As mentioned in Chapter 7, there are several ways to measure the quality of a research degree programme. One suggestion is to look at student achievements after graduation. This is a good idea, but from our experience is rarely done in any depth, and is rarely collated, as a certain amount of updating is required to achieve satisfactory data. However, these data would be very valuable for marketing to attract new students.

For MPhil/PhD students most of the reported feedback relates to an individual's experience and because it is usually anonymous, it would be difficult to relate this to a specific doctoral programme if student feedback was collected from a mixed cohort, such as from a school and not a department. This is in contrast to other research degrees, such as the MRes or professional doctorate, which relate to a course and are managed by a course leader. This is also true for feedback by an external examiner or examiners who are able to give general comments on a course, unlike that of a PhD external examiner, who can only really give feedback on the performance of the student being examined including their thesis, viva and their supervision.

As we also discuss in Chapter 2, it seems clear that at the very least, different questionnaires need to be provided for the different types of research degree students as well as trying to find ways for individual supervisors to receive feedback, especially from overseas students.

In addition to a questionnaire, the 'cohort' nature of PhDs with Integrated Studies, professional doctorates and MRes also lend themselves to feedback via forums and staff–student meetings that are focused on their experience of the specific programme.

Finally, feedback from students and on programmes is only as good as it can be relayed back to where problems (and possible solutions) may lie. Although feedback is often easier rising through different levels of university committees and certainly has some benefit at the top regarding institutional overviews, in our opinion, it is usually more difficult passing back down to individuals, partly because of anonymity issues. Unfortunately, there are no obvious easy solutions to this problem.

Good examination practice

For the majority of research degrees, a thesis written on the research work performed, is initially examined and subsequent to this, a viva is held in which the student is usually questioned on the content of the thesis. Of course, for MRes and professional doctoral students there will be the additional requirement for assessment of taught modules. Also, unlike PhD degrees, in which a viva is almost always obligatory, for MRes programmes, a viva may be discretionary and could include the examination of taught course material. The latter may also be true in the viva examination of professional doctorates, although the viva itself is usually obligatory and the nature of the exam would be more like a PhD.

For a PhD by publication, the nature of the viva will probably be a little different, with emphasis placed on how much of the work published has actually been done by the candidate (and whether they understand it) and less direct emphasis on the quality of the work, unless the publications themselves are from low-quality journals.

Interestingly, recent developments for doctoral students include a recommendation that they undergo a practice viva before the viva examination proper. Perhaps we should be offering the same for MRes students?

Processes for complaints and appeals

These processes are institution wide, apply equally to all research degree programmes and if complaints are not resolved at the institutional level, they are then referred to countrywide practices. It is understood that there may well be institutional differences and instances where the appeal or complaint relates to the taught component of the degree, but with the introduction of the QAA (2004) Code of Practice, together with the Office of the Independent Adjudicator at about the same time, institutions have been encouraged to meet the national requirements for these processes.

Conclusion

Even though there are now many different kinds of postgraduate research degree programmes, academics on the whole, perhaps not surprisingly, tend to focus on the management of conventional MPhil/PhD students. This means that other research degree programmes can be neglected, although research master's and professional doctoral programmes tend to be looked after by departmental course management teams rather than by institutional bodies. Instead, it would seem that particular attention needs to be paid to Joint PhD programmes and where institutions allow PhDs by publication.

With professional doctorates, entry requirements are different from just possessing a good bachelor's degree, with professional experience and expertise being especially relevant. It is therefore presumed that admissions for such programmes would be managed by the course team, rather than postgraduate research admissions officers in a department or school.

Induction is also an area where even with MPhil/PhD students, provision can be patchy and inadequate. As induction is important for all research students to help them get established in the institution more quickly, it is highly desirable that it should be implemented for all relevant students in the most efficient manner.

In general, there tends to be separate institutional publications for research students and those students on taught courses. However, professional doctorate students would actually benefit from both, whereas MRes students would probably not gain a great deal by looking at information for research students, as theirs is a different type of degree. Therefore, consideration should be given to whether there is sufficient provision of publications to cater for all types of students, bearing in mind the particular teaching element in some courses. For example, a programme or course handbook for hybrid programmes such as a professional doctorate is recommended to make sense of any special features and ensure that students know the essentials for their particular programme.

Supervisory arrangements and monitoring are other areas where significant differences occur between the many different research degree programmes. Also, perhaps greater effort needs to be made in supervisor development for those who are not supervising MPhil/PhD students. In these cases peer support may be particularly relevant due to the specialist nature of the programmes.

Since the early 2000s there has been some progress made on the quality and quantity of feedback obtained from research students on their research programmes, although problems still arise in obtaining feedback from overseas students. As well as debating whether questionnaires provide the best sort of feedback, other areas for improvement include getting feedback to individual supervisors and obtaining data on student destinations after graduation.

To meet demands of funding bodies, there is a need to be aware of the many different types of research students and programmes and the resulting complications in obtaining completion rates.

Finally, the vast majority of research students have to pass a viva to be awarded their degree, but it is worth remembering that the nature of the viva itself can differ, depending on the type of research degree being examined.

Talking points

- Are all doctorates considered equal, or are PhDs still considered to be the flagship in doctoral education?
- Is there too much emphasis on MPhil/PhD degree programmes in the QAA (2004) Code of Practice precepts and not enough consideration of other research degree programmes?

Key text

Wisker, G. (2001) *The Postgraduate Research Handbook: Succeed with your MA, MPhil, EdD and PhD*. Basingstoke: Palgrave Macmillan.

11

Future directions and conclusions

What do PhDs do? • Postdoctoral workers as supervisors • Pedagogy of research supervision • The future of supervision • Report on the review of research degree programmes: England and Northern Ireland • Conclusion

In this book we have specifically concentrated on the main issues surrounding the precepts of the QAA (2004) Code of Practice and how they impact on postgraduate research supervision relating to MPhil/PhD students. We have also considered these precepts with regard to other types of research students, such as those undertaking an MRes and, for example, professional doctorates.

As well as trying to conclude the content of the previous chapters we were keen to discuss new ideas and proposals in the broader field of research supervision, such as future employment of PhD students, postdoctoral workers as supervisors, the pedagogy of supervision, supervisor development and continuing professional development, and the most recent QAA review of research degree programmes; these topics form the basis of this chapter.

What do PhDs do?

One of the major considerations for the future of research degrees, especially the PhD, is to understand what research students do with it regarding employment. This will help shape the nature of research degrees in the future so that the needs of students are more closely matched by the demands of employers. The latest figures show us that the total number PhD students registered in the UK has gone up every year between 2002 and 2007, numbers have risen by 11 per cent between 2001 and 2005 (UK GRAD 2007) and that PhD programmes are as popular as ever. Approximately half of all UK PhD graduates went into the education sector and just over one-third were employed as researchers (both within and outside academia). After education, health and social work (approximately 16 per cent) was the next most popular destination, followed by manufacturing (approximately 15 per cent), finance, business and IT (approximately 9 per cent), and public administration (approximately 5 per cent). The overall rate of employment as higher education (HE) lecturers was 14 per cent, so it is clear that only a relatively small proportion of current PhD graduates become academic members of staff. This has obvious repercussions, in that the majority of PhD graduates are not employed in universities and require different employment-related skills. Of course, this is a generalization, and there are major differences in employment destinations between the different sectors, such that only 6 per cent of PhD graduates in physical sciences and engineering are employed as HE lecturers, while about 28 per cent of PhD graduates in arts and humanities are employed in the same position. However, the overall finding is that although the PhD is the basic requirement for an academic position in the HE sector, most PhD graduates are not employed as academics.

Postdoctoral workers as supervisors

In some areas, such as science and engineering, where the work is often laboratory based, postdoctoral researchers may have a role in the day-to-day supervision of research students (Delamont et al. 2004: 78). An important question is whether postdoctoral workers should be doing this at all. Clearly, if supervision of research students is not mentioned in the contract of employment then they do not need to do it. However, for many postdoctoral researchers the supervision of research team activities as described in their job summary will mean that this task may fall within their work remit. Successful supervisory experience may also be regarded as an important part of their own career development – one that could help them to achieve subsequent career goals. The next question is how much supervision is required, and how this relates to the work of the supervisory team. In some institutions postdoctoral workers are not allowed to be formally named as part of a supervisory team. However, this situation is changing, and increasingly the important (in some cases, central) contribution of postdoctoral staff to the supervision of research students is being formally recognized by institutions and funding bodies, such as research councils.

Typically, in a laboratory with several research students, it is often not possible for a supervisor to be able to supervise these students on a day-to-day basis, and this role falls to the postdoctoral worker. The latter can be described as a bridge between the student and supervisor. Postdoctoral workers can also act as trouble-shooters and help boost the morale of students whose work is not progressing well. As postdoctoral workers can get to know the students quite quickly they can also serve as (perhaps unofficial) mediators in any difficulties in the supervisor–student relationship.

One major problem, however, is that postdoctoral workers rarely receive any professional development or training in how to manage research students. The realization that this situation is not good enough has now led to a new law on science education in the USA (Lederman 2007). Applications for National Science Foundation (NSF) grants that include funds for postdoctoral workers have to describe the mentoring and professional development activities, provided through the research projects, and require the NSF to evaluate those activities as a factor in its grant review process.

As well as the poorly defined institutional status of postdoctoral workers, other areas of concern are length of contract, lack of uncertainty about the future, lack of resources and lack of support and training. Consequently, many are dissatisfied with their situation and look for alternative areas of employment on a regular basis. This means that there is often significant turnover of postdoctoral workers in a laboratory, which is not ideal for supervising research students. This is also unattractive for supervisors, as the more experienced postdoctoral workers are usually seen as valuable in training of research students as well as training of new postdoctoral staff.

What is obvious from the above is that in the relevant subject areas, contracts of employment need to clearly specify the tasks of a postdoctoral worker, and the institution needs to carefully consider its responsibilities towards research students. Appropriate development of this role should then be encouraged by the institution for the good of the research student as well as the postdoctoral worker's career.

A pilot study at the University of Sheffield has seen the introduction of a PhD advocate scheme for senior postdoctoral workers of more than three years' experience. In this scheme, postdoctoral workers mentor students on an informal basis, as these workers are seen as less intimidating to students than academic staff and more able to relate to pastoral needs. Here the student may approach the postdoctoral worker at any time, and the worker advises the student on where to obtain help or further advice and/or may accompany the student to meetings if required. It must, however, be stressed that this scheme is additional to the supervisor and pastoral tutor and is not a replacement. It will be monitored over a period of a few years and will be assessed to see whether it brings with it any advantages.

It is felt that the utilization of postdoctoral workers as supervisors of research students is a controversial and neglected area, and the topic needs to be addressed sooner rather than later.

Pedagogy of research supervision

Traditionally, the supervision of research students has been part of the research function of academic staff. However, there has been growing recognition that while being active in research is a necessary condition for research supervision, it is not the whole story, and supervisors need skills relating to the supervisory process. Moreover, supervision is increasingly considered to be a form of teaching, which Brown and Atkins (1988: 115) state is 'probably the most subtle and complex in which we engage'. Therefore, to be considered an effective supervisor one needs to be an effective teacher.

If we reflect on the knowledge and skills that academic staff require for effective supervision, two models have been proposed. The first is called the researcher-administrator model (Manathunga 2005), which is determined by a knowledge and understanding of the regulatory and administrative environments, and means that the supervisor has to have research expertise, knowledge of the institutional regulations as well as knowledge of what the institution requires from its supervisors. However, this model takes no account of the relationship between the supervisor and student, which is important in helping to support the latter to become an independent researcher who is able to make an original contribution to knowledge in their specialist subject. This second model is called the researcher-administrator-teacher model (Pearson and Brew 2002) and suggests that expertise in supervision can be associated to a specific type of teaching. Therefore, if teaching plays a role in research supervision, and if one considers the literature on teaching and learning, it becomes apparent that there will be different supervisor styles that relate to the type of teaching approach which a supervisor adopts. In a study by Gatfield (2005), he refers to four main styles and calls them 'laissez-faire', 'directorial', 'contractual' and 'pastoral', which depend on the amount of support the supervisor provides to the student and how structured the research programme is. From this, one can deduce that students have preferred learning styles, and it has been suggested (Malfoy and Webb 2000) that as long as the learning style of the student and teaching style of the supervisor match, there should be fewer difficulties in the supervisor–student relationship. It would therefore appear that supervisors should be aware of different teaching and learning styles, as they could practically relate to more effective supervision. Exploring these and other related issues would seem like obvious topics for supervisor development programmes.

The future of supervision

There is no doubt that the research supervision environment has changed since the early 1980s, with increasing numbers of students, many of whom are from overseas, demands for timely degree completion rates (and penalties for those who are late), a wider diversity of research degrees and the development of the research degree programme, and a comprehensive list of supervisor and institutional requirements, which have been discussed in detail in this book.

As larger numbers of students now qualify with a doctorate, and with no significant increase in academic staff recruitment, there is a realization, as already discussed in this chapter, that the majority of these students will not enter academia, and that they must pursue other careers. This has repercussions for what a PhD is for, and what can be done to make it more appropriate for a broader range of careers. Reeves (2007: 161) makes the point that 'the PhD experience should result in a portfolio of skills for life, not simply a hardbound manuscript that sits in a library'. The concept of the Research Training Programme, in which students acquire lifelong skills, then seems to be a good move in the right direction and is not something that must be avoided at all costs, as some rather naive and outdated supervisors have portrayed.

Pressures on the supervisory process have also resulted from the above changes and from a culture that seems to be moving towards performance management both at institutional and personal levels. What seems to be increasingly important is the concept of supervisor development or training. However, as Reeves (2007: 155) points out, 'there is the obvious problem of getting supervisors to embrace training'. Another issue concerns that of the training itself as 'the problem with training supervisors is that it requires other academics to do it because academics are often reluctant to accept expertise in people other than themselves' (Reeves 2007: 155).

For inexperienced supervisors of research students, apart from having a more experienced supervisor mentor who is there to make sure all goes well for at least the first doctoral student, there is a requirement to attend the institution's certificated course on postgraduate research supervision or equivalent or possibly a course on teaching and learning which includes a research supervision component. What may be more difficult to achieve is meeting the demands of the growing concept of continuing professional development (CPD), where all academics, including those who may be very experienced, update their knowledge of research supervision on a regular basis. Certainly at a small number of institutions pressure has been placed on all supervisors to attend such a supervisor development programme, as this will keep supervisors in good standing and allow them to keep on supervising. Failure to attend may compromise their right to supervise and to apply for related research funding.

Similarly, there have been developments with supervisor accreditation, as we illustrate in some detail in Appendix 1, with the TAPPS scheme. It would seem that as the subject of research supervision grows in its own right as a specialist topic and which may impinge on research funding, and as penalties may be significant for institutions where completion rates are poor, there is a likelihood that CPD activities and the desire for supervisor accreditation will be more widespread. Indeed, the fact that some institutions now reward excellence in research supervision illustrates the growing recognition of its importance.

Report on the review of research degree programmes: England and Northern Ireland

The QAA in 2007 reviewed research degree programmes (RDPs) in England and Wales in the light of the Code of Practice introduced in 2004 and the following principal findings represent the most up-to-date developments in the field.

Selection, admission and induction

- A number of institutions indicated that, although training for RDP admissions was not mandatory at present it was planned or under consideration.
- More than 20 per cent of institutions were asked to give further consideration to certain aspects of their selection, admissions and induction processes.

Supervision

- For Precept 11, institutions expect principal supervisors to be research active, hold a doctorate (although a number of institutions have special arrangements for supervisors who do not) and have the experience of supervising at least two research students to successful completion. Most institutions expect their supervisors to be full-time permanent members of academic staff and some explicitly state this as requirement.
- As well as some institutions offering a dedicated qualification such as a Postgraduate Certificate in Research Degree Supervision, many others provide access to training by staff development units. As a way of creating incentives for supervisor development, one institution runs a competition for best student–supervisor relationship, based on nominations, while another has introduced a Vice-Chancellor's Award for Excellence in Doctoral Supervision.
- Many institutions now have formal arrangements for the training of new and established supervisors and a small number have regular events including update seminars, master classes, and annual supervisors' conferences or away-days for established supervisors. One institution even includes good supervisory practice as a key criterion for promotion to reader and professor.
- In the monitoring of and review of supervision in some institutions, the annual progress review is being conducted by two independent assessors excluding the supervisor. Interestingly in two institutions, there is a formal review of supervisory practice and the supervisory team when a thesis is failed or requires major revisions.
- In many institutions there is still work to be done engaging many established supervisors in supervision development programmes. In a few institutions, they are required to take an appropriate training course at least every two years as a condition of being allowed to continue to serve as a supervisor.

- Few institutions specify a minimum frequency with which students and supervisors should meet but at least every four to six weeks is typical of those that do. Similarly, few, if any, mention what special arrangements are in place for supervising part-time or distant research students.
- In the context of Precept 14, there was variability between institutions particularly in terms of workload allocation models. Supervisory load is usually taken into account but there is no generally agreed load for a typical supervisor. There were also variations in institutional maxima on the number of research students a principal supervisor is allowed to supervise.
- Many institutions expressed a need for the formalization of supervisory team arrangements and feedback mechanisms on supervisor performance.

Progress and review arrangements

- The use of a third party monitoring system which enables students to discuss their research degree studies with a third party who is neither their supervisor nor their head of discipline is to be encouraged. Also the integration of skills development with academic progress in annual review was praised.
- The lack of consistency between departments or faculties within a single institution in the conduct of annual reviews requires attention.

Development of research and other skills

- Many institutions have appointed, or plan to appoint, a research training programme manager or coordinator (usually funded by Roberts money) to deliver appropriate training centrally and to coordinate training in faculties and schools. (Following the SET for success review of research and training (2002), the UK government, through the research councils, has provided funding to support the development of training opportunities and post-doctoral researches, which is known as Roberts money.)
- Many institutions expect training needs analysis evidence to be included in the annual progress review process.
- Many institutions have recently introduced personal development planning (PDP) tools which are online or paper based. A few institutions have plans to integrate records of skills training into the Registry information system, to facilitate the creation of transcripts of skills training as records of achievement.
- Many institutions made special arrangements to enable part-time, distant and overseas students to access appropriate training in research and other skills for example, by delivery at weekends and residential weeks.
- In a few institutions, skills training was still being planned but not fully in place at the time of the RDP review. In most institutions, provision for the development of research skills is better developed than that for generic skills and that uptake by students follows the same trend.

- Not all institutions have formal procedures for monitoring student uptake of, and participation in, research training. Also many institutions do not explicitly define the amount of training they expect their students to engage in, with some not requiring the ten days training per year regarded by research councils as appropriate.
- There was diversity of practice relating to the training of research students who teach. In some institutions, such training is required before the student is allowed to teach, whereas in others the training is encouraged but not required.
- While most institutions have now formalized research training programmes, it was concluded that many of them could be further enhanced to make them more fit for purpose. Specific areas for improvement included better embedding of skills development within RDPs, developing more formal and/or compulsory programmes of skills development, and better alignment of programmes with the requirements of the Research Councils UK (2001) Joint Statement of Skills.
- A few institutions were required to use induction sessions to raise awareness of institutional requirements or expectations relating to research training and to provide appropriate information about research training to students.

Feedback mechanisms

- There was evidence of a wide variety of means of obtaining student feedback including student forums, postgraduate societies or research student committees as well as the more usual questionnaires. Institutions often have some process for collating and analysing reports from external examiners and some pro formas seek an opinion on the institutional processes as well as the candidate's performance.
- A number of institutions elicit research student feedback via online processes for discussion, an annual anonymous student satisfaction survey, the opportunity for research students to provide feedback directly to the Board of Graduate Studies as part of the annual review process, the communication of student evaluation and university response via the regular newsletters and mechanisms for obtaining feedback from recent RDP graduates.
- There was much variation not only for receiving feedback between institutions but also in the formality and efficacy of these mechanisms. Because of these, 25 per cent of institutions were asked to improve the latter.
- A large number of institutions were asked to consider their arrangements for securing feedback from stakeholders other than current research students, such as employers, sponsors, supervisors and recent graduates. Other areas of concern at a number of institutions were the absence of an appropriate level of student representation on senior institutional committees dealing with research degree matters and the lack of staff–student liaison committees dedicated to research students at departmental level.

- Some institutions have found that the return rate of student questionnaires is disappointingly low and are exploring the use of focus groups as one means of obtaining feedback.
- There was a tendency for research students to be overlooked in certain regards, in some institutions with relatively small numbers of research students but very large undergraduate populations.

Assessment

- Although some institutions include the appointment of an independent non-examining chair to help ensure consistency between different vivas and in providing an additional viewpoint if the conduct of the viva should become the subject of a student appeal, others rejected the practice on the grounds that with very large graduate schools the resulting additional workload would be unacceptable. It remains to be seen how best to assure that the viva voce process is fair and transparent in the absence of an independent chair.
- It was thought valuable to offer a mock viva and to provide training sessions or workshops to assist students to prepare for their viva. The Freedom of Information Act 2000 has prompted a more universal disclosure of the final (joint) report to both student and supervisor.
- Some other areas of good practice include: a requirement for new internal examiners to attend the Internal Examiners' Briefing session; the use of an inquiry panel to review students failing to achieve the target award to see if any lessons could be learnt; the use of independent moderators to overcome problems that might arise from a relatively small research base; the clarity of the guidelines for the conduct of the research degree examinations; the requirement to review supervisory practice when a thesis requires major revision prior to resubmission; the arrangements for note-taking in an oral examination.
- Regarding Precept 22, the criteria used by institutions to assess various research degrees such as professional doctorates, MPhil, MRes and doctorates through publication, must be clear and readily available to students, staff and external examiners.
- A significant number of institutions were asked to review their practice of allowing a supervisor, member of a supervisory team or an external collaborator in the research to act as internal examiner. It would appear that the practice of formulating the membership of such examining bodies is variable across the UK and needs further consideration.

Complaints

- In a few institutions there were a small number of examples of good practice including: clarity of procedures; clarity of information about procedures; the training and briefing of staff who deal with complaints; the existence of separate complaints regulations for applicants and the development of improved policy as a result of use of the complaints procedure.

- Many institutions did not define an indicative timescale for research student complaints.
- Few institutions routinely monitor and report the number and outcomes of complaints by research students, although some are putting systems in place to do this. For those institutions that monitored complaints, the maximum number reported was four complaints between 2002 and 2007.
- The most common areas that required further consideration were: to ensure that complaints are dealt with in a timely manner; to more clearly define the formal complaints process for students; to make the process more readily available to students; to make more explicit what constitutes the basis for an appeal.

Appeals

- Few institutions routinely monitor and report the number and outcomes of appeals, although some are putting systems in place to do this. A handful of institutions mentioned that they receive an average of two or three appeal cases each year.
- A number of institutions were asked to review their arrangements concerning: clearly defining timescales for appeals procedures; ensuring that appeals are heard in a timely manner; reviewing their arrangements for appeals against progression decisions; to define more clearly the decisions process; to make more explicit the grounds that may form the basis of an appeal; to adapt the standard institutional appeal procedure specifically for use by research students; to consider whether having a member of the supervisory team as a member of the review panel is compatible with the need for impartiality and to review the status of students in their pre-registration period.

It is clear therefore from the summary of the above review findings that although there is still a certain amount of flexibility in postgraduate research provision, institutions are working hard to meet the demands of the precepts.

Conclusion

As we said at the start of this book, it was never our intention to 'bureaucratize' research supervision. Instead, we have used the precepts as a framework to support supervisor development. While the pros and cons of specific approaches to supervision remain open to debate, some have been persuasively endorsed in recent publications.

The core questions about supervision remain deceptively simple:

- What is research supervision – what do you do?
- Why do you supervise in this way?
- How do you know when that works or not?

The sea change in this area is the development of a literature to inform our answers to these questions. However, that literature is still developing, and the precepts provide a framework for supervisors to generate their own answers.

Appendix 1

Training and Accreditation Programme for Postgraduate Supervisors (TAPPS) as a national accreditation scheme, Bologna process and European Charter for Researchers

TAPPS • Bologna process • European Charter for Researchers

TAPPS

Since the formation of the Institute for Learning and Teaching in Higher Education (ILTHE), it has been possible for academic staff to gain recognition for professional activities related to teaching. With the merger of the ILTHE in 2004 to form the Higher Education Academy (HEA), it is now possible to gain the same professional recognition from the latter body.

A related development has been the creation of the TAPPS scheme for the training and professional recognition of postgraduate supervisors (www.iah.bbsrc.ac.uk/TAPPS/index.html), which is also recognized by the HEA. TAPPS was started in 1998, was initially designed for the biological sciences and is accredited by the Biotechnology and Biological Sciences Research Council (BBSRC), but it is flexible enough to make it suitable for other fields of study.

The purpose of TAPPS is to provide a framework and process for the development, professional accreditation and support of postgraduate research supervisors. Accreditation of a research supervisor by TAPPS is based on assessment of a claim for accreditation, which must be supported by a portfolio of evidence relating to the individual's supervisory practice over a period of at least three years (Figure A.1). This framework is designed to promote good practice, and to recognize the individual postgraduate supervisor's experience and practice as teacher and mentor.

An accredited research supervisor will be expected to demonstrate that they can:

1 Develop or agree a programme of research that is suitable for a research degree.
2 Recruit and select an appropriate student for the research programme.
3 Plan and agree an appropriate research supervisory process and team.
4 Use an appropriate range of teaching and supervisory skills to ensure students' education, attainment and professional development.
5 Provide appropriate support to individual students on academic and pastoral issues.

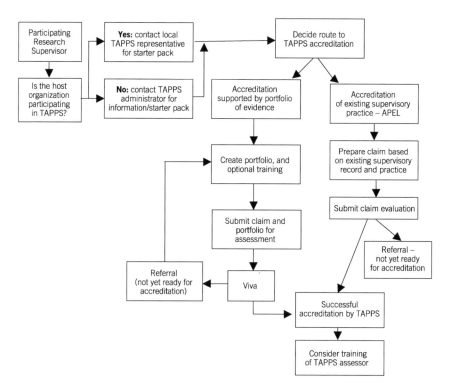

Figure A.1   Routes to TAPPS accreditation.
Source: Institute for Animal Health

6 Use an appropriate range of methods to monitor and assess student progress and attainment.

7 Reflect on their own practice, assess and plan for their future needs and continuing development as a research supervisor or research worker.

It is too early to predict what sort of impact TAPPS will have on the quality of research supervision in the UK as currently only a small number of universities have adopted the scheme. However, the idea is to be applauded if it is able not only to raise the profile of research supervision but also to improve standards.

Bologna process

The Bologna process proposes that the European Higher Education Area (EHEA) is developed as a means of promoting mutual recognition of qualifications, demonstrating transparency of systems and allowing for easier mobility of staff and students across higher education in Europe.

One of the key features of the Bologna process involves the development of a national qualifications framework in each country and the development of criteria and procedures to be used by each country to verify that its national framework is compatible with an overarching qualifications framework for the EHEA (details at www.bologna-bergen2005.no/Docs/00-Main_doc/050218_QF_EHEA.pdf).

The framework for the EHEA consists of three main cycles. Each cycle has a generic descriptor of the typical abilities and achievements associated with completion of that cycle. Doctoral programmes are the third cycle of the Bologna process (Table A.1) where the core component is the advancement of knowledge through original research.

Addressing the criteria and procedures for verification allows each country engaging with the Bologna process to illustrate both the robustness of their quality assurance systems and the links between the qualifications which comprise their national framework and the three EHEA qualification cycles. The process is one of self-certification by each country.

The target is that verification of compatibility with the EHEA will be completed by all Bologna countries by 2010.

Salzburg Principles

In 2005, a meeting was held in Salzburg to debate on the third cycle of the Bologna process concerning doctoral programmes and research training. The main outcome was to reach agreement on the establishment of a set of ten basic principles (sometimes known as the Salzburg Principles

– www.eua.be/eua/jsp/en/upload/Salzburg_Report_final.1129817011146.pdf)
as follows:

1 The core component of doctoral training is the *advancement of knowledge*
   through original research. At the same time it is recognized that doctoral
   training must increasingly meet the needs of an employment market that
   is wider than academia.
2 *Embedding in institutional strategies and policies*: universities as institutions
   need to assume responsibility for ensuring that the doctoral programmes
   and research training they offer are designed to meet new challenges and
   include appropriate professional career development opportunities.
3 *The importance of diversity*: the rich diversity of doctoral programmes in
   Europe – including joint doctorates – is a strength which has to be under-
   pinned by quality and sound practice.
4 *Doctoral candidates as early stage researchers*: should be recognized as pro-
   fessionals – with commensurate rights – who make a key contribution to
   the creation of new knowledge.
5 *The crucial role of supervision and assessment*: in respect of individual doctoral candidates' arrangements for supervision and assessment should be
   based on a transparent contractual framework of shared responsibilities
   between doctoral candidates, supervisors and the institution (and where
   appropriate including other partners).
6 *Achieving critical mass*: doctoral programmes should seek to achieve critical mass and should draw on different types of innovative practice being
   introduced in universities across Europe, bearing in mind that different
   solutions may be appropriate to different contexts and in particular across

Table A.1 Cycles of the Bologna process using Scotland as an example

EHEA qualification cycles	*Qualifications within The Framework for Qualifications of Higher Education Institutions in Scotland*
First cycle qualification	Scottish bachelor's degree
Short cycle qualification within or linked to the first cycle	Diploma of Higher Education
Intermediate awards within the first cycle	Certificate of Higher Education/Graduate Certificate/Diploma
Second cycle qualification	Master's Degree/Integrated Master's Degree/ MPhil degree
Intermediate awards within the second cycle	Postgraduate Certificate/Diploma
Third cycle qualification	Doctoral degrees including doctorates by research

Source: QAA Scotland

larger and smaller European countries. These range from graduate schools in major universities to international, national and regional collaboration between universities.

7 *Duration*: doctoral programmes should operate within appropriate time duration (three to four years full-time as a rule).

8 *Promoting innovative structures*: to meet the challenge of interdisciplinary training and the development of transferable skills.

9 *Increasing mobility*: doctoral programmes should seek to offer geographical as well as interdisciplinary and intersectoral mobility and international collaboration within an integrated framework of cooperation between universities and other partners.

10 *Ensuring appropriate funding*: the development of quality doctoral programmes and the successful completion by doctoral candidates requires appropriate and sustainable funding.

In a more recent report (European University Association (EUA) 2007) it was stated that there was a great need to develop new supervision practices in doctoral training. In particular, arrangements need to be developed based upon a transparent contractual framework of shared responsibilities between doctoral candidates, supervisors and the institution, and, where appropriate other partners as mentioned in the above Salzburg Principles. Attention should also be paid to ensuring multiple supervision arrangements, the continuous professional skills development of academic staff (as typified in the UK by the QAA (2004) Code of Practice), and performance reviews of supervisors.

The importance of ensuring good supervision needs to be properly recognized as a task of staff supervising doctoral candidates, should be included in their workload and task descriptions, and thus also taken into consideration in academic career structures and decisions on promotion. In some universities, workload models have been developed to ensure that a supervisor dedicates enough time in support of each doctoral candidate.

European Charter for Researchers

The European Charter for Researchers (European Commission 2005) is a set of principles and requirements which specifies the roles, responsibilities and entitlements of researchers as well as of employers and/or funders of researchers. The aim of the Charter is to ensure that the nature of the relationship between researchers and employers or funders is conducive to successful performance in generating, transferring, sharing and disseminating knowledge and technological development, and to the career development of researchers. Supervision and supervisory duties are mentioned in the Code as follows.

Relation with supervisors

Researchers in their training phase should establish a structured and regular relationship with their supervisor(s) and faculty or departmental representative(s) so as to take full advantage of their relationship with them. This includes keeping records of all work progress and research findings, obtaining feedback by means of reports and seminars, applying such feedback and working in accordance with agreed schedules, milestones, deliverables and/or research outputs.

Supervision and managerial duties

Senior researchers should devote particular attention to their multifaceted role as supervisors, mentors, career advisers, leaders, project coordinators, managers or science communicators. They should perform these tasks to the highest professional standards. With regard to their role as supervisors or mentors of researchers, senior researchers should build up a constructive and positive relationship with early stage researchers, in order to set the conditions for efficient transfer of knowledge and for the further successful development of the researchers' careers.

Supervision

Employers and/or funders should ensure that a person is clearly identified to whom early stage researchers can refer for the performance of their professional duties, and should inform the researchers accordingly. Such arrangements should clearly define that the proposed supervisors are sufficiently expert in supervising research, have the time, knowledge, experience, expertise and commitment to be able to offer the research trainee appropriate support and provide for the necessary progress and review procedure, as well as the necessary feedback mechanisms.

Complaints and appeals

Employers and/or funders of researchers should establish, in compliance with national rules and regulations, appropriate procedures, possibly in the form of an impartial (ombudsman-type) person to deal with complaints or appeals of researchers, including those concerning conflicts between supervisor(s) and early stage researchers. Such procedures should provide all research staff with confidential and informal assistance in resolving work-related conflicts, disputes and grievances, with the aim of promoting fair and equitable treatment within the institution and improving the overall quality of the working environment.

Eurodoc

There are many European associations that are interested in doctoral programmes. In particular, eurodoc (www.eurodoc.net) is the federation of the national associations of PhD candidates and young researchers in Europe. In 2006 it introduced its Charter to promote effective supervision in Europe. Only in France and the UK are there significant and detailed standards on supervision and training. Therefore, it was felt that there was a need for a Charter that each European country could develop. The Charter will focus on the following important areas:

• Mechanisms to ensure good supervisor–student relations are built
• Suitable training for supervisors
• Comprehensive complaints and feedback mechanisms.

Appendix 2

Case studies for supervisor development programmes

Case 1: Charlie's first year • Case 2: Amanda's dilemmas – examining a PhD thesis • Key text

These cases are the copyright of John Wakeford and are chosen from his file of over 100 actual but anonymized accounts by students and supervisors, who were paid a fee for the copyright. They are published here with his generous permission. John Wakeford uses them in the training of postgraduate research students and supervisors at the Missenden Centre and elsewhere. By 2009 the whole portfolio should be published online by University College London.

The two cases we have selected focus on issues arising at the start and end of the doctoral process. These cases work particularly well when supervisors discuss each stage separately. To prompt discussion there are questions after each 'act' and 'episode'.

Case 1: Charlie's first year

Act 1: The very beginning

I did not know I was going to the University of Barchester until about one month before the start of the new academic year. When I heard that I had been awarded a one-year faculty studentship I was so relieved. Pauline, the departmental officer, thought that I might not be pleased with just the one year, but after five near misses of PhD studentships of one kind or another, it felt so good just to know what I was going to be doing. Obviously, I was also very excited. I had found out the news while at work (secretarial temping for a marketing company in London) but when I got home even better news was waiting. On my answerphone was Pauline saying that somehow more money had become available and that now I had three years' funding. With this news and the fact that I was about to go on a two-week holiday abroad, I was simply on top of the world. However, it did mean that I only had just two weeks to sort out what I knew was going to be one of the biggest changes in my life.

First, I had the difficult task of finding somewhere suitable to live. I did make inquiries about campus accommodation but I was much too late. The accommodation office sent me some details of rooms available, but not knowing Barchester at all made looking virtually impossible. Luckily a friend of mine from Middlemarch Metropolitan University (where I had done my first degree) had a sister living nearby. So I went to stay with her. I met this complete stranger off the bus and she put me up for a couple of nights while I attended the induction week and searched for somewhere to live. It was very important to me to find somewhere which would not be a problem when my partner came to stay. The flat I found was great except for three snags. First, it was two bedroomed, therefore, I needed to find a flatmate, as I could not afford the rent on my own; second, it was totally unfurnished, and third, I could not move in for two weeks.

Life seemed hectic, new and exciting but it also felt very scary at times. I could not believe that here I was miles from home and on my own. What on earth was I doing. I was in the north of England and my partner, family and friends were all down south. On top of this, I was the only external applicant in my department. I did not know anyone nor even the way around the campus and here I was just about to start a PhD having come straight from my undergraduate degree. Experiencing all these changes at once and having had so little time to prepare left me feeling rather stressed.

On a more positive note I had found Sue, my colleague who I was sharing an office with, and she seemed very nice. Also the other postgraduates in the department had left me a note welcoming me to Barchester which felt good. Then on the second day of the induction week I bumped into my co-supervisor who then promptly told me that he was going to be away abroad for most of the first term but that he would arrange to see me before he went. Immediately following this, the Postgraduate Tutor, who had interviewed me some five months back, came around the corner. After welcoming me he then informed me that my main supervisor was going to be on sabbatical for two terms. Sue just looked at me and said later that she could not believe it. I nearly burst into tears. Too much was happening too fast. I was left feeling totally disorientated and very alone.

Q1 Comment on the department's policies on recruitment, selection and induction as experienced by Charlie.

Q2 What should Charlie do now?

Act 2: Researching sensitive issues

I had not anticipated the extent of the effects that my research area could have on me. Here I was researching an emotive and highly sensitive topic, childhood sexual abuse, and I had gone and left my total support network in London. I knew, however, that I had not lightly chosen this area of study, having already devoted much time on this subject at undergraduate level, including my dissertation. Which I must say was the best thing I had ever done. However, I believe I could not have guessed totally the implications that this research might have, perhaps not only for myself but also for my supervisor. Remembering back to my interview, I distinctly felt the interviewer's (Postgraduate Tutor) discomfort in asking me about my own experiences of childhood sexual abuse. He first apologised that my intended supervisor (a female) was not able to be present at the interview through sickness. I knew that he would mention this issue. After all I had not hidden this fact from my application, and it was his job to ensure that I was capable of doing the research in question.

Further moments of awkwardness came when issues of self were raised during supervision sessions. This again was unavoidable given that I had chosen to conduct my research from a feminist perspective, where my own standpoint is of significance within the research. To best illustrate the above I would like to share the following.

I attended a three-day course: 'Doing Fieldwork' at the University of Coketown. Of particular interest to me was the workshop on using story telling as an interview technique. A personal sideline to this was that I had struck up a friendship with an older male delegate who also happened to be a psychiatrist. Now whether it was because he was older or in a position of power I don't know but I found his attraction to me had stirred up a lot of old feelings connected with my own childhood abuse. In an attempt to understand this, I wrote down, in the form of a story narrative, what had happened and how I had felt. I found this exercise to be extremely useful.

The following supervision session, I talked about the possibilities of incorporating the use of 'stories' into my research. I had some concern about the idea of showing my 'story' to my supervisor, but to illustrate my point I decided to go ahead. However, I felt rather embarrassed and ashamed at the same time. Several weeks passed before I heard anything back from my supervisor and during that time I had been regretting leaving him the 'story'. I knew that it was OK to experiment with different ideas, after all I was only in my second term of my first year. However, because the 'story' was personal I felt I had made myself vulnerable in some way. The struggle in finding the balance between researching an area which is not only sensitive but also directly of relevance to me, and trying to establish oneself as a competent researcher in an academic environment was proving to be an issue which I had not prepared myself for. I believe one of the problems was as a result of having come from being in psychology (my first degree) to an applied social science department.

I was now feeling extremely nervous about my supervisor's response (even though I liked my supervisor and felt that I could talk to him). My supervisor came into my office and sat down. He looked puzzled and said he was not quite sure why I had left him the 'story' to look at. I explained again that it was simply to illustrate the technique of using stories. He looked relieved, and commented to the effect that he had thought I was trying to tell him something in an indirect way, about how I might be feeling in our supervision sessions, as he was an older man and in a position of power. I assured him there was no hidden agenda and thanked him for his concern. However, I still felt rather silly and embarrassed.

Q1 Comment on the supervisor's situation and response to Charlie's research problems.
Q2 What should Charlie do now?

Act 3: Too much work and too little money

Around the beginning of the summer term, one of the academics in my department approached me to see if I would be interested in doing a joint project with her. The project was to involve the analysis of over 1000 letters written by victims of childhood abuse. Given that the project was directly related to my research I jumped at this golden opportunity. However, there were several drawbacks. To begin with I could not get over the fact that the project was much larger than my own PhD in terms of the number of participants involved (which is actually now working out to about 1500 to my approximate 40), and we only had approximately three or four months to complete the project unlike the three years for a PhD. I started to feel that this might be a mission impossible. On top of this, I was being given very little in terms of financial reward. At first this was not a problem, after all I knew that it had the prospects of many long-term benefits, for example, the use of the data for my own research and publications. However, by the end of the summer term, my studentship was completely exhausted and I didn't know how I was going to manage until the new academic term in October.

My financial situation was worsened due to other circumstances. I have a joint account with my partner who had only just finished his undergraduate degree in Middlemarch. I also studied for my first degree in Middlemarch and having come straight onto a PhD we have considerable debts. So despite my studentship being more money than my LEA grant, I was this year in effect subsidizing my partner. We have, and still are constantly struggling financially, paying back debts of one sort or another, as well as having two places to rent, and although my partner immediately found work after his exams, it has not been consistent. Therefore, I was faced with having very little spare time, due to the commitments I made to the project, to try and find other (paid) work. Furthermore, I did not only have the project to do, I was also involved in designing four questionnaires for a local Rape Crisis Centre; I had a 5000 word essay on reliability and validity to write for my Advanced Qualitative Course; and after asking for the possibility of some teaching (to earn some money) I was given a lecture to do, for which I have to prepare for October and of course the list goes on, that's without such things as literature reviews.

I have been feeling totally overwhelmed. The word that comes to mind is flooding. To make matters even worse, my partner, while having been accepted at Coketown University for his PhD, was unable to secure funding. The added worry that this has given on top of everything else has made the summer extremely tough. At times I feel so stressed that to concentrate on anything has been impossible. I have been receiving some support through a student counsellor. However, what I feel I really need is a holiday with my partner, but with no time or money, a holiday has been out of the question.

By the time the deadline came for the analysis of the letters and the report to be completed we had coded only 400 letters (out of 1500) and had inputted onto the computer database even less (120 out of 1500). So there is still a very long way to go and despite working flat out I feel that I have hardly made a difference. At the beginning the letters (which range from 1 page to 30 pages) were taking at the most 5 hours to code. Of course we have got a lot quicker with practice. The latest problem for me has been in not having a computer with a big enough memory to take the database. It is very important that I can have access to a computer in my office, due to the sensitive nature of the letters where confidentiality is so very important. At present I feel very frustrated and so very tired. However, I never think about giving up because I know that my partner and I have come too far, both having returned to education as young but mature students. I also know that I am in a very fortunate position with many excellent opportunities and furthermore, at the end of the day it is my choice to be doing the PhD. However, I just wish that things could be easier.

Q1 What support can supervisors really give?
Q2 What should Charlie do now?

Team task

Provide some guidance for

- postgraduate research students
- supervisors
- institutions.

Case 2: Amanda's dilemmas – examining a PhD thesis

Episode 1

I have been a lecturer at the University of Barchester for nine years now, but my only experience of the examination of a PhD thesis was my own – the viva for which was almost ten years ago.

On the plane on my way home from a conference my colleague and friend Kate from the Department of Health Studies asked me if I would be the internal examiner for a PhD that she had supervised. She told me about the topic. Although my research expertise is in health and illness, this research was not in my specific field.

I felt flattered that she had asked me, but my main concern was that the period running up to the viva was also the period during which I expected to be in the final stages of writing a book for which there was a tight deadline. I explained this. Kate replied that she was very keen that I took on the job and perhaps the viva could be delayed slightly to allow me to get the book completed.

Q1 What factors should be taken into account in identifying potential examiners for a doctorate?
Q2 How should Amanda respond to Kate's invitation?

Episode 2

In the event I felt I had little choice but to say 'Yes', particularly as Kate pointed out that at this stage in my career it was about time that I took on this responsibility. Apart from anything else, it would be good experience and stand me in good stead when asked to be an external examiner.

Not long after arriving back in Barchester I happened to mention to my head of department (HoD) that I had agreed to be the internal examiner for a PhD – imagining that he would be pleased at the recognition it conferred both on my status as an academic, and also on the department.

I was therefore surprised by his negative reaction. Although he would not of course stand in my way of accepting, his advice was 'don't touch it with a barge pole'. He went on to tell me, based on his own experience and his observations of others' experiences, how many things could go wrong. First he said that as I had never examined a PhD before I might be rejected by the Postgraduate Studies Committee as unsuitable, and this rather than furthering my career would undermine my credibility. Second, it would be a huge amount of work for no reward – at least financial. He also pointed out that being close friends with the supervisor was potentially problematic. Supposing I felt that the thesis should fail, would I feel able to say so and would this risk our friendship? Such a response would by definition be critical of her supervision. He also raised other issues about the possibility of me disagreeing with the external – whom I knew to be a very senior academic. Kate had mentioned that they had collaborated on a large research project and co-authored several publications.

Q1 How independent should examiners be of the supervisor, student and other examiner/s? What relationships would make a candidate unacceptable?
Q2 What should Amanda do now?

Episode 3

Having been thoroughly unnerved by my HoD's reaction, I thought the best course of action was to preempt the Postgraduate Studies Committee finding me 'unsuitable'. I called the Secretary of the Committee to suggest myself that I might be unsuitable as I had had no previous experience of PhD examining. I hoped thereby to be able to tell my friend Kate that, although I would have loved to do it, it was out of my hands and that she unfortunately needed to find another examiner.

On the contrary the Secretary responded that my inexperience would simply mean that a chairperson would have to be appointed to oversee the viva, and, if this was arranged, there was no reason why I should not be the internal examiner. My heart sank.

Q1 What preparation should be provided for PhD examiners?
Q2 What should Amanda do now?

Episode 4

I rang Kate to tell her about the need for a chair. I just hoped that she might say that it would be easier to find another internal. But a few hours later she phoned me back saying that she had managed to find a senior colleague who had agreed to chair the viva. There was apparently no way out – and I still had to tell my HoD.

After my classes on the following day Kate surprised me by asking me whether I had realized that it was up to me to arrange the viva and coordinate between the different parties.

I found the logistics worrying, especially as I knew that not only was the student from overseas but also that she had specially requested that Kate be at the viva. This seemed to pose more problems than the usual two examiners and one home student. Although Kate gave me their email addresses, it seemed strange that when the student, external examiner and chair were already in frequent communication with her, that it would be me that had to arrange the meeting. In the event finding a suitable and mutually convenient time for the five of us was every bit as time consuming as I had anticipated.

Q1 How should vivas be organized in your institution? By whom?
Q2 What should Amanda do next?

Episode 5

A couple of weeks later I received an enormous parcel in the internal mail – it was the thesis – along with the form of appointment and details of regulations and duties. So, having read the regulations I signed and returned the form and then set the thesis aside unread until I had finished writing the book – and the current mountain of marking. I had committed myself to being internal examiner without even looking at the thesis. It then sat on the corner of my desk engendering feelings of anxiety every time I caught sight of it.

Three or four weeks later, just after Christmas, I sprained my ankle and was confined to the house for a week. This I felt was a golden opportunity to read the thesis. It took me ten days of careful reading and making notes. Although it was in my general area of 'health', the student had used a theoretical perspective quite different from those with which I am familiar. Thus many of her references were new to me.

Nevertheless I ploughed through trying to make intelligent criticisms for the report. It seemed to me, unfamiliar as I was with the theoretical approach (Foucault rather than Habermas) that it *probably* did fulfil the criteria for a PhD though I did have grave reservations about the very limited scope of the fieldwork, the structure and the coherence of the overall argument. Individual chapters were well constructed and argued, but I was not convinced that they were sufficiently well integrated to make a coherent whole.

Q1 How can an examiner determine whether a thesis is of PhD standard?
Q2 What should Amanda do next?

Episode 6

Kate and I had often discussed the work of her research students. She had had others who had caused her concern, but, as far as I could recall, this candidate was apparently not one of them. She had even said at one stage, when talking about one of her problematic students, that she wouldn't suggest that I acted as examiner for him. It seemed to me that the implication was that the student I was to examine was in her view 'unproblematic'.

I have great respect and admiration for Kate's academic and teaching skills. Thus I put my reservations about the thesis down to my own inexperience as an examiner. As the last – indeed the only – PhD thesis I had read was my own, I presumed that I had 'forgotten' that such work represents a very early stage in an academic career and concluded that I had been expecting work of too high a standard.

Nevertheless I sent in my examiner's report which raised the issues about which I had concerns, but I did not feel that I should indicate my reservations about the thesis' suitability for the award of PhD. In addition, I thought, as the viva is also part of the examining process, perhaps the student would offer a convincing defence of her work.

Q1 What should be included in the examiners' pre-viva reports?
Q2 What should Amanda do now?

Episode 7

Kate and I had from the start explicitly agreed not to talk about the thesis. This was difficult sometimes when we met, as practical arrangements had to be made and it was tempting to share my reservations about the thesis at these times. I felt as though I was misleading her into thinking that all was well, when clearly it might not be. I sometimes felt a little dishonest, possibly implying that all was well when in reality I was harbouring major reservations.

In the weeks running up to the viva, Kate and I continued to meet socially. On one occasion when discussing the room to be used for the viva, she mentioned out of the blue that as examiner I must put our friendship aside, and that, if I had criticisms of the thesis, I must not feel constrained about voicing them in the viva.

Q1 How should Amanda respond to Kate?
Q2 Is there anything else she should do at this stage?

Episode 8

In my response I decided to tell her that I had already submitted my report and that I did feel there were some aspects of the thesis that needed defending, but I felt it inappropriate to go into more detail. I then 'forgot' about the thesis and applied myself to the daily obligations of teaching, marking and writing.

I was just thinking of resurrecting it in preparation for the viva when, a week before the due date, I had an email from the external asking me to arrange his accommodation and book a hotel room for him. This caught me by surprise. Was this also included in my list of duties? I had the feeling that it was over and above what an internal might be expected to arrange. The secretary of the Postgraduate Studies Office confirmed that this was not part of my obligation and that the external would have been sent a list of approved accommodation with the other papers. So I emailed a diplomatic message to the external to this effect, and offered the services of the student's department should he require further assistance.

But five days before the viva I had an email from him saying that he had concerns about the thesis and asking me to ring him. My heart sank yet again.

Q1 What contact should there be between examiners before the viva?
Q2 What should Amanda do?

Episode 9

I decided to call him. From a lengthy discussion he appeared not to have written his report, but he raised as problems all the reservations I had had about the thesis, and some more, and said that he did not feel that in its present state the student could be awarded a PhD for the thesis. I felt vindicated but concerned.

As we were speaking I remembered that some years ago Kate had told me of a previous viva at which the student (and she) had been taken by surprise by the examiners' criticisms and she had felt that this had been a very unsatisfactory experience for all parties. I was therefore worried that she would feel attacked at the viva if we withheld our concerns until then.

So I asked him whether she should be warned beforehand. When he heard that Kate would be at the viva, he suggested that I phone her to alert her to the problems. That increasingly familiar sinking of the heart reappeared. I could just hear my HoD saying 'I told you so . . .'.

Q1 What should a supervisor and student know of the examiners' views or decisions before the viva is held?
Q2 What should Amanda do in response to the external examiner's suggestion?

Episode 10

I feared that the implications of me telling Kate about our concerns could be interpreted as a personal criticism of her judgement and supervision. Nevertheless I rang her – all probably highly irregular – and told her about my discussion with the external and our reservations about the thesis.

Her immediate reaction was to remind me that the viva was part of the examination process and that the outcome should not be preempted – the student might after all be able to defend the thesis against our criticisms. But during the conversation it became clear that she was surprisingly *un*surprised. She told me that the student was quite headstrong and difficult to steer away from her pre-commitments and that Kate herself had not in fact seen the final version of the thesis as submitted, and assumed that her comments on the student's final draft would have been incorporated.

She warned me that the student might be quite aggressive if criticized in the viva. I assume that, although the issue was never raised between us, she did not warn the student that the viva might be difficult.

And at this point Kate offered to send me a copy of the comments on the final draft she had sent to the student and suggested that I also send them to the external.

Q1 What account should the examiners take of the supervisor's views in coming to their decision?
Q2 So what should Amanda do now?

Episode 11

... which I did. (Reading her six pages of typed, single-spaced comments I suspected that even if they all been heeded we would both still have had reservations about the thesis, though perhaps not as many.)

I spent the weekend dreading Monday morning. The arrangements were that the external, who had stayed in Barchester overnight, would meet me in Kate's room at 9.30. The viva was scheduled for 11, to be followed by lunch with Kate, the chair and the second supervisor. The external was late. So Kate and I had half an hour to explore how the viva was to be handled. Once the external examiner had arrived we spent the hour deciding how to address the discussion and discovered that not only did our views of the thesis correspond, we had also made similar notes and observations while reading the thesis.

In the event the viva was not the ordeal I had feared. Despite not having a copy of her thesis with her the student acquitted herself well. But in my view there was little chance that, however well she had done, resubmission would not be the outcome. The viva lasted for nearly two hours and was an exhausting process for all concerned. At the end the student and Kate left the room while the chair remained and the external and I discussed the outcome.

Q1 What makes a good viva?
Q2 Are there any rules to be followed?

Episode 12

We agreed to recommend that, in the light of her performance, she be given a year to rewrite and resubmit for a PhD.

When we had come to this agreement, we called Kate and the student back in. The external told the student what had been decided and what would be required to achieve a PhD. Although looking upset, she was clearly relieved that we believed that she could achieve a PhD rather than only an MPhil.

Incidentally, although we did not in the end wish to fail the thesis, the form provided by the university did not appear to allow us this option. There were two columns, each of which had three options. The first column offered the options of (a) awarding the PhD forthwith, (b) subject to grammatical and typographical corrections or (c) subject to some textual revisions. The second column offered the options of (a) resubmission within 12 months for the degree of PhD, (b) to award an MPhil forthwith or (c) to resubmit for an MPhil. What examiners would do if they believed the thesis to be unsalvageable was unclear.

I called Kate the next evening. She told me she thought that the viva had been fair and well handled. I felt relieved.

The saving grace for me of this harrowing process was that the external, the supervisor and I all shared the same opinion of the thesis. To some extent the process and the fact that the external and I reached similar views independently has given me confidence in examining at this level. I now have the resubmission to look forward to, but can *at least* make one addition to my CV.

Q1 Has the student any grounds for appeal under your regulations?
Q2 What assistance might a PhD candidate expect from supervisors and examiners during the period allowed for rewriting?

Postscript

Exactly a year to the day after the student had been given 12 months to rewrite, the amended thesis arrived in my pigeonhole at the university.

Fortunately it was during the Easter vacation, so at least I had time to read it. This reading proved even more time consuming than the previous year's as I had not only to read the resubmitted thesis, but also constantly refer to the original to 'spot the difference' and to the examiners' requirements which had long since been forgotten by me. However, after a week's effort I was satisfied that the student had complied with the required amendments and I completed the form for the Postgraduate Studies office to that effect recommending that the PhD be awarded forthwith.

A month later I had an email from the external examiner saying that he had just read the thesis and had written his comments (which were attached) and if they concurred with mine he would submit them. If they did not we would have to discuss the matter. Luckily the comments were almost identical, and he also recommended the student be awarded her PhD.

Q1 Discuss the external examiner's communication.
Q2 Evaluate Amanda's performance as an examiner and compare it with the team's experiences elsewhere.

Team task

List the issues that students, supervisors and examiners should be aware of in your institution.

Key text

Eley, A. and Jennings, R. (2005) *Effective Postgraduate Supervision: Improving the Student/Supervisor Relationship*. Maidenhead: Open University Press.

Appendix 3

Precepts and explanations

Institutional arrangements • The research environment • Selection, admission and induction of students • Supervision • Progress and review arrangements • Development of research and other skills • Feedback mechanisms • Assessment • Student representations • Complaints • Appeals

Reproduced with permission from the Quality Assurance Agency for Higher Education (2004) *Code of Practice for the Assurance of Academic Quality and Standards in Higher Education, Section 1: Postgraduate Research Programmes*. Also at: www.qaa.ac.uk/academicinfrastructure/codeOfPractice/default.asp

Institutional arrangements

Institutions offering postgraduate research programmes will safeguard the academic standards of such programmes, putting in place arrangements that will enable them to be delivered successfully according to national and, where relevant, international expectations. They will wish to assure themselves that they provide appropriate support and guidance to enable research students to complete their programmes and, for students, supervisors, examiners and other staff involved in research degree programmes to fulfil their responsibilities, as indicated in other sections of this document.

Precept 1

Institutions will put in place effective arrangements to maintain appropriate academic standards and enhance the quality of postgraduate research programmes.

This objective is amplified through the requirements of the other precepts in this section.

Precept 2

Institutional regulations for postgraduate research degree programmes will be clear and readily available to students and staff. Where appropriate, regulations will be supplemented by similarly accessible, subject-specific guidance at the level of the faculty, school or department.

Institutional regulations can cover:

- Requirements for admission to the programme
- Procedures for considering claims for the accreditation of prior experiential and/or prior certificated learning (AP[E/C]L)
- The academic and procedural requirements for particular postgraduate research awards
- The requirements for progression, including monitoring and review arrangements for the award and the minimum and maximum periods within which the programme may be completed
- Assessment methods, requirements and procedures, including the criteria for achieving the award
- The institution's procedures for dealing with research misconduct, including plagiarism
- Complaints and appeals processes.

Institutions will wish to review such regulations regularly and update them when necessary, to take account of developments and innovation.

Precept 3

Institutions will develop, implement and keep under review a code or codes of practice applicable across the institution, which include(s) the areas covered by this document. The code(s) should be readily available to all students and staff involved in postgraduate research programmes.

Institutions should use both external and internal guidance when developing their own codes of practice for research programmes. Such codes are considered an integral part of institutional quality assurance mechanisms and are valuable in assuring the quality and maintaining academic standards of research programmes. Guidance at faculty, school or departmental level, for example in handbooks, can provide useful additional advice for students and staff.

Institutions will wish to bring their codes of practice to the attention of students as early as possible, and certainly no later than induction.

Precept 4

Institutions will monitor the success of their postgraduate research programmes against appropriate internal and/or external indicators and targets.

Institutions have their own views of what defines success in the broad subject areas in which research programmes are undertaken, where appropriate guided by national and international expectations. In setting targets and monitoring indicators, institutions will wish to take into account the different needs and study patterns of different types of students and the diversity of their research programmes.

Factors that an institution may consider when collecting evidence to evaluate the success of its postgraduate research programmes (normally as part of an annual monitoring process) may include:

- Submission and completion times and rates
- Pass, referral and fail rates
- Withdrawal rates
- The number of appeals and complaints; the reasons for them, and how many are upheld
- Analysis of comments from examiners
- Recruitment profiles
- Feedback from research students, employers, sponsors and other external funders
- Information on employment, destinations and career paths of former students.

There should be formal opportunities for institutional, faculty and departmental committees and groups to consider statistical and other information relating to postgraduate research programmes and to act upon it. Student involvement in these processes is beneficial.

The research environment

In each research environment a range of factors, appropriate to the subject and types of students and research programmes involved, and including one or more of the examples below, can be used to demonstrate 'high quality'. National and international reference points also provide subject-specific benchmarks appropriate to individual disciplines.

Precept 5

Institutions will only accept research students into an environment that provides support for doing and learning about research and where high quality research is occurring.

Examples of factors that can be used to indicate high quality research include:

- Demonstrable research achievement or output in the subject, such as: journal publications; books; work produced in other media, including performing arts, sculpture, fine art and design
- Sufficient numbers of staff, including postdoctoral researchers, and research students (either within the institution or included in collaborative arrangements)
- Clinical research achievements
- Knowledge transfer and the application of research techniques and solutions to practical problems (such as those funded by employers)
- In some research environments, the ability to attract external funding.

Emergence of new research groups normally occurs when an environment that demonstrates research of high quality is already being achieved.

The research environment, which may be located in or across one or more institutions, will be adequate for the conduct of the kind of research in question and capable of supporting the type and range of students being recruited, and their changing needs and requirements as the programme develops. The environment should be enabling and instructional, and be conceived as a place of learning as well as of research productivity.

Features of an environment well suited for doing and learning about research (see (a) below) are supported by other characteristics that encourage research achievement (see (b), p. 196). There are some other features that help to assure the quality of the research environment (see (c), p. 196).

(a) An appropriate environment in which to do and learn about research might include the following:

- Opportunities and encouragement to exchange and develop ideas with people at appropriate levels who are also engaged in doing and learning about research and pursuing established research programmes
- Ready access to academic colleagues and others able to give advice and support
- Adequate learning and research tools including access to IT equipment, library and electronic publications
- Opportunities for students to develop peer support networks where issues or problems can be discussed informally (this could include access to social space provided for the purpose)

- Supervision (see also the section on Supervision below) that encourages the developments and successful pursuance of a programme of research
- Guidance on the ethical pursuit of research and the avoidance of research misconduct, including breaches of intellectual property rights
- An emphasis on the desirability of developing: research-related skills that contribute to the student's ability to complete the programmes successfully (including, where appropriate, understanding related to the funding of research and its commercial exploitation); personal and, where relevant, employment-related skills
- Availability of advice on career development, where relevant.

Such a learning environment will also enable research students to make judgements requiring creativity and critical independent thought, accepting that uncertainty is a feature of conduct of research programmes. This environment should enable students to grapple with challenges that develop intellectual maturity and encourage a high level of reflection on the student's own learning about research as well as on research outcomes. Institutions that fund or otherwise support postgraduate-run initiatives, for example journals, conference organization and attendance, often find this valuable in helping students develop professional skills.

(b) Components of an environment supportive of research achievement might include the following:

- The pursuit of high quality research in cognate areas by a community of academic staff and postgraduates
- Supervisors with the necessary skills and knowledge to facilitate the successful completion of students' research programmes
- Access to the facilities and equipment necessary to enable students to complete their research programmes successfully.

Institutions who wish to put in place explicit expectations that are clear and readily accessible to students and supervisors concerning timely submission and successful completion periods. Such expectations are likely to be influenced by research council requirements where relevant, and by the mode of study of the student, either full-time or part-time. They are also likely to vary according to the needs of subjects and individual students.

(c) In addition, institutions may wish to provide the following:

- Access to welfare and support facilities that recognize the particular nature of research degree study
- The opportunity for effective student representation, and for addressing students' feedback including complaints
- Sufficient implementation and monitoring mechanisms to ensure that

where a project is undertaken in collaboration with another organization, the standards of both organizations are maintained.

Selection, admission and induction of students

Precepts 6 to 10 and the accompanying explanations highlight to all concerned the importance of clear admissions and induction procedures and requirements, and the need for fair and consistently applied admissions policies.

Precept 6

Admissions procedures will be clear, consistently applied and will demonstrate equality of opportunity.

Institutions will make clear and accurate admissions information readily available to applicants and staff involved in the admissions process. Institutions are advised to make this information available on their website and in printed form.

Institutions should also make provision for staff responsible for admissions to be aware of and understand legal requirements relating to the processes and the need to conform to such legislation. In respect of equal opportunities, institutions will wish to put in place monitoring arrangements to satisfy themselves that:

- Appropriate attention is paid to legislation and guidance available internally and externally
- An effective support infrastructure is in place for students with special needs
- Students are made aware of opportunities to apply for additional or special funding and how to apply for such funds.

Precept 7

Only appropriately qualified and prepared students will be admitted to research programmes.

Students will be expected to have a sufficient level of English language competence. This should be identified by a process that is consistently applied by the institution. For doctoral research, students will be expected to have one or more of the following:

- A degree normally with class 2.1 or equivalent in a relevant subject

- A relevant master's qualification or equivalent
- Evidence of prior professional practice or learning that meets the institution's criteria and good practice guidelines for the accreditation of prior experiential and/or certified learning (AP[E/C]L).

Precept 8

Admissions decisions will involve at least two members of the institution's staff who will have received instruction, advice and guidance in respect of selection and admissions procedures. The decision-making process will enable the institution to assure itself that balanced and independent admissions decisions have been made, that support its admissions policy.

The instruction, advice and guidance provided by institutions will enable those involved in admissions decision-making to fulfil their role effectively and efficiently. Admissions staff will need to consider how interviews with applicants might be used as part of the admissions process (including arrangements for assessing the suitability of those based overseas and working at distance).

In addition to familiarizing selectors with the institution's admissions policies, institutional guidance will normally cover the use of references and other information used to assess the suitability of a candidate to undertake postgraduate research.

Institutions will wish to put in place suitable criteria for assessing student qualifications and preparedness, including consideration of any claims made for the accreditation of prior learning gained through professional practice or other appropriate work experience or study.

Important factors to be considered are the student's motivation and potential to complete the programme.

The student's ability to complete the programme may be affected by financial support, and for this reason institutions may wish to assure themselves that students have sufficient funding in place for the duration of the programme. It is equally important to ensure that students are made aware at the earliest opportunity of the financial implications of registering for the programme.

Guidance provided by the institutions should enable selectors to be aware of issues concerning international students, including the assurance of language proficiency and the importance of providing opportunities for candidates to improve their language proficiency by taking advantage of in-house or other training. Staff and applicants will need to be aware of the minimum proficiency levels set by the institution, with appropriate reference to external guidance, such as that provided by the International English Language Testing System (IELTS).

For quality assurance purposes and to help selectors, institutions should provide clear guidance on the balance of responsibilities between staff in local units and central postgraduate administration.

Precept 9

The entitlements and responsibilities of a research student undertaking a postgraduate research programme will be defined and communicated clearly.

The institution's offer to successful candidates for research degrees will normally be expressed in a formal letter that is specific to the individual applicant. This constitutes a contract between the student and the institution. The terms of the letter are binding on the institution and, upon acceptance, on the student. The letter will normally refer to or enclose other information, for example, references to institutional web pages, supplemented by printed information where necessary.

The letter and enclosures normally refer to:

- The expected total fees, including extra charges (such as 'bench' fees) which will be levied, and any other expenditure on practical items relevant to the individual student
- The expected period of study for which the student is enrolled
- The requirements which the institution places upon the research student (for example, attendance, progress reports, contact with supervisors) and arrangements for enrolment and registration
- References to the institution's regulations, student handbook, sources of funding and other relevant information for a research degree programme, all of which will normally be available via institutional web pages
- The responsibilities being accepted by the student for their academic studies and candidacy for a research degree
- If known, the requirements and conditions of any sponsor
- An outline of any opportunities to undertake teaching or other duties and any conditions associated with these (for example, training for teaching) to be defined in principle at the beginning of the student's programme unless already part of his/her funding arrangements
- Reference to practical information, for example, concerning accommodation and financial or travel information.

Other information can be provided separately, perhaps as part of the induction process. For example, handbooks (printed or electronic) may include details of health and safety procedures, regulations concerning plagiarism and good practice in research and guidance on research ethics. It is also important that students are aware of the institution's expectations of them in relation to personal conduct and academic performance.

The institution's policies, practices and requirements with respect to intellectual property rights (including arrangements, where relevant, with external commercial or industrial organizations with their own intellectual property rights arrangements) will need to be clearly expressed to applicants and any relevant third party.

Institutions should assure themselves that students are made aware of their responsibilities at the beginning of their programme. Students' responsibilities normally include:

- Taking responsibility for their own personal and professional development
- Maintaining regular contact with supervisors (joint responsibility with supervisors)
- Preparing adequately for meetings with supervisors
- Setting and keeping to timetables and deadlines, including planning and submitting work as and when required and generally maintaining satisfactory progress with the programme of research
- Making supervisors aware of any specific needs or circumstances likely to affect their work
- Attending any development opportunities (research-related and other) that have been identified when agreeing their development needs with their supervisors (see explanation with Precept 10)
- Being familiar with institutional regulations and policies that affect them, including the regulations for their qualification, health and safety, intellectual property, and ethical research guidelines (see also Precept 5(a) above and the bullet points under Precept 10 below).

Precept 10

Institutions will provide research students with sufficient information to enable them to begin their studies with an understanding of the academic and social environment in which they will be working.

Institutions will ensure that an induction programme, the timing and content of which reflects the diversity of needs of specific groups of research students (including part-time and newly arriving international students) is delivered at the most appropriate levels (institution, faculty, school or department, or a combination).

The information to be provided as part of the induction programme can usefully include:

- General information about the institution and its postgraduate portfolio in the relevant subject(s)
- The institution's registration, enrolment, appeals and complaints procedures, assessment requirements and research degree regulations
- The names and contact details of the student's supervisor(s) and information about how supervisory arrangements work
- The institution's research ethics and codes and those of relevant professional bodies and discipline groups, including consideration of issues concerning authorship and intellectual property
- The institution's expectations of the independence and responsibilities of the student

- Student support and welfare services such as counselling and advice centres
- A summary of the facilities that will be made available to the student, including the learning support infrastructure
- Relevant health and safety and other legislative information
- Where appropriate, a brief outline of the proposed research programme(s), together with the normal length of study and the facilities that will be made available to the student
- Reference to the challenges that will typically face research students during the course of their studies and where guidance may be sought in the event of difficulties
- Any opportunity for the student representative body to introduce themselves, including specific postgraduate representation
- Social activity, including that provided specifically for postgraduates
- Opportunities for postgraduates to be represented by the student body
- Details about opportunities and requirements for skills development.

It can be helpful if institutions provide students with an introductory pack, providing details about where they can find essential information.

Other information is likely to include details of supervision arrangements, including evaluation, monitoring and review procedures. During the induction process, students will be provided with details of opportunities that exist for meeting other research students and staff, and for developing scholarly competence and independent thought.

The student should meet his/her supervisor at the earliest opportunity, to agree on their plans for the programme including the following:

- The initial objectives of the research, taking account of the sponsor's requirements where appropriate
- The development and general educational needs of the student, measured against the Research Councils UK (2001) *Joint Statement of Skills* if appropriate
- The means by which the student will communicate progress to the supervisor(s) and how they will arrange regular meetings
- Monitoring of progress in the research and training aspects of the programme.

(See also the section on Supervision that follows.)

Supervision

It is important to establish systematic and clear supervision arrangements. These include: the need to provide students with opportunities for access to regular and appropriate supervisory support; encouragement to interact with other researchers; advice from one or more independent source (internal or external); and arrangements that protect the student in the event of the loss of a supervisor.

These four principles are covered in more detail by the following precepts. They provide a framework for the minimum standards required by institutions in providing supervisory arrangements for research students.

Precept 11

Institutions will appoint supervisors who have the appropriate skills and subject knowledge to support, encourage and monitor research students effectively.

All supervisors need appropriate expertise for their role. They will wish, and institutions will require them, to engage in development of various kinds to equip them to supervise students.

New supervisors will participate in specified development activities, arranged through their institutions, to assure their competence in the role.

Institutions will expect existing supervisors to demonstrate their continuing professional development through participation in a range of activities designed to support their work as supervisors. Supervisors should take the initiative in updating their knowledge and skills, supported by institutional arrangements that define and enable sharing of good practice and provide advice on effective support for different types of student. Mentoring relationships are one example of how support can be provided for supervisors.

To assure consistency of supervision, institutions will wish to encourage supervisors working in industry or professional practice to participate as appropriate in any developmental activities offered by the institution.

Precept 12

Each research student will have a minimum of one main supervisor. He or she will normally be part of a supervisory team. There must always be one clearly identified point of contact for the student.

Supervision arrangements will depend on the structure for research student support that exists within the institution and any guidance provided by the relevant research council, where appropriate.

Involvement with a supervisory team can provide valuable staff development and grounding in the skills required to become an effective research supervisor. A supervisory team can give the student access to a multifaceted support network, which may include: other research staff and students in the subject; a departmental adviser to postgraduate students; a faculty postgraduate tutor; or other individuals in similar roles.

Between them, the main supervisor and, where relevant, other members of the supervisory team, will ensure that research students receive sufficient support and guidance to facilitate their success.

At least one member of the supervisory team will be currently engaged in research in the relevant discipline(s), so as to ensure that the direction and monitoring of the student's progress is informed by up-to-date subject knowledge and research developments.

Breadth of experience and knowledge across the supervisory team will mean that the student always has access to someone with experience of supporting research student(s) through to successful completion of their programme.

In all cases, a student should have an identified single point of contact, normally the main supervisor. It should be clear to the student who the relevant contact is if the main supervisor is not available. This will normally be an additional, designated member of academic staff able to provide advice and support. To avoid misunderstandings, the names, contact details and responsibilities of the main and any other supervisor(s) should be provided to students at registration and be readily available throughout their programme.

As and when a main supervisor is not able to continue supervising the student, an appropriate supervisor will be appointed to assume the role.

Institutions will wish to take a view on how long a main supervisor may be absent before a permanent replacement is appointed. In determining this period, institutions will be influenced by the importance of providing breadth and continuity of supervision for the student. In some circumstances, it will be appropriate for another supervisor to assume the role of main supervisor, while a replacement main supervisor is found.

It is important that, if a student/supervisor relationship is not working well, alternative independent sources of advice are available to the student. By mutual agreement between the student and the institution and, where permitted, by the terms of any sponsorship agreement, supervisory responsibilities can be changed, at the request of either the student or a supervisor.

Students will have sufficient opportunities for contacting and receiving advice and guidance from their supervisor(s) throughout their programme, irrespective of their geographical location. Reasonable accessibility of supervisors is a priority and institutions should assure themselves that students and supervisors are aware of its importance.

Precept 13

Institutions will ensure that the responsibilities of all research student supervisors are clearly communicated to supervisors and students through written guidance.

It is important that supervisor(s) and students are fully aware of the extent of one another's responsibilities, to enable both to understand the supervisor's contribution to supporting the student and where the supervisor's responsibilities end.

Depending on institutional and research council guidance, supervisory responsibilities may include:

- Providing satisfactory guidance and advice
- Being responsible for monitoring the progress of the student's research programme
- Establishing and maintaining regular contact with the student (where appropriate, guided by institutional expectations) and ensuring his/her accessibility to the student when he/she needs advice, by whatever means is most suitable given the student's location and mode of study
- Having input into the assessment of a student's development needs
- Providing timely, constructive and effective feedback on the student's work, including his/her overall progress within the programme
- Ensuring that the student is aware of the need to exercise probity and conduct his/her research according to ethical principles, and of the implications of research misconduct
- Ensuring that the student is aware of institutional-level sources of advice, including careers guidance, health and safety legislation and equal opportunities policy
- Providing effective pastoral support and/or referring the student to other sources of such support, including student advisers (or equivalent), graduate school staff and others within the student's academic community
- Helping the student to interact with others working in the field of research, for example encouraging the student to attend relevant conferences, supporting him/her in seeking funding for such events; and where appropriate to submit conference papers and articles to refereed journals
- Maintaining the necessary supervisory expertise, including the appropriate skills, to perform all of the role satisfactorily, supported by relevant continuing professional development opportunities.

Supervisors will be sensitive to the diverse needs of individual students, including international students, and the associated support that may be required in different circumstances. An awareness of the range of support available (as referred to above), and how students can access it, is an important part of the supervision process.

Institutions will ensure that students and supervisors always have access to relevant documents concerning the above responsibilities: electronically, in paper form, or both.

Institutions may find it helpful to include in their code(s) of practice (see Precept 3 above), guidance on the minimum frequency of contact advisable between students and supervisors. Such codes can also include details of procedures for dealing with extensions and suspensions of study, which students and supervisors may find helpful.

Precept 14

Institutions will ensure that the quality of supervision is not put at risk as a result of an excessive volume and range of responsibilities assigned to individual supervisors.

In appointing supervisors, institutions need to be aware of and guided by the overall workload of the individual, including teaching, research, administration and other responsibilities, for example, external examining duties and other professional commitments, such as consultancy or clinical responsibilities. Institutions are encouraged to find ways of showing their support for supervisors' valuable contribution to the research environment.

Supervisors need time to provide adequate contact with each research student and to fulfil the responsibilities listed under Precept 13 above. Supervisors and students should agree between themselves the level of interaction required and what constitutes sufficient time, in terms of quality as well as quantity, to devote to the supervisory role.

When a student needs advice or guidance, supervisors should be able to respond within a reasonable timescale.

Progress and review arrangements

Regular and structured interaction is necessary between students and supervisors, as part of the support provided to enable students to progress satisfactorily. Institutions should make it as easy as possible for students and supervisors to be aware of the requirements of the progress and review process, including knowledge of their respective responsibilities.

Precepts 15, 16 and 17 cover all types of review of student progress, including meetings that take place between the student and the supervisor(s), and other individuals, such as members of an annual review panel. There are two distinct types of review: meetings that deal with formal review of the student's progress and forward planning, and informal meetings where the student and members of the supervisory team meet to discuss general matters. Both are covered below.

Precept 15

Institutions will put in place and bring to the attention of students and relevant staff clearly defined mechanisms for monitoring and supporting student progress.

The main purpose of the monitoring process is to provide overall support for the student to complete the research programme successfully within an appropriate timescale. The purpose and frequency of monitoring arrangements need to be clear from the outset, so that both the student and the supervisor can plan adequately for them, prepare relevant documents and consult other individuals as appropriate. Should a student's progress not be satisfactory, the monitoring process should include ensuring that support is available for the student to make improvements.

Arrangements made between the student and the supervisor may allow some flexibility, if both are satisfied that adequate support is being provided for the student and there are sufficient opportunities for formally monitoring progress. As well as providing opportunities for formal interaction, institutions should make it clear that students and supervisors are expected to meet informally, and frequently enough to address the student's need for general guidance.

Students and supervisors are jointly responsible for ensuring that regular and frequent contact is maintained and there will be times when the student, as well as the supervisor, needs to take the initiative. The nature and frequency of contact between student and supervisor(s) will vary, depending on the duration of the programme, the way the research is being conducted and the amount of support needed by the student.

Taking account of these variables, the following should be agreed by and clear to both student and supervisor(s) from the start of the programme:

- The minimum frequency of scheduled meetings between student and supervisor, or supervisory team, and the purpose of such meetings
- Guidance on the nature and style of the student/supervisor interaction, including discussions about academic and personal progress.

Institutions will wish to put in place opportunities for seeking independent advice should the student/supervisor relationship break down, and to ensure that students are aware of these (see also Precept 12).

Precept 16

Institutions will put in place and bring to the attention of students and relevant staff clearly defined mechanisms for formal reviews of student progress, including explicit review stages.

Institutions will wish to establish processes for reviewing student progress involving individuals independent of the supervisor(s) and the student. Such processes will operate less regularly than meetings between student and supervisor(s) and may involve, for example, an annual review by a panel or other institutionally specified body such as a research degrees committee. A significant progress review would normally be undertaken at specific points in a research student's programme, for example, when completing probationary periods of training or transferring from a research master's to a doctoral degree. The student should be present at the review. The target dates of expected review stages throughout the programme, such as those referred to above, should be agreed by and clear to both student and supervisor(s).

Institutions will wish to assure themselves that the following are clear to students and supervisors from the beginning of the programme:

- The implications of the possible outcomes of review meetings
- The criteria to be used for making decisions about the extension, supervision or termination of a student's registration
- The circumstances in which the student appeal mechanisms may be used.

Institutional regulations will specify the minimum and maximum periods within which the student can complete the research programme. Bearing these in mind, decisions about transferring the student's registration to a doctoral qualification should take place when there is sufficient evidence to assess the student's performance. This may be part of the annual review process. The student will normally provide as a minimum a written submission, considered by a panel that includes the student's main supervisor, and some members who are independent of the supervisory team. In most cases, there is likely to be an oral presentation by the student, with questions put by panel members.

Precept 17

Institutions will provide guidance to students, supervisors and others involved in progress monitoring and review processes about the importance of keeping appropriate records of the outcomes of meetings and related activities.

Guidance in this area might take the form of advice about the kind of records that need to be kept in relation to the different types of meeting and review. For example, the information that is recorded after an informal meeting that takes place regularly between the student and his/her supervisor is likely to be different from and less detailed than the formal record of a meeting to consider an application to transfer to a doctoral degree or a meeting of an annual review panel. In some institutions it is considered good practice for students to keep the record of regular, 'routine' meetings with supervisors. Supervisors, as well as students, should keep copies of records of supervisory meetings.

Institutional guidance on record-keeping should be easily accessible at all times to students, supervisors and others involved in the progress and review processes. This may be facilitated by the introduction of electronic logs, such as can be made available through institutional portals, perhaps as part of personal development planning.

Development of research and other skills

The importance of acquiring research and other skills during research degree programmes is recognized by students, academic staff, sponsoring organizations, employers and former students. These skills improve the student's ability to complete the research programme successfully. Development and application of such skills is also understood to be significant in the research graduate's capability for sustaining learning throughout his or her career, whether in an academic role or in other employment. Research students are encouraged to recognize the value of transferable skills in enabling them to take ownership and responsibility for their own learning during and after their programme of study.

Precept 18

Institutions will provide research students with appropriate opportunities for personal and professional development.

Research students need support to develop the research, subject-specific, communication and other skills they require to become effective researchers, to enhance their employability and assist their career progress after completion of their degree. These skills may be present on commencement (for example in the case of some mature students), explicitly taught or developed during the research programme.

In providing research students with opportunities for developing personal and research skills, institutions will wish to pay particular attention to the differing needs of individual postgraduates, arising from their diversity. It is expected that a range of mechanisms will be used to support learning and that they will be sufficiently flexible to address those individual needs. For example, the development needs of research students already employed to undertake research may be different from those of other students. The emphasis in formal training should be on quality, relevance and timeliness.

Institutions will wish to consider embedding opportunities for skills development in research degree programmes. Depending on the needs of the subject and the student, personal and professional development opportunities for research students will either be spread across the duration of the research degree or will be provided at the beginning of the programme, the aim being to maximize the effectiveness of training in developing skills, both research and generic.

In deciding which elements of research and skills development to make mandatory, institutions will wish to take into account advice from research councils and other sources. It will not necessarily be appropriate for all students to undertake such development; for example, mature students who may be studying for their own interest in the subject may not need to acquire skills for employment.

To ensure students' needs are being met, institutions will find it helpful to review on a regular basis the training in research and generic skills provided for their students, as part of the quality assurance mechanisms for research programmes.

Opportunities for skills development can be provided either by the institution offering the student's research programme, or by other institutions, perhaps through regional or other collaboration.

Precept 19

Each student's development needs will be identified and agreed jointly by the student and appropriate academic staff, initially during the student's induction period; they will be regularly reviewed during the research programme and amended as appropriate.

The UK Research Councils and the Arts and Humanities Research Board (AHRB) play an important role in setting standards and identifying best practice in research training. In their *Joint Statement of the Skills Training Requirements for Research Students*, they have set out the skills that doctoral research students they funded are expected to have on completion of their programmes.

Institutions will wish to use their experience of structured training and education to establish personal and professional development opportunities for the benefit of students. The extent to which research students are required to take advantage of these opportunities will normally be negotiated through the supervision process, taking account of subject and individual needs.

Where postgraduate students are provided with opportunities for teaching (for example, acting as demonstrators in laboratories or teaching small groups), appropriate guidance and support will be provided. If the student's teaching activity also extends to assessing students, training will reflect this. It is helpful for postgraduates to be part of a larger teaching team, so they can benefit from the support and mentoring provided by experienced teachers.

Precept 20

Institutions will provide opportunities for research students to maintain a record of personal progress, which includes reference to the development of research and other skills.

It is accepted as good practice for students to reflect on their learning, supported by frameworks developed by institutions for recording personal development. National guidelines (currently the QAA (2001) *Guidelines for Higher Education Progress Files*), suggest that PDP for students should operate across the whole higher education system. Research students may find it useful to use the PDP tools provided by their institutions to record their personal progress and development, including reference to research and other skills. Planning for skills development and checking that necessary guidance and support has been provided should form part of the process of personal development planning.

Students who, on entry to the research programme, are unfamiliar with keeping records of their progress and development are likely to need additional guidance and support.

Institutions may also wish to implement some form of recognition of the acquisition of transferable skills in parallel with, or as part of, the academic assessment of the student's progress.

Feedback mechanisms

Collecting and acting upon feedback from students, staff, examiners and others involved in research programmes is a fundamental part of the quality assurance process, at institutional and subject levels. Precept 21 and accompanying text outline how institutions may wish to approach this activity.

Precept 21

Institutions will put in place mechanisms to collect, review and, where appropriate, respond to feedback from all concerned with postgraduate research programmes. They will make arrangements for feedback to be considered openly and constructively and for the results to be communicated appropriately.

Institutions will wish to establish and operate constructive feedback procedures that are as representative as possible of the views of all those involved. These include feedback mechanisms for:

- Current students and recently completed research degree graduates
- Supervisors, review panels and internal examiners
- Research administrators
- External parties, including external examiners, sponsors, collaborating organizations, employers and, where possible, alumni.

(See also list of suggested evaluation factors in bullet points accompanying Precept 4.)

Separate arrangements should exist for obtaining individual and collective feedback, for example, through a student forum. Individual feedback mechanisms should enable students to provide confidential views if they wish.

Institutions should use the feedback in an appropriate format in their quality assurance processes as part of the regular review of academic standards. The feedback and review cycle should normally occur at least annually.

Information about action taken in response to feedback should be made easily and promptly available to those involved.

Assessment

Assessment processes for research qualifications are quite different from those for taught awards and usually include come kind of oral examination. The following three precepts and explanations address the most important elements of assessment for research students and qualifications.

Precept 22

Institutions will use criteria for assessing research degrees that enable them to define the academic standards of different research programmes and the achievements of their graduates. The criteria used to assess research degrees must be clear and readily available to students, staff and external examiners.

In setting criteria for assessing different types of research programmes, institutions will wish to refer to the qualification descriptors for doctoral and master's degrees in the *Framework for Higher Education Qualifications* (QAA 2008b) or their equivalent. They will also find it helpful to refer to the qualifications nominated in these documents, including the guidance on the use of titles for research programmes of different kinds. Thought will also need to be given to the assessment criteria to be used in different subjects such as the performing or visual arts and for different types of research programmes, including professional doctorates and doctorates by published work.

Applying assessment criteria for postgraduate research degrees helps institutions to safeguard the academic integrity of such programmes and awards, internally and externally. Making assessment criteria available to research students will give them the insight they need into what the institution expects. Criteria should enable students to show the full extent of their abilities and achievements at the level of the qualifications they are aiming for. Practical advice for students is also helpful, for example, on word limits and what is meant by 'originality' and other similar terms.

When making an award at a different level from the qualification for which the student has been assessed (for example, giving a master's award to a PhD candidate), institutions will wish to use assessment criteria that enable examiners to confer the alternative award for positive achievement by the student.

Precept 23

Research degree assessment procedures must be clear; they must be operated rigorously, fairly and consistently; include input from an external
examiner and carried out to a reasonable timescale.

Although there is some variation between institutions and between different
types of research degree, the most common features of research degree assessment procedures in the UK system are as follows:

- The student is examined on the basis of an appropriate body of work and an
  oral examination (viva voce).
- As a minimum, two appropriately qualified examiners are appointed for
  the purpose, at least one of whom is external to the institution. When more
  than two examiners are appointed, the majority are generally from outside
  the institution.
- None of the student's supervisors should be appointed as an examiner.
- It is exceptional to appoint as internal or external examiners researchers
  who have had a substantial direct involvement in the student's work or
  whose own work is the focus of the research project.
- Examiners submit separate, independent written reports before the viva and
  a joint report after it.

In meeting this precept, the institution will want to consider carefully:

1 The criteria to be used in appointing examiners, including how many examiners are to be appointed. Some institutions appoint additional external
  examiners where the research student is also a member of staff or, in cases
  where the thesis is highly interdisciplinary. Other issues include how to
  establish that the examiners have relevant qualifications and a clear understanding of the task; in what circumstances and with what support an
  inexperienced examiner might be appointed; and what guidance is to be
  given to the examiners.
2 The preparatory period prior to the viva. Institutions will wish to consider
  ways of making sure that the examiners have the information and conditions they need to identify the areas to be explored at the viva. Those
  institutions which do not at present ask their examiners to produce separate
  reports might consider whether to change their practice. Thought needs to
  be given to the procedures for handling such reports, including to whom
  they should be submitted and when.
3 The way in which the viva is to be conducted. Institutions will wish to
  satisfy themselves that the processes enable the viva to meet agreed criteria
  for fairness and consistency. Some institutions now appoint an independent, non-examining chair; this is thought to be good practice, not least
  in ensuring consistency between different vivas and in providing an

additional viewpoint if the conduct of the viva should become the subject of a student appeal. Where the appointment of an independent chair is not feasible, institutions should find alternative ways of assuring fairness and consistency, acceptable to the student, that enable them to know the viva is conducted in an appropriate manner. Institutions might also consider whether the student's supervisor should be present, with the student's agreement, and, if so, on what basis; whether other people should be present (e.g. current research students); and whether it would be helpful to ask for an account of how the viva was conducted.

4 How to handle cases where the examiners are unable to reach a consensus view on the outcome.

5 How and when the result is to be communicated to the student. This will involve: giving thought to the range of assessment outcomes open to the examiners, including referral or awarding a qualification different from the one for which the student has been examined; the nature and source of guidance to be given if a student is asked to revise and resubmit the thesis; and the various parties who need to be notified of the result (e.g. the student's sponsor).

6 The criteria to be used for selecting external examiners when they have had previous affiliations with the awarding institution.

The institution will also need to consider how it assures itself that the research programme assessments carried out in its name meet the criteria set out in this precept. For example, it may want to have a system for reading the examiners' report(s) similar to that in place for reading external examiners' reports at undergraduate and taught master's levels. Additionally, it may also want to keep a 'log' to ensure that the process is being conducted promptly: undue delay is unfair to the student.

Precept 24

Institutions will communicate their assessment procedures clearly to all the parties involved, i.e. the students, the supervisor(s) and the examiners.

The main official source of information on research degree assessment is often the institution's regulations. These are often written in semi-legal language because they may be used in formal complaints and appeals processes. The institution may therefore need to supplement regulations to provide students and staff with a clear understanding of the assessment process and its implications. In doing so, it may help to think through the process as the student experiences it. This will include providing detailed information on timings and deadlines; the assessment process itself; the time taken to reach a decision; and the potential outcomes of the assessment.

In particular, students should be warned of the penalties for plagiarism and should be reminded of the significance of declaring that the material being presented for examination is their own work.

The viva can be an especially challenging event in the research student's career and she/he may well need support in preparing for it. The institution will want to consider providing written guidance and/or making arrangements for the student to undergo a 'mock' viva or other similar experience.

Institutions will also need to think about whether and, if so, when, students should routinely be given copies of the report and, if so, whether this should be the final report only or the final report and the separate independent reports prepared before the viva. Depending on the institution's policy in this respect, examiners may need to be informed in advance that their reports will be made available to the candidate. Whatever the institution's agreed procedure, it should be applied consistently in all cases to assure equality.

Student representations

It is in the interests of students and institutions to resolve problems at an early stage. To facilitate this, institutions should ensure that students and staff know the difference between informal ways of making representations and routes they can use to make formal complaints or appeals. It is also important to distinguish between complaints, which are defined as being representations about general matters (including conduct) and appeals, which are against specific outcomes or decisions. Institutions are advised to develop their own definitions of complaints and appeals and generally to assure themselves that staff and students are aware of the different types of representations and procedures.

Precept 25

Institutions will put in place and publicise procedures for dealing with student representations that are fair, clear to all concerned, robust and applied consistently. Such procedures will allow all students access to relevant information and an opportunity to present their case.

Institutional procedures for addressing student representations at various levels (institution, faculty, school or department) will be clearly and openly publicized to research students. They will apply equally to all research students including those who are part-time, off-site, registered on collaborative programmes or on visiting programmes. Students should be made aware of the final stage in any complaint or appeal, if all other possibilities have been exhausted, including the opportunity to make representations to the Office of the Independent Adjudicator for Higher Education, which provides an independent scheme for the review of student complaints and appeals.

The importance of resolving any problems at an early stage should be made clear to students and staff. All concerned should be made aware of the stages and processes, informal and formal, through which representations can be made.

Institutions will assure themselves that schools or departments have accessible mechanisms that apply when students are not able to resolve difficulties informally with their supervisor(s). Impartial person(s) with suitable experience (whose role should be widely publicized) will be appointed, to whom students can take their complaints. This is essential to assist in resolving problems at an early stage.

Complaints

Precept 26

Independent and formal procedures will exist to resolve effectively complaints from research students about the quality of the institution's learning and support provision.

Institutions will wish to implement complaints procedures that are appropriate for use by research students.

These should include an indicative timetable for dealing with different types of complaints: some may need to be dealt with more quickly than others.

The need for students to discharge their responsibilities in relation to pursuing a formal complaint will be highlighted. On receipt of a formal complaint, students will be informed promptly of the actions that will be taken.

Appeals

Precept 27

Institutions will put in place formal procedures to deal with any appeals made by research students. The acceptable grounds for appeals will be clearly defined.

All appeals procedures will be clear, impartial and well publicised to protect the rights of all those concerned. They should be dealt with fairly and in a timely manner.

Institutions will wish to define clearly the grounds for an appeal and how to lodge an appeal. This information will be clearly communicated to all research students. Further to this there should be clear explanation of the appeals process including:

- How decisions are taken to grant an appeal hearing
- The constitution of an appeal panel and the relation of its members to those involved in the original assessment decision
- How records are maintained of an appeal hearing
- The mechanisms for communicating the results of an appeal hearing to interested parties.

References

Advisory Board of the Research Councils (ABRC) (1996) *The Nature of the PhD: A Discussion Document*. London: Office of Science and Technology.

Anderson, J. (1988) *The Supervisory Process in Speech-Language Pathology and Audiology*. Boston, MA: College Hill Press & Little, Brown.

Bandura, A. (1977) Towards a unifying theory of behaviour change. *Psychological Review*, 84: 191–215.

Becher, T., Henkel, M. and Kogan, M. (1994) *Graduate Education in Britain*. London: Jessica Kingsley.

Brown, G. and Atkins, M. (1988) *Effective Teaching in Higher Education*. London: Methuen.

Buckton, L. (2008) Student complaints and appeals: The practitioner's view. *Perspectives: Policy and Practice in Higher Education*, 12: 11–14.

Burnham, P. (1994) Surviving the viva: Unravelling the mystery of the PhD oral. *Journal of Graduate Education*, 1: 30–34.

Caffarella, R. S. and Barnett, B. G. (2000) Teaching doctoral students to become scholarly writers: The importance of giving and receiving critiques. *Studies in Higher Education*, 25: 39–51.

Craswell, G. (2007) Deconstructing the skills training debate in doctoral education. *Higher Education Research and Development*, 26: 377–391.

Cryer, P. (1998) *Developing Postgraduates' Key Skills*. London: Society for Research into Higher Education.

Deech, B. R. (2007) Adjudicating student complaints: The first three years of the Office of the Independent Adjudicator for Higher Education. *Education Law Journal*, 8: 233–237.

Delamont, S., Atkinson, P. and Parry, O. (2004) *Supervising the Doctorate: A Guide to Success*, 2nd edn. Maidenhead: Society for Research into Higher Education and Open University Press.

Elbow, P. (1973) *Writing without Teachers*. Oxford: Oxford University Press.

Eley, A. and Jennings, R. (2005) *Effective Postgraduate Supervision: Improving the Student/ Supervisor Relationship*. Maidenhead: Open University Press.

European Commission (2005) *European Charter for Researchers and the Code of Conduct for the Recruitment of Researchers*. Brussels: European Commission.

European University Association (EUA) (2007) *Doctoral Programmes in Europe's Universities: Achievements and Challenges*. Brussels: EUA.

Farrington, D. and Palfreyman, D. (2006) *The Law of Higher Education*. Oxford: Oxford University Press.

Gatfield, T. (2005) An investigation into PhD supervisory management styles: Development of a dynamic conceptual model and its managerial implications. *Journal of Higher Education Policy and Management*, 27: 311–325.

Golde, C. M., Jones, L., Bueschel, A. C. and Walker, G. E. (2006) The challenges of doctoral program assessment: Lessons from the Carnegie Initiative on the doctorate.

In P. L. Maki and N. A. Borkowski (eds) *The Assessment of Doctoral Education: Emerging Criteria and New Models for Improving Outcomes*. Sterling, VA: Stylus.

Gough, M. and Denicolo, P. (2007) *Research Supervisors and the Skills Agenda: Learning Needs Analysis and Personal Development Profiling*. London: Society for Research into Higher Education.

Green, H. G. and Powell, S. D. (2005) *Doctoral Study in Contemporary Higher Education*. Buckingham: Open University Press.

Gurr, G. M. (2001) Negotiating the 'Rackety Bridge': A dynamic model for aligning supervisory style with research student development. *Higher Education Research and Development*, 20: 81–92.

Harland, T. and Plangger, G. (2004) The postgraduate chameleon: Changing roles in doctoral education. *Active Learning in Higher Education*, 5: 73–86.

Hart, C. (1998) *Doing a Literature Review*. Thousand Oaks, CA: Sage.

Higher Education Funding Council for England (HEFCE) (2003) *Improving Standards in Postgraduate Research Degree Programmes: Formal Consultation*. Available at www.hefce.ac.uk/pubs/hefce/2003/03_23.htm, accessed 6 January 2009.

HEFCE, SHEFC, HEFCW and DENI (1998) *Research Assessment Exercise 2001: Key Decisions and Issues for Further Consideration*, RAE 1/1998, July.

Higher Education Policy Institute (HEPI) (2006) *The Academic Experience of Students in English Universities*, HEPI Report 27. Available at www.hepi.ac.uk, accessed 23 December 2008.

Hinchcliffe, R., Bromley, T. and Hutchinson, S. (2007) *Skills Training in Research Degree Programmes: Politics and Practice*. Maidenhead: Open University Press.

Hole, C. (1997) *Research Supervision: The Case for a Code of Good Practice*, Briefing Paper 47. Sheffield: Universities' and Colleges' Staff Development Agency.

Jackson, C. and Tinkler, P. (2007) *A Guide for Internal and External Examiners*. London: Society for Research into Higher Education.

Johnston, S. (1997) Examining the examiners: An analysis of examiners' reports on doctoral theses. *Studies in Higher Education*, 22: 333–347.

Kamler, B. and Thomson, P. (2006) *Helping Doctoral Students Write: Pedagogies for Supervision*. London: Routledge.

Krashen, S. (2002) Optimal levels of writing management: A re-analysis of Boice (1983). *Education*, 122: 605–608.

Lederman, D. (2007) Professional development for postdocs. *Inside Higher Ed*. Available at http://insidehighered.com/layout/set/print/news/2007/08/20/postdoc, accessed 23 December 2008.

Lee, A. (2008) How are doctoral students supervised? Concepts of doctoral research supervision. *Studies in Higher Education*, 33: 267–281.

Lee, A. and Boud, D. (2003) Writing groups, change and academic identity: Research development as local practice. *Studies in Higher Education*, 28: 187–200.

Lewis, P. and Hall, G. (2007) Evaluation and review of skills training programmes for research students. In R. Hinchcliffe, T. Bromley and S. Hutchinson (eds) *Skills Training in Research Degree Programmes: Politics and Practice*. Maidenhead: Open University Press.

Loumansky, A. and Jackson, S. (2004) Out of the frying pan into the viva. *Journal of International Women's Studies*, 5: 22–32.

McCulloch, A. and Stokes, P. (2008) *The Silent Majority: Meeting the Needs of Part-time Research Students*. London: Society for Research into Higher Education.

McGrail, R. M., Rickard, C. M. and Jones, R. (2006) Publish or perish: A systematic review of interventions to increase academic publication rates. *Higher Education Research and Development*, 25: 19–35.

Mackinnon, J. (2004) Academic supervision: Seeking metaphors and models for quality. *Journal of Further and Higher Education*, 28: 395–405.

McVeigh, C., Moyle, K., Forrester, K., Chaboyer, W., Patterson, E. and St John, W. (2002) Publication syndicates: In support of nursing scholarship. *Journal of Continuing Education in Nursing*, 33: 63–66.

Maki, P. L. and Borkowski, N. A. (eds) (2006) *The Assessment of Doctoral Education: Emerging Criteria and New Models for Improving Outcomes*. Sterling, VA: Stylus.

Malfoy, J. and Webb, C. (2000) Congruent and incongruent views of postgraduate supervision. In M. Kiley and G. Mullins (eds) *Quality in Postgraduate Research: Making Ends Meet*. Adelaide: Advisory Centre for University Education, University of Adelaide.

Manathunga, C. (2005) The development of research supervision: 'Turning the light on a private space'. *International Journal for Academic Development*, 10: 17–30.

Morley, L., Leonard, D. and David, M. (2002) Variations in vivas: Quality and equality in British PhD assessments. *Studies in Higher Education*, 27: 263–273.

Morss, K. and Murray, R. (2005) *Teaching at University: A Handbook for Postgraduates and Researchers*. London: Sage.

Mullen, C. A. (2001) The need for a curricular writing model for graduate students. *Journal of Further and Higher Education*, 25: 117–126.

Mullins, G. and Kiley, M. (2002) It's a PhD, not a Nobel prize: How experienced examiners assess research theses. *Studies in Higher Education*, 26(4): 369–386.

Murray, R. (1998) *The Viva* (video and notes). Glasgow: University of Strathclyde.

Murray, R. (2003a) Students' questions and their implications for the viva. *Quality Assurance in Education*, 11: 109–113.

Murray, R (2003b) Survive your viva. *Guardian*, 16 September.

Murray, R. (2006a) *How to Write a Thesis*, 2nd edn. Maidenhead: Open University Press.

Murray, R. (2006b) Writing articles, books and presentations. In N. Gilbert (ed.) *From Postgraduate to Social Scientist: A Guide to Key Skills*. London: Sage.

Murray, R. (2009a) *How to Survive your Viva: Defending a Thesis in an Oral Examination*, 2nd edn. Maidenhead: Open University Press.

Murray, R. (2009b) *Writing for Academic Journals*, 2nd edn. Maidenhead: Open University Press.

National Academic Recognition Information Centre (NARIC) (1996) *International Guide to Qualifications in Education*, 4th edn. London: British Council and Mansell.

National Committee of Inquiry into Higher Education (NCIHE) (1997a) *Higher Education in the Learning Society*, Dearing Report. Hayes, UK: NCIHE Publications. Available at https://bei.leeds.ac.uk/Partners/NCIHE, accessed 23 December 2008.

National Committee of Inquiry into Higher Education (1997b) *Report of the Scottish Committee*, Garrick Report. Hayes, UK: NCIHE Publications. Available at https://bei.leeds.ac.uk/Partners/NCIHE, accessed 23 December 2008.

National Postgraduate Committee (NPC) (2005a) *NPC Guidelines on Including Postgraduates in the Institutional Audit Process*. Available at www.npc.org.uk/postgraduate factsandissues/postgraduatepublications, accessed 23 December 2008.

National Postgraduate Committee (2005b) *National Survey on User Perception of Personal Development Planning for Postgraduate Research Students*. Troon, Scotland: National Postgraduate Committee of the United Kingdom.

Neumann, R. (2005) Doctoral differences: Professional doctorates and PhDs compared. *Journal of Higher Education Policy and Management*, 27: 173–188.

Nyquist, J. D., Manning, L., Wulff, D. H., Austin, A. E., Sprague, J., Fraser, P. K. et al. (1999) On the road to becoming a professor: The graduate student experience. *Change*, 31: 18–27.

Paltridge, B. and Starfield, S. (2007) *Thesis and Dissertation Writing in a Second Language: A Handbook for Supervisors*. London: Routledge.

Park, C. (2003) In other (people's) words: Plagiarism by university students – Literature and lessons. *Assessment and Evaluation in Higher Education*, 28: 471–488.

Park, C. (2005) New variant PhD: The changing nature of the doctorate in the UK. *Journal of Higher Education Policy and Management*, 27: 189–207.

Park, C. (2007) *Redefining the Doctorate*, Discussion Paper. York: Higher Education Academy.

Partington, P., Brown, G. and Gordon, G. (1993) *Handbook for External Examiners in Higher Education*. Sheffield: Universities' and Colleges' Staff Development Association.

Pearce, L. (2005) *How to Examine a Thesis*. Maidenhead: Open University Press.

Pearson, M. and Brew, A. (2002) Research training and supervision development. *Studies in Higher Education*, 27: 138–143.

Phillips, E. M. (1992) The PhD: Assessing quality at different stages of its development. In O. Zuber-Skerritt (ed.) *Starting Research: Supervision and Training*. Brisbane: Tertiary Education Institute, University of Queensland.

Phillips, E. M. and Pugh, D. S. (2005) *How to Get a PhD: A Handbook for Students and their Supervisors*, 4th edn. Maidenhead: Open University Press.

Pololi, L., Knight, S. and Dunn, K. (2004) Facilitating scholarly writing in academic medicine: Lessons learned from a collaborative peer mentoring program. *Journal of General Internal Medicine*, 19: 64–68.

Powell, S. (2004) *The Award of PhD by Published Works in the UK*. Lichfield, UK: UK Council for Graduate Education.

Powell, S. and Brown, K. (2007) *Access to Doctoral Examiners' Reports*. Lichfield, UK: UK Council for Graduate Education.

Powell, S. and Green, H. (eds) (2007) *The Doctorate Worldwide*. Maidenhead: Society for Research into Higher Education and Open University Press.

Powell, S. and Long, E. (2005) *Professional Doctorate Awards in the UK*. Lichfield, UK: UK Council for Graduate Education.

QAA (1999a) *Code of Practice for the Assurance of Academic Quality and Standards in Higher Education: Postgraduate Research Programmes*. Gloucester: Quality Assurance Agency for Higher Education.

QAA (1999b) *Code of Practice for Assurance of Academic Quality and Standards in Higher Education: Students with Disabilities*. Gloucester: Quality Assurance Agency for Higher Education.

QAA (2001) *Guidelines for Higher Education Progress Files*. Gloucester: Quality Assurance Agency for Higher Education.

QAA (2004) *Code of Practice for the Assurance of Academic Quality and Standards in Higher Education. Section 1: Postgraduate Research Programmes*. Available at www.qaa.ac.uk/academicinfrastructure/codeofpractice/section1/postgrad2004.pdf, accessed 23 December 2008.

QAA (2006) *Institutional Audit: A Guide for Student Representatives*. Available at www.qaa.ac.uk/students/guides/instauditguide06.asp, accessed 12 January 2009.

QAA (2007a) *Code of Practice for the Assurance of Academic Quality and Standards in Higher Education. Section 5: Academic Appeals and Student Complaints on Academic Matters*.

Available at www.qaa.ac.uk/academicinfrastructure/codeofpractice/section5/default. asp, accessed 23 December 2008.

QAA (2007b) *Report on the Review of Research Degree Programmes: England and Northern Ireland. Sharing Good Practice.* Gloucester: Quality Assurance Agency for Higher Education.

QAA (2008a) *Frequently Asked Questions for Students.* Available at www.qaa.ac.uk/ students/faqs.asp, accessed 12 January 2009.

QAA (2008b) *Framework for Higher Education Qualifications in England, Wales and Northern Ireland.* Available at www.qaa.ac.uk/academicinfrastructure/fheq/EWNI08/default. asp, accessed 12 January 2009.

Race, I. (2007) Professional learning through reflective practice: The UEA experience. In R. Hinchcliffe, T. Bromley and S. Hutchinson (eds) *Skills Training in Research Degree Programmes: Politics and Practice.* Maidenhead: Open University Press.

Reeves, J. (2007) Getting beyond supervision. In R. Hinchcliffe, T. Bromley and S. Hutchinson (eds) *Skills Training in Research Degree Programmes: Politics and Practice.* Maidenhead: Open University Press.

Research Councils UK (RCUK) (2001) *Joint Statement of the Skills Training Requirements for Research Students.* London: RCUK.

Roberts, G. (2002) *SET for Success: The Supply of People with Science, Technology, Engineering and Mathematics Skills.* Report of Sir Gareth Roberts' Review, Higher Education Funding Councils for England, Scotland and Wales. London: HM Treasury.

Roberts, G. (2007) Foreword. In R. Hinchcliffe, T. Bromley and S. Hutchinson (eds) *Skills Training in Research Degree Programmes: Politics and Practice.* Maidenhead: Open University Press.

Samuels, A. (1973) The student and the law. *Journal of the Society of Public Teachers of Law,* 12: 252–265.

Scott, D., Brown, A., Lunt, I. and Thorne, L. (2004) *Professional Doctorates: Integrating Professional and Academic Knowledge.* Maidenhead: Society for Research into Higher Education and Open University Press.

Swift, J. and Douglas, A. (1997) *The Viva Voce.* Birmingham: Birmingham Institute of Art and Design.

Sutherland-Smith, W. (2008) *Plagiarism, the Internet and Student Learning.* London: Routledge.

Tannen, D. (1995) *Talking from 9 to 5.* London: Virago.

Taylor, S. and Beasley, N. (2005) *A Handbook for Doctoral Supervisors.* London: Routledge.

Thorley, L. and Gregory, R. (1995) A broader education for research students: Changing the future. In B. Smith and S. Brown (eds) *Research Teaching and Learning in Higher Education.* London: Kogan Page.

Tinkler, P. and Jackson, C. (2004) *The Doctoral Examination Process: A Handbook for Students, Examiners and Supervisors.* Buckingham: Society for Research into Higher Education and Open University Press.

Torrance, M., Thomas, M. and Robinson, E. J. (1993) Training in thesis writing: An evaluation of three conceptual orientations. *British Journal of Educational Psychology,* 63: 170–184.

Trafford, V. and Leshem, S. (2002) Starting at the end to undertake doctoral research: Predictable questions as stepping stones. *Higher Education Review,* 35: 31–49.

Trafford, V. and Leshem, S. (2008) *Stepping Stones to Achieving your Doctorate: Focusing on your Viva from the Start.* Maidenhead: Open University Press.

UK Council for Graduate Education (UKCGE) (1996) *The Award of the Degree of PhD on the Basis of Published Work in the UK*. Lichfield, UK: UKCGE.

UK Council for Graduate Education (2002) *Report on Professional Doctorates*. Dudley, UK: UKCGE.

UK GRAD (2007) *What Do PhDs Do? Trends, a Commentary on 2004–2006 survey of PhD Graduates. Key Changes and First Destination Trends?* Cambridge: CRAC Ltd (Careers Research and Advisory Centre).

Universities' and Colleges' Staff Development Unit (USDU) (1994) *Staff Development in Relation to Research*. USDU Task Force 3 Occasional Green Paper no. 6. Sheffield: USDU.

Walker, G. E., Golde, C. M., Jones, A., Bueschel, C. and Hutchings, P. (2008) *The Formation of Scholars: Rethinking Doctoral Education for the Twenty-First Century*. San Francisco, CA: Jossey-Bass.

Wisker, G. (2001) *The Postgraduate Research Handbook: Succeed with your MA, MPhil, EdD and PhD*. Basingstoke: Palgrave Macmillan.

Wisker, G. (2005) *The Good Supervisor: Supervising Postgraduate and Undergraduate Research for Doctoral Theses and Dissertations*. Basingstoke: Palgrave Macmillan.

Wisker, G., Robinson, G., Trafford, V., Creighton, E. and Warnes, M. (2003) Recognising and overcoming dissonance in postgraduate student research. *Studies in Higher Education*, 28: 91–105.

Index

HOW TO DESIGN AND DELIVER ENHANCED MODULES
A CASE STUDY APPROACH

Diana Medlicott

- Would you like to make the modules you teach more engaging?
- Do you want to deliver enjoyable and effective learning?
- Are you interested in a model that has been proven to work?
- Would you like to evaluate the quality of what you deliver?

This book is key reading for university and further education tutors who want to engage and motivate their students, and create learning environments that cater for diversity whilst producing more successful outcomes.

Based on experience, the author provides practical expertise on:

- Challenging the standard module structures
- Maximising attendance, enthusiasm and commitment without compromising quality
- Putting supported assessment and feedback at the heart of learning
- Providing appropriate support for all students
- Increasing self-esteem, confidence and independence in learning
- Evaluating the success of the module

The book has two sections – the first focuses on design, and the second on delivery and evaluation. It details practical ideas for seminars, lectures, assessment, feedback and student support that readers will be able to apply immediately to their own teaching practice. As such, the book provides key reading for all those interested in improving student learning and retention.

Contents
Part one: Designing the enhanced module – Introduction – Who are my students? – Design principles – Designing attendance support – Designing support for learning and assessment – Designing opportunities for feedback – Designing assessment tasks – Designing seminars – Designing lectures – Part two: Delivering and evaluating the enhanced module – Introduction – Delivering attendance support – Delivering support for learning and assessment – Delivering feedback – Delivering assessment – Delivering seminars – Delivering lectures – Enjoyment, self-awareness and reflection on feedback – Evaluation and continued enhancement – Conclusion – Appendix one: Attendance support policy – Appendix two: Attendance support – enquiry into absence – Appendix three: Assignment feedback form – Appendix four: Example of a team collaborative activity – Appendix five: Self-awareness quiz – Appendix six: End-of-module letter to students with poor attendance records – Appendix seven: Pre-module questionnaire – Appendix eight: Best/worst mini-questionnaire – Appendix nine: Post-module question-naire – References – Bibliography – Index.

June 2009   144pp
978-0-335-23397-7 (Paperback)   978-0-335-23396-0 (Hardback)

STEPPING STONES TO ACHIEVING YOUR DOCTORATE
FOCUSING ON YOUR VIVA FROM THE START

Vernon Trafford and Shosh Leshem

- What criteria are used to assess the scholarly merit of a thesis?
- What is the level of conceptualization that is expected in doctoral theses?
- How can you prepare to defend your thesis?
- What is the most effective route to achieving your doctorate?

The starting point to achieving your doctorate is to appreciate how your thesis will be examined. The criteria that examiners use, the questions they ask in vivas and their reports provide templates against which theses are judged. So, why not start from this endpoint as you plan, undertake, write and defend your research?

This book focuses specifically on how you, as a doctoral candidate, can raise your level of thinking about your chosen topic. Doing so will improve the quality of your research and ultimately contribute to knowledge. It also explores the nature of conceptualization which is sought by examiners in theses. As a candidate, the book provides those essential characteristics of doctorateness that examiners expect to find in your thesis.

The book will also appeal to supervisors, examiners and those who conduct workshops for doctoral candidates and supervisors.

This practical book includes extracts from theses, examiner reports and cameo accounts from doctoral examiners, supervisors and candidates. It also contains numerous visual models that explain relationships and processes for you to apply and use in your doctoral journey.

Based upon contemporary practice, Stepping Stones to Achieving your Doctorate is an essential tool for doctoral candidates, supervisors and examiners.

Contents

List of examples – List of figures – List of tables – List of tasks – Acknowledgements – Introduction – The end is where we start from – What is doctorateness? – Architecture of the doctoral thesis – Exploiting the literature – Thinking about research design – What's in a word? – How to conclude your thesis in one chapter – The abstract – The magic circle: Putting it all together – Preparing for the viva – Dynamics of the doctoral viva – Epilogue: Arriving back at where we started – References – Index – Author name index.

2008   264pp
978-0-335-22543-9 (Paperback)   978-0-335-22542-2 (Hardback)

EFFECTIVE POSTGRADUATE SUPERVISION
IMPROVING THE STUDENT-SUPERVISOR RELATIONSHIP

Adrian R. Eley and Roy Jennings

- What kind of problems are encountered while undertaking postgraduate study?
- How are these problems best avoided or resolved?
- How can the student/supervisor relationship be improved?

This practical guide is based on a series of successful workshops on postgraduate supervision and presents the most frequently encountered difficulties in the student/supervisor relationship. Detailed but concise case studies offer realistic solutions to the thirty issues discussed, including:

- Conflict
- Culture
- Distance
- Funding
- Isolation
- Language
- Management
- Plagiarism
- Priority
- Time
- Transfer
- Write-up

Each case study raises important questions to generate discussion, and suggests solutions and preventative measures. The book also includes a section that shows how the case studies can be used in a teaching workshop setting.

Effective Postgraduate Supervision is essential reading for supervisors of postgraduate degrees including those at masters and doctoral level as well as prospective and current postgraduate research students.

Contents
Foreword – Preface – Acknowledgements – Contributors – Introduction – An Issue of isolation – An issue of conflict – An issue of non-compliance – An issue of plagiarism – An issue of time – An issue of language – An issue of writing – An issue of scrutiny – An issue of transfer – An issue of progress – An issue of judgement – An issue of distance – An issue of teaching – An issue of management – An issue of culture – An issue of funding – An issue of appeal – An issue of stability – An issue of ownership – An issue of availability – An issue of health – An issue of direction – An issue of contract – An issue of priority – An issue of write-up – An issue of viva preparation – An issue of identity – An issue of alleged fraud – An issue of collaboration – An issue of procedure – Conclusions – Key questions – Appendix 1: Answers to the key questions – Appendix 2: Use of student/supervisor issues in a workshop setting – Bibliography – Index.

2005   208pp
978-0-335-21707-6 (Paperback)   978-0-335-21708-3 (Hardback)

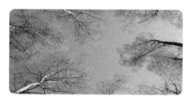